Break It Down with Michael

This Junkie's Path to Becoming a Spiritual Warrior

by Michael Haynes

Written by a recovered addict, Break it Down with Michael explores how belief systems and our past experiences and attachments control our behavior every day, without us even being aware of it. Raw experiences are shared to illustrate how belief systems can be identified, tackled, and changed in real time to create a better spiritual condition.

Michael's lack of filter and candid humor is a refreshing way to approach radical life change for anyone and everyone—addict or not! We are all plagued by belief systems that run in the background of our minds and hold us captive. This book is a road map for changing our attachments and beliefs with immediacy.

Prepare yourself to laugh, cry, get angry, and have visceral reactions to the topics in this book. That's the point—stretching your comfort level for lasting spiritual change.

Break It Down with Michael
This Junkie's Path to Becoming a Spiritual Warrior
by Michael Haynes

Published by SkillBites LLC
https://skillbites.net/

ISBN: 978-1-952281-57-0 paperback
ISBN: 978-1-952281-58-7 eBook

Contents

Contents

Dedication

My wife, Susie, for 34 years of patience to let me change to a better man on my own terms with God and Spirit.

Special Dedication to my friend and mentor, Easton Wren. The one who drove me to write and publish my writings. I am grateful for our partnership and his participation in where this project will lead. Love you, Easton.

Michael Eugene Dolphin, for teaching me how to change all my belief systems to let them be guided by Spirit.

Beth Krueger, for being my guide and mentor.

Alisa Carter, for being my mentor, guide, and book partner.

Bill Phillips, my brother, friend, and guide, for going through the last 40 years and helping me get through down times.

Preface

This book is about how I went to war with my belief systems. I needed change, and through the work outlined in this book, it came when all other types of avenues failed. Belief systems are the things I fight to know and be right about. They are how I must judge everyone else's belief systems to be wrong. They encompass my patterns of continuing to act and think how I have been acting and thinking for 25 years, five years, or six months ago.

I came to the realization that I could not continue believing the same things that I had believed my entire life, and I hated that. However, I was out of options. I had been a drug addict for the better part of four decades and needed to pull out all of the stops. I was desperate for change. The way I was behaving and the things I was saying were being rejected in all avenues of my life. I found out that, to my surprise, people are allowed to get tired of how I treat them. And they were. Then I wondered why this was happening. I could see the answer even though I didn't want to.

I faced an existential crisis. Why do I think I don't need to change? Why is it so easy to blame everyone else? I acknowledged that the only way I could see out of the darkness was to change everything about what I believed and thought about everything in my life. This is where my spiritual warriors were created. I couldn't do this alone, so I imagined great warriors to assist me in tearing down my soul to allow my Spirit to emerge.

At 14 years clean and sober, I still think the way I always have. It is second nature for me to be a controlling, intolerant, angry person. The difference is that I now have the option to be a decent, principled, spiritual person. I have the choice today to service principles instead of myself. I had never been able to access this until I was ready.

This book is how and why I shift. My mental, emotional, and physical life depends on this shift every single day. Through the eyes of a spiritual warrior, I proceed through my existence. I am forever attempting to do things a little better than yesterday. This includes finding harms I cause and amending this directly to those I hurt along the way.

The topics included in this book are merely translations of my collected experiences of changing things that I never thought I could. I found I was driven to share how I was able to shift from dark belief systems within me.

There is no truth to anything I say, but if something rings true for you, it is yours. Bon voyage.

Introduction: Michael's Story

I admit it, I'm abrasive. I'd be lying if I said I didn't appreciate this aspect of my personality. I view it as a talent. I would rather be a dickhead than a pansy. Before we get into the meat of this book, it is prudent to understand my history. I love my defects. I love to hate and I love to be defiant. I love to lie. It is what I've always told myself. I'm unsure if this will give me any authority of the subject matter, but my opinions and experiences have been shaped throughout my life which was filled with addiction, trauma, and mental illness.

I walked out of my parents' house when I was 15 years old. I had reached the point where the brutal environment in which I was living became untenable. My father's physical abuse and chronic womanizing pushed me out into the real world. I didn't think it could be worse than anything I had already experienced. My father fucked anything that walked and my mother did nothing.

My mother meant little or nothing to me. She pretended that everything was all right when this was unconscionable. She imagined she didn't see the bruises, invented internal excuses that made her deaf to my cries, and deflected when she didn't hear the moans of the whores my father brought home echoed down the hall. I never had respect for my father. There was a time when I respected her, but I lost it because she pretended as though nothing was out of the ordinary. Maybe it was ordinary for us, though, but I knew I didn't want to be a part of that lifestyle anymore. I was certain she knew the truth even though she denied it all.

I was a by-product of Jesuit school and a heavily Catholic upbringing, which supremely backfired, to say the least. My religious foundation was worth something—I had someone to pray to when the ass whoopings became torture. However, God never afforded me what I really needed—a reliable out. So, when I departed, I knew it was for good. I was on my own and left to my own devices.

I refused to do anything for that woman, my mother, the older I got. Of course, this made more trouble for yours truly. I got whooped because I lied. I lied about doing chores she had asked me to complete or anything else that I thought would get me in trouble. My dad got too lazy to beat me every day. I lied so much he couldn't keep up. Saturday was christened "belt-whooping day". I would get hit for all the lies and the things I didn't do up to their standards. I would get an average 30 belt whooping each Saturday, but I learned to come prepared. I would wear two pairs of jeans, thermals, and four pairs of underwear so the blows would be softened. I admit that my defiance began as a small seed, but my resentment and their behavior watered and fed it until it was a beast. Basically, I couldn't win for losing and I felt that if I was going to lose, it would be on my terms.

When I left, I didn't have much of a plan. I did some couch surfing with friends until I met a man. He was named Don, a neighbor of sorts, who seemed like a good option. I found out promptly that he was a super pedophile. I had resigned myself to my decision of absconding from home and I saw this man as a relatively easy way out. I didn't care that he did sexual things to me. I didn't care that I was being used. After all, I was using him, too. We traded—sexual shit for drugs, whiskey, and a place to live. I was able to live with him and get all my needs met while I did the same for him. I didn't see it as that bad at the time—it was what I had to do to survive. I considered it a fair trade. At least it was a trade I was responsible for. My life hadn't been my own for years and this way, I had some freedom to choose.

I was with Don for 5 months. No one knew what he truly was, just me. He befriended my parents and they met to discuss me. They made a collective decision that I was using too many drugs. What's laughable is that Don provided much of them to me. Of course, no one knew that, either. I was sent to rehab at 15. Somehow, I had become the problem. An abusive father, a neglectful mother, and a pedophile neighbor all decided I was the issue.

I was shipped off to a brand-new treatment center. It offered horses, cows, chickens, and outdoor labor. I loved it. I gained 50 pounds in that time and morphed from a string bean to a real boy. I remember the first time a girl looked at me—never before had a girl looked at me! It was exhilarating and new. I made an abrupt decision, one that I stood by for decades: I became a real whore. I took advantage of the three months there, to say the least.

I never intended to stop using drugs. I went because I had no choice, being a minor. After I left rehab, I was introduced to the needle. My ultimate daily goal was to have methamphetamines coursing through my veins all day, every day. I ran with seven other guys, and we cooked and shot meth one hundred percent of the time. We hotel hopped and sold drugs. My life was crazy and fun. Don't believe people who say using wasn't ever fun. It was. That continued for a long, long time—that's why I never stopped. Yeah, there were consequences, but they didn't hold a candle to the enjoyment of meth.

When I was 17, I stole a car. This action wasn't without purpose—I had to get to Dallas to get money from my mom to pay my dealers so I wouldn't get beaten to death. I needed it more than the guy it belonged to, because he probably wasn't going to die if he didn't drive it that day. Once I finished that task, I decided that I liked the car. I made an executive decision to keep it. I put it in the backyard under a tarp. I could have been smarter here. One morning, around 3 am, the police broke down the door, pulled me out of bed, and arrested me. I was naked, but at least I had an attorney.

The judge sentenced me to two years at a residential treatment facility. It was a program for juveniles that were in trouble and needed reform. Calling it treatment is a poor representation of what it really was. It was an in-your-face bootcamp-style facility where they broke you down mentally, emotionally and spiritually. One day, the staff accused me of being dishonest about something. I did lie a lot, but I don't recall lying about anything in this specific instance. Of course, I argued; I was a supreme hair splitter. I was made to sit in the corner for a week and write down everything I had lied about. I made up a bunch of shit, like accidentally touching a girl's butt, to make the staff think I was trying hard. The main thing I did lie about, though, was Don. When I brought this as the part of the list, the response was lacking. There was no empathy or compassion for me as a victim of abuse. As a part of my punishment, they brutalized me with their words in front of the entire community. My dishonesty around experience with sexual trauma had become my fault, my problem, my cross to bear. I got this message everywhere I turned—from my father, to my mother, to my abuser, to the people who were supposed to help me, and back again. Starting then, I was made to start every sentence with "I'm a liar". As in, "I'm a liar, could I have some toilet paper? We ran out." Other kids and staff would goad me into talking to them just to take enjoyment out of me embarrassing myself.

I couldn't do it anymore after four months and I left. I had been moving up in the ranks and getting more responsibility. I was becoming a community leader when the entire liar issue happened. I couldn't take the cruelty of how the tides had turned, and I was finished. I have a history of running and when I realized I could, I did.

I went back to my dad's and got a job with his girlfriend's fine jewelry business. My boss was a lady named Suzanne. She embodied hardcore principles; do shit right, proper everything, Miss Manners. 'There is a right way to do everything' and 'don't talk back to me' were her slogans. I talked back, I got in trouble constantly. I couldn't help myself; it was a hobby. It was fun. For some reason she endured, and even grew to like me. All the older ladies there did.

When you leave the place where a judge tells you stay, it follows that you're going back to see the judge and he's going to be mad. The ladies, including Suzanne, that I worked with accompanied me to court to speak in my favor. I had worked with them for six months. Instead of five years in the penitentiary, he sentenced me to five years of super intensive supervision probation. I was fine with that; I had dealt with worse.

Then, I met a woman. I was 19, she was 31. I had a place to live, and she had a car—it just made sense that we got married. Her parents were powerful insurance brokers and had a lot of clout in several arenas, including political and financial, in the state. I would mow my father-in-law's yard and he began to teach me about speaking and how to interact with people. I never had any social training, and this was invaluable.

We were married for a year. She wanted a child, so I gave that to her. My youngest child's name is Anthony, he is in the Navy, a life timer. Despite my and my ex-wife's lack of understanding and foresight, he is an incredible man with a family of his own and a work ethic that I couldn't have understood at his age.

Then, I got my dream job. I was 19. I worked for a stamp company delivering stamps all day, smoking weed in a really nice company car. Time of my life, so I thought. That's where I met her. She was the head of the accounting department. She was married at the time, as was I. Having said all that, she looked at me one day, out of the blue, and told me that we were going to get married one day. She was right—we've now been married for over 30 years.

I was 23 by the time we were married. From that age until I was 44, we shot dope. There were other facets of life, like working, children (she had a son as well), but everything centered around dope and sex. We lived a fast life most of the time, although we tried to be the best parents we could.

When I was 44, my wife decided to enter rehab. She had tried to kill herself and almost succeeded a couple of times. She provided me with an ultimatum—get sober or 'get the fuck out of the house'. She had rehab and a support system—I had nothing. I didn't go to treatment, and I had no outlets. There were no sober people that I knew of, and I thought that getting sober was a joke. I was in the house that I shot dope in for two decades and I was alone. Thankfully, I knew I didn't want to be alone or homeless, so I said fuck it, I might as well give it a shot. I visited her at the treatment center. She told me that if I didn't go to Cocaine Anonymous that day, I should work on packing my shit.

I went to the meeting. I happened to meet a woman who was able to hook me—she's the only reason I kept showing up. She was the only person who could get through to me, although I don't really know why. It isn't even important. I heard her like I had never heard anyone else, and something clicked.

What was shocking about when I stepped in sobriety was that all my dark thoughts and feelings came out, too. I hoped these ruminations would just automatically turn into something else, so I began to pray and ask God questions about what I expected. He laughed. I thought, 'this is why I gave up on God, because I thought He would remove the urge to think and feel the way I always did'. Me, master of the game, as I always thought I was. So one day, God revealed himself to me in my room. He looked kind of like Gandalf sitting on the couch. He was eating Cheetos and he had two pompoms. He sat up, waved the pompoms at me, and said, 'go Michael!' He said that his job was only to give me the courage to change everything I didn't want to, and that I would be given a path through principles to walk through every old feeling, belief system, and habit. He told me that I will do everything or die. Humility and integrity would be acquired, and I needed to find my purpose in this. There are always two options: quit or find gratitude within me and move forward. 'Consider that all this will be half as hard as you think it is', He told me.

At about nine months sober, I met a man who changed my life. To say we were different would be an understatement. He's an old Black Panther motherfucker and I'm a white republican. We got into a lot of shit one day, but over everything, I respected him. We never spoke about politics again, ever, after that. There was no need. I knew that he had been through the same shit I had and had put together years of sobriety. I knew I could learn from him. He taught me that I had options—if I wanted them. I could be decent, or not, but I had to decide who I wanted to be, in that moment and every day since. It wasn't because I really wanted to, it was a necessity.

I found within myself that with any addiction there's a deep underlying force that will not stop driving me to continue the cycle. I called mine my dark dude. I could never tell the truth about it to anyone, except someone with the same addiction. My motive was to somehow justify the addiction and not feel alone by sharing it. It did not matter how I got into the addiction, all I knew was that I was just very committed to it. The only way to get out was to die. Until I found sobriety.

I came to quit blaming my past for what I became because one day me and my Spirit got together and found a face and voice to obey. I only love this stuff only half as much as I think I do. So I began to pretend that maybe I didn't love these defects. We started to pretend and act like doing the opposite might be cool. I asked God to make the principles cool sometimes, especially when I don't think that they are.

We addicts are mad dogs. People that shoot dope no matter what, fuck no matter what, steal no matter what, and have opinions no matter what. We don't give a fuck about who we hurt, really, and we aren't going to hold back. It isn't that we don't care, it's that we have no ability to keep ourselves from being ourselves to you and hurting you as a by-product. The funny part is that we offend and we hurt, but we're offended and hurt no matter what about everything and by everything. I have found that is because we like it. It gives us permission to hit back. There is no room for compassion or tolerance where we come from. We just have no capacity to be able to do that for anyone. Our self-pity is a monster, but we have pity for no one. I was able to understand these core truths about myself in doing the work that this book is based upon. I couldn't change it until I admitted it was all accurate. Mike made it cool for me to think this way; that these things everyone always told me were awful were assets and had kept me alive. I didn't have to be ashamed.

I was willing to put a principle in whatever issue I thought I had, shove it in, and sit there long enough to wait to see what happened. He taught me that I had two options: either get up or stand down in real time. That's all that matters—here and now, don't think, just do the right goddamn thing. This is a story about a major junkie, liar, and thief and the path he took to becoming a decent, honest person.

We ran the streets using for so long, it seemed like we ruled shit forever. Coming into this Spiritual process of having been a junkie up until the moment I got here and based on all the people I fucked over, lied to, and the manipulation with how I got my way, the God piece said I should just be aware. I need to remember that when I have all the I'm-supposed-to-get-some-shit-moments, the fact I'm alive means that I have already cashed all those moments in. I'm cut off, tapped out. I don't get to be that guy who gets it for free. I did earn all of them and now they've run out. I'm learning how to give shit away, at least to pretend to, and at the same time recognizing who I work for. God let me do whatever the fuck I wanted before. I can keep doing that, keep getting what I got before, but He's looking for people to step up into angels to take care of His kids. Who else better trained for that shit than people who would have no part of it to begin with?

I'm letting you know from jump that there really is no truth to anything I say. It's just a path. We all have to find our way, today. Someone, Mike D., had to be given permission from a part of me I did not know existed to shut up, get up, and write out my spiritual principled instruction for a day. All the subjects I write about come so naturally and are mandatory to survive and excel in the game; myself and other committed drug addicts included. Pretending for a moment that I did not really need to believe I was crippled by something, for example blame; pretending to not blame in a moment is what I chose to practice for the past 14 years. It's just something I do because I've grown weary of me and how I like to act. I think I will continue tomorrow.

PART I:
The Essentials

Discipline Warrior

Belief Systems

My belief systems stem from what I think I know up to this point in my life. They are bred from what I have seen, been through, and interpreted. Belief systems tell me how much or how little I will care or do for anything outside of myself. The only way I will change a belief that I know is true and works for me is if I get in enough pain. I usually just pick up someone else's belief system and call it mine. It's easier than trying to think of it myself. The other option is that I move through my own shit to get to the principle I need to produce change from within. Obviously, this is the more mature way of going about it.

My defects, as they call them in the 12 step rooms, are an accumulation of most of my belief systems. I had to search for the core of why I think I have to believe certain things. These belief systems are where I really believe who I have to be when certain situations come in to play.

When I came into shifting these beliefs in sobriety, my irit said, 'good job getting here and not dying. However, these will not do because there are no principles that you have that are acceptable. You have just been surviving. How is that surviving thing working for you? You, Mr. drug addict, are going to have to find a way to crush or lay aside everything you think about in your belief systems as they are now. You must ask the spirit of God to allow you to have an open mind and a new experience. You might want to consider new experiences in these areas: your opinions, arrogance, jealousy, self-pity, control, defiance, hatred, and all the persistent reasons you justify having to act on these things.'

The big belief system I recognized I had to scrutinize was that I had no intention of wanting to be a good guy. I was still getting something out of what I had become in the game. I had contracts with myself where I committed to my dark dude to disrupt as many lives as possible. I did this while justifying defending myself. I kept these beliefs alive and well by only spending time with and around people that had the same beliefs. This had to change for me to find it cool to change within myself and to heal.

After addiction when I moved into sobriety, it was terrible to find that within my thoughts and feelings were embedded opinions and beliefs that I knew were true. Even if they weren't, I took them as gospel. They were about everything and anything. I asked myself, why this, why that, why do I need to do this or why will I never do that? All the answers I gave myself to the questions I asked came from the past somewhere. The new principles I was living out of caused me to ask myself why these old belief systems were still relevant. Whatever happened before had no ability to provide guidance for me now, in the path of change. Even though I believed in my way of doing things, I knew my belief systems were killing me. By myself, in the night, when I begged my Spirit to come into me and make it easy to change something, I knew something had to give so that I would shift. Things like self-pity, doing nothing for anyone, complaining, and blaming were ruling my life.

Spirit said, do you really think you can change these on your own? The thinking you know cannot allow you to change anything because it is not supposed to work that way. It can't work that way—you're thinking got you here, dumbass. (Spirit talks to me like a friend, which I appreciate.) Change comes with a willingness and desperation to do so, plus a moment of sacrificing everything I think I know. When I do one thing that I normally refuse to do, I am told that a new belief system is happening within me. It had already been created without me knowing. My action has, in the moment, kicked out each belief system on some level that I ever had. When I do one of these things, this Spirit and principles of change within me reign supreme.

All my belief systems notice and acknowledge this is a change of heart within a person that refused to do this. A major example is allowing my wife have the room with believing something I disagree with and instead moving to her side and sparing her my opinion. Asking my opinion to leave the room for the lifetime and asking it to vaporize completely is a change I didn't think I could accomplish.

Inventory

How this affects my...
Self-esteem - I scream in the middle of the night with no one there because I can't go on with these old belief systems that I bring to the table, but I'm really not willing to change based on my actions
Pride - I don't change or sacrifice for anyone if I don't have to; my crappy life says I need to try
Security - Dealing and shifting what I think and feel to Spirit world principles would be easier if everyone else around the world would go first and never question me (How stupid is that, how scary how much I believe that will happen)
Ambition - I am stuck in believing that other people need to change their opinions, beliefs, and values to fit what is best for me
Men - Men are meant to be broken; I am tired of being so angry and unbendable with men
Women - All my belief systems with women turned out to not be true, it was me and how I tried to use them; I learned they are different species and I should treat them as such; when I had the courage to stop treating them like men, the relationship changed
Pocketbook - I don't want to change my belief systems and behavior around getting and having money, I'd like to keep this greedy part of myself in rotation

My Part

How Am I...
Dishonest - I never let people know how dishonest and vindictive I am; I call people out and try to ruin reputations of people that do the same dishonest things that I do

Selfish - I'm smug and proud of the belief systems that I think still work for me
Self-seeking - I have no respect for people unless they like me and support my way of doing things
Afraid - To lay out all my defects and belief systems; I think I'm embarrassed these but I'm not capable of that

5 Fears

1. Fear of practicing principles on purpose because I'm shallow and don't have the courage to pretend to be embarrassed
2. Fear of the unknown
3. Fear of trying to kill myself and pain (but I'm proud of that, too)
4. Fear of the judgments about myself not being true
5. Fear of being capable of being a better person than I think I am

Resentment to God

For meeting me at the bottom and talking to me, for suddenly making it possible to find me, I really did not want this

Corrective Measures

1. Find two small belief systems that are not working and write inventory on them
2. Write a lay aside prayer about specific troublesome belief systems

Attachment Warrior

Attachments

Attachments are my belief systems. They are things that I like to I call my way of doing life, no matter what. I get attached to people and what they should do for me, to things that need to please me, to owning and controlling things that I deserve to keep. Where I really get attached is with the flow of money. My opinions seem even more than attachments—I viciously protect and justify them.

I noticed that they don't change as to how I think or believe I can get away with behaving. My motive is that I never let go if I want something or someone. A part of me says I will stalk you until you surrender to my will for you. This happens in marriage, relationships, money, arguments. All areas of my life are dictated by what I believe and am attached to.

This is how it was for a drug addict in the game. This way of living has followed me into sobriety. It is alive and well within me today, always running in the background. Without principles, this way of living will take over; it is hardwir.

I do not like to admit it, but attachments are very satisfying in the process of getting what I want. I would never say that attachments don't cause me pain or there's no guilt attached when it comes to causing others pain if I get what I want. Sometimes I feel guilty, but not that often. When I do, I easily sweep it under the rug or squash it like a bug.

It's hard to itemize my attachments. With Mike, I could not see them at first. I called them goals. These were things I strove to be or the things to hunt down and get at all costs. I listed all I could, and then included the many he pointed out. I put them all into a four-column piece of inventory. He forced me to take a principle and pull it into each attachment when completing the corrective measures.

For example: My attachment to being a predator and using or taking advantage of a woman. What would it look like if I was humble for once and took no as an answer? My wife says "no" is a complete sentence. What if I dropped in a huge amount of brotherly love and understood sex isn't due to me?

Another example is thinking of a time I had a conversation with my boss that I did not like. What would it look like if I brought my spiritual integrity into one of these conversations and let him know he was right, especially when I think I disagree?

My attachments seem to be hardwired into what I feel, what I think I need, and especially into the things I won't do or should not have to do. So, the question from Spirit is: why do I need to have attachments? The answer: because I think I do or because I love them as they are. Maybe the answer is that I honestly don't know.

Needing to be attached because I always have will not do on the path with principles that I'm traveling. This is how it was put to me when I got sober: I am welcome to go back to a life and belief systems where I thought they worked at any time. The problem is that I begin to see my attachments in my feelings and thoughts. It is insanely overwhelming.

I don't think I agree with what you call my attachments, as I go into them one at a time. I see how hard I fight to keep things that hold me back, as opposed to letting them go. I think it is so challenging to let things go that I tell myself I can't. This isn't true, come to find out.

I'm attached to the outcome of everything. I expect people to let me make them do things only for me. I expect my wife to agree with me and my opinions often, but she won't. I get attached to the thoughts that I have constantly running through my head. It's exhausting.

Sometimes I believe there are things I should not have to do, like take out the trash. But no one ends up doing it but me. How mad do I want to get? My other option is to take the trash out. It takes 30 seconds and solves the problem. Why am I obsessed with the idea that other people have to? People in traffic need to know to get out of my way. People need to listen and agree with me in every scenario. When they don't, I think I need to lose my mind. I found out that this was an option I chose to take every day, repeatedly. I liken it to stabbing myself in the neck with an icepick over and over again.

Burning down my attachments has created a neutral space in the lifetime of a con. It is a journey my Spirit says we must take and continue every day until I die. Otherwise, left unchecked, I'll be back in the game in no time.

Inventory

How this affects my...
Self-esteem - I pride myself in the people and things I'm attached to and keeping them as my own
Pride - The more people want to keep something, the better I feel about taking it
Security - I get insanely insecure when I get caught taking what you are attached to
Ambition - My ambition directs me to do as little as possible; things should come to me naturally
Men - My attachment to men is thinking I deserve everyone's respect and loyalty; I want to be at the top of the food chain
Women - If women would only act like me, all their problems would be solved; I'm attached to lying to and cheating on women
Pocketbook - I always believe I should get more; I'm attached to money making me feel good or bad; I'm infatuated with money all day until I'm not

My Part

How Am I...
Dishonest - I lie about how serious my attachments are to what I think, feel, and do
Selfish - I know exactly how I think things are supposed to be; I know how I will react and if I'm really OK with what is or isn't

Self-seeking - I react when people have attachments to what they expect me to do for them and when they expect me to do it
Afraid - To let go of the belief system deep within me that hard work and the Spirit of principles through me will prove enough

5 Fears

1. Fear of seeking all my attachments and cutting them loose with Spirit's help
2. Fear of not hanging on to things
3. Fear of being of service to others unconditionally
4. Fear of having old belief systems
5. Fear of following marching orders through God without question

Resentment to God

For not letting me keep the way I do things even though they are killing me

Corrective Measures

1. Identify two belief systems that are extreme and pretend they aren't through action for one day
2. Let someone else's attachment be greater than yours

Control Warrior

Control

The great illusion! Both in my earlier life and now, control is what I was always scrambling for and it was continually out of reach. I fought for control since the time I left home as a teenager. The same fight for control changed from being abused to drug addiction to a sober life with principles, living by the dictates of my Spirit and the Spirit of God.

I must see the control in order to stand down and see what principle has to be called for and executed in these moments. I must be in the emotion and situation where I am actively engaged and trying to force control to and then act my way out of it through principles of pretending to act like a good guy to actively change.

When I'm trying to control or not be controlled, my dark side pops up. My self-motives start kicking ass and taking names in every aspect of my life. I have always felt that my urge to control wasn't something I could regulate—I had no power over this monster that ruled me. It's ironic, to be controlled by a controlling nature.

I'm trying to control anything, until I'm not. My internal thoughts and feelings torment me and it's almost as if I have no power whatsoever to change. I am locked in a prison, and someone is going die if I don't get out. I came into the recovery world to find a new purpose. I wanted to explore the idea that my Spirit could get big enough to come into the deep fibers of what I exhaust myself into doing every minute of every day.

Then there's the whole control world of my massive sexual nature and obsessions. That's an entirely different topic.

I started writing pieces of inventory like, "why is control mandatory in me?", "why do I have to get offended when I don't have control?", and "why does it please me so much when I have control and why do I get so fucking angry when I don't have it?"

I found deep in this dark place that there is a part of me that wants to get offended when I cannot con people to give me what I want to control. Having to be offended, even when I'm not actually offended is a contract I didn't know I had. Sometimes I think I'm offended until I stop and look at the situation from 20 feet in the air and realize that I don't care about the thing I am supposedly offended about and that I just use this to get what I want. I searched and came to find out what hell that is. I asked for my deep Spiritual Father to come into these spaces and kill some of this stuff when I give Him permission. I must ask myself: why does what I think matter so much and can I ever escape my bullshit concerning all of this?

I realize my control was self-taught. I never had much control over life's lessons, but I had to make decisions and acquire belief systems that would get me by. It seemed that there was always someone standing in the way of the principles, to learning or doing the 'right' things.

I believe I have power with what I think to have control. The chase for control makes me feel ok. I get into a headspace where I truly think that what I think and feel has merit. I stand so firmly in that idea that I set myself up for depression, jealousy, and obsessions. I become preoccupied with the idea that something is going make me feel better, I'm going to find it, and control it when I do.

Spiritual power begins to manifest in my behavior and how I make right the wrongs of what I've said or done to people. My Spirit gives me the courage to stand down and not need to control anything, moment by moment. I don't have power either way, because needing control has power over me like no other. My Dark Dude will never let me get above the illusion that control is mandatory and must be sought. Spirit gives me the courage to see the damage and futility that control does to me and my relationships and allows me to change myself, one situation at a time. I had to become content with being in the flow of what is happening in the present. That's about as good as I need to be.

Inventory

How this affects my...
Self-esteem - I demand to have control, only to find out I don't have control; I fuck things up when I think I have control; this loop drives me crazy
Pride - I think I am better when I can control what people can and can't have from me
Security - Even when I'm out of control, I believe I'm in control
Ambition - I have to have control to not think I'm a weak piece of shit
Men - I go out of my way to control men so they cannot control me first
Women - I have to give women more control than I like in order to be in a relationship that I want (sucking up is another form of control)
Pocketbook - I should be able to control how much money I make or get

My Part

How Am I...
Dishonest - I don't tell people my motives so it makes it easier for me to control the narrative and relationship
Selfish - I will not let people get over on me or control me
Self-seeking - I have to have the upper hand in any relationship; I have convinced myself I cannot be weak and not having control equates to weakness
Afraid - Of sacrificing myself for the good of others or God's kids; of not having control even though I have little

5 Fears

1. Fear of allowing other people to be right
2. Fear of being wrong and looking weak/stupid
3. Fear of letting my Spirit face these things for me

4. Fear of surrendering this behavior to my Spirit and the Spirit of God and the principles
5. Fear of what I do reflecting and mandating who I am

Resentment to God

For giving me control and taking it away

Corrective Measures

1. List 4 big controls I think I have (opinions, justifications, rationalizations, etc.)
2. Get to two people I assert control over in some way and let them know I can and will do better

Path Warrior

Demands

What are demands?

Demands come from the deepest part of my inner insane asylum. It's where my entitlement, self-centeredness, selfishness, and identity are locked away until I open the doors and let them loose. Sometimes I like to unlock the doors just to see what will happen, what havoc my demands will ensue. Other times, the lock is picked by people or events in my life pushing my buttons. I like to pretend that I'm a victim when this happens, but that's just another con I like to run.

I can't even tell you where my demands come from, they're just here. They are alive in my thoughts, feelings, and belief systems. Some examples are: I think women should find me attractive, I think men need to agree with me, my kids need to do what I say, employers need to pay me more, cars need to get out of my way, my wife should appreciate me, listen to what I tell her to do, and blow me.

I do have an idea where they started. This thinking and feeling shit starts the ball rolling and then I push to do of whatever it takes to make what I want to happen come to fruition. My demands can be based around the smallest thing I fight for, or it could be a mountain. The consistency lies in the demands themselves, not what they are today.

Coming from the meth world, all my demands and the defects that accompany it followed me. Everyone has the option to do what I demand or not, even though I pretend they don't. I'm the only one that actually takes them seriously and holds shit against people for not behaving accordingly.

Mike started to break down the bad news when I started to get sober: this shit won't do, that I'm an idiot with these demands, and it will never cut it to be who I was before. He told me I probably wasn't that important today (or ever) to push on people the way that I had been. In Spirit world, maybe it isn't a bad thing to push on people, because it equates to unpushing in the moment of pushing. Is that some bullshit or what? I didn't want to listen or accept what he was telling me because I didn't know who I was without making demands.

I had him break down all my illusions, one at a time. This included the illusion of how important I think I am and all the shit that I do when I'm in con mode (steal and lie to get what I demand and justify the behavior). This doesn't even scratch the surface of what a demand looks like inside me. Mike said that this would be a great time to go ahead and lose my mind, time to start working directly through Spirit and principles and do a complete brainwash. He said that everything before now must be recreated. We started with a few questions: why do I have demands? Who do I think I am, a self-important, self-righteous prick, to think that I am entitled to demand things of others?

Next was to walk down the path of what to do with these demands. I wasn't exactly ready, but here we go. Why am I not listened to? Why do I lose my shit when people don't listen to me? Why do I feel like I'm supposed to be the one who people drop what they're doing to do what I want on every whim? Why do I feel like I have a right to demand to be listened to? Where does all the force and energy behind this come from and why am I just now dealing with it today? Why are these rules just for drug addicts? Why do you have to be a junkie first to go down this road? Why not you, and why me?

Spirit said whether you listen to me or not, it's really just the same thing. A different experience with different consequences, just the same coin with two opposite sides. Get my way, don't get my way; whether I'm right or wrong, different experience for each. Now we're just splitting hairs.

My part is that I do whatever it takes. I demand to not be less than. I demand to not be wrong, and even more extreme, for other people to agree with me constantly. Mike asked me, what it would it look like if I put some humility, the kind I had never seen before, right into the middle of any of these demands? Spiritual humility means that I'm not afraid of being wrong, I'm not afraid to not be demanding, and I'm not afraid of having no expectations right now, because I do have all of these. Mike told me to sit down with him and a pen, and I let him show me what a four-column piece of inventory looked like on demands. So, we did.

Inventory

How this affects my...
Self-esteem - I need people to shut the fuck up and do what I want; I expect no demands be made of me, just do what I say
Pride - Making demands gives me that feeling of power; I make demands so I can get pissed off when they aren't met
Security - I expect people to demand as little of me as possible to be ok
Ambition - People don't tell me no, most of my resentments come from no, and then I have to double-down on my demand
Men - I love telling men "no"; criticizing men all day is as important as breathing
Women - I expect women to want to be with me, to give into me sexually, I demand women to not say "no", I like women more the more they say "yes" to me
Pocketbook - I expect shit for fre; I shouldn't have to use my money; employers should pay me more than I deserve, and then I still won't be happy

My Part

How Am I...
Dishonest - I lie about my demands and expectations because I know they're unreasonable
Selfish - I know my demands are one-sided, but I'm not able to care

Self-seeking - I don't really care about the effects of what I say and do to people; my demands are just something to do and if it hurts you, too bad, so sad
Afraid - of not being able to allow the Spirit and principles to become important to me, to stand up within me, and give me the courage needed to shift

5 Fears

1. Fear of being alone
2. Fear of not caring about anyone but myself
3. Fear of radically changing my belief systems
4. Fear of not being defiant
5. Fear of not having the courage to find my purpose

Resentment to God

Fear of not being put in my place, not letting Him drive principles and spiritual dictates into me in this life

Corrective Measures

1. Make amends to two people that I have daily demands on to find out what I can do to make it right
2. Allow one person to be right that I think is wrong everyday

Self-Will Warrior

Entitlement

Entitlement and everything that comes with it is my most brutal belief system. Keep in mind, deep down, I am incredibly lazy and get jealous of what anyone else has. I don't know where this belief system comes from. I lived on this belief system of entitlement in the drug lifestyle the entire time I was in the game. Entitlement comes up today with the same enthusiasm. My dark dude and his entitlement has to be handled by my Spirit dude every day. I'm entitled until the one minute that I am not. I'm not killing people with my entitlement, until I am. Which is most of the time when I act this way. Whether I am or not only shows my behavior, not in what I say or feel.

My first three answers when I'm asked to do something are: I want to get paid more, I'm not doing that, I shouldn't have to. Gut reaction, I'm not a giving person. After I get past those thoughts, principles and Spirit tell me that the next three answers are: maybe, I'll get ready, or yes. Granted, it takes me about 14 or 15 bullshit responses in my head until I agree because I really don't want to. This happens even when I'm asked to just take the trash out or do some mundane task at work that I don't think falls under my job description.

When it comes to the Spirit stuff, I entered the 12-step process and was told that I was going to have to prepare to say yes and do what anyone asked of me. This also meant that I had to be available to be asked. I am a chronic avoider and if I can tell you're even thinking about making eye contact with me to ask me a question, I bolt. I'm a master of the Irish Goodbye.

The rage in me said that there was no way I could do this, that I would rather die than do things I didn't want to. This is where the influence of my sponsor came in. He said to do what I didn't want to every single day, and I listened. Without question, I hated every minute of it. Trust me, when I was available, people did ask. What I didn't realize until later, was that every time I was asked and agreed, it gave me little opportunities to change my cold, black heart. After some time, I began to be a little grateful for having the heart and breath to be useful. I was never useful before and it was a surprising but welcome change.

My sponsor also told me that I had to spare these people my opinions of what I thought about what they had asked me to do. He said that I can't brag to anyone about what I did because otherwise, I don't get the humility package that Spirit will give. There was no glory, no fame, no props. If I fished for compliments or recognition, it voided the contract. While it pissed me off, I agreed. I had limited options and knew I had to change everything about what I had believed up until this point.

Inventory

How this affects my...
Self-esteem - I have no guilt or shame for my vast entitlement
Pride - People should see how special I am and should want to do things for me, even though my entitlement makes me hard to be around
Security - People should never criticize me in order for me to be OK
Ambition - People should embrace my bullshit even though I have no tolerance for theirs
Men - I'm the alpha male; I'm always right; my feelings must be protected at all costs
Women - Women oh owe??? me no matter how horrible I have treated them; I think I own women as a race
Pocketbook - I deserve more for doing less; I believe I should be able to take anything I want; I deserve it all and no one else does

My Part

How Am I...
Dishonest - I have to keep my entitlement inside; people might argue with me or give me consequences like break off relationships
Selfish - My belief system that I keep says I deserve it all and others don't, I truly believe this and it runs the show
Self-seeking - I fool people into thinking I care about them until it's time to take something; I'm entitled for you to trust me
Afraid - Of finding out that I don't deserve anything; that people don't owe me; and I have to grow up and do it myself

5 Fears

1. Fear of being honest and humble
2. Fear of not being entitled
3. Fear of gaining people's respect and trust
4. Fear of allowing my belief systems to be changed
5. Fear of not being afraid to change

Resentment to God

For not agreeing with the ways and motives for taking whatever I want from whoever I want

Corrective Measures

1. Don't ask anyone for anything for one day, do it all yourself
2. Do something for someone else without asking for feedback or a reward

Expectations

My expectations are massive. They take up so much room in my life that they drive me to insanity. I do insanity really well, though, so much so that I think I love it. I must—or else why do I keep coming back around to these arbitrary rules I have set for myself and others?

As a part of the spiritual enema that I had chosen to embark upon, I had to find out where expectations came from within me. When I looked around, I realized that I had set expectations of everything and everybody. It didn't matter who you were or what situation I was in, I had already decided what needed to happen or not happen. When things didn't go my way, my response was always justified anger. It scared the shit out of me.

I had to define what expectations were before I could even decipher how they played a role in my life. Expectations come from where I come from—in the game. The importance here, though, is that everyone has their version of the game. If it isn't drug addiction, it's any number of iterations in the game of life. It could be popularity and bullying, home life, or past romances. The specific game isn't what defines having expectations—this is a given. Everyone has expectations. Your version of the game, whatever that is, sets you up for having individualized expectations and how you will move forward with them throughout your life.

I found that expectations are preset. What I feel or do has already been determined ahead of time, based upon the belief systems I have poured energy into for years. Looking in the past, I could see that my expectations were exactly the same as before. Nothing had changed, contrary to my thoughts and high opinion of myself. What was really noticeable was that I had an expectation paired with an opinion ready for the draw in each imaginable situation. I wasn't really living out of free will—it was all a deck pre-loaded constructs that I pulled from daily. This was mandatory to not lose my mind in the daily grind of what my life had become, and I was still perfecting this habit in the present. I was here, in the present, sober and stable, living by the same rules of the jungle.

Mike was able to direct me to sit still and write about these preloaded thoughts. I became willing to think about pretending that I didn't have predetermined expectations, just one thought and one person at a time. I saw that I continually think that I am incredibly important and create standards that I force people to live up to. If they fail, which is inevitable, I gleefully punish them. I had thought that these standards were the truth, but they are just a lie that I taught myself in the game.

The energy and anger that is created from not getting my way consumes me the moment that I step into it. To get, to have, to take, to fuck, etc. If I look back, I had expectations way before I started using substances. They were different than the ones I have in sobriety, but the existence of expectations was just as strong and present in my day-to-day life.

So, where do expectations come from? You might not like the answer. It isn't a black and white issue. That doesn't even matter, although most people think it should. Expectations originate from whatever, wherever, or whoever I think they come from. I could go to hours of therapy and decide that my family of origin taught me to have certain expectations and ideas about life. I could then blame everyone else for everything I've ever done. Maybe therapy helps some people achieve the level I needed to get to, there is no shame in that. However, I didn't have much of a choice. I either had to change expectations drastically or else I was going to go back to drugs and die. I didn't have a slow road option—it had to happen, and fast.

If I wanted to make headway, I had to admit the truth. This was the brutal, painful experience of ripping off the biggest band aid ever in the worst way possible. There is no concrete explanation for expectations. The only thing that I could come up with that rang true was that I tried an expectation on, liked it, so I kept it. Each expectation that I have, I have chosen to continue manifesting every day. I have put a lot of effort into continuing this pattern. Each minute of each part of my life is where expectations come from, right down to the point where I expected God to save me somehow without me doing jack shit.

I expect so much and give so little in many ways in my life. Some of these forms are money, sex, and doing just about anything for anybody that doesn't get me what I want. I got to the point where I sat back and asked myself: How did that become so normal? It was inherent in me, like breathing. I couldn't seem to stop and realized that it wasn't a conscious choice because I don't do anything but that. But when I understood what I was doing, it entered into my conscious mind, and I had to decide what to do with it. It was a brand-new concept and I noticed it everywhere I turned. I saw that either I'm angry because I'm not getting it (whatever it is) or I'm trampling on other people with joy in getting what I think I want. The kicker, the blind spot, is that it's deep within my nature to not do a goddamn thing that other people expect me to do, especially in addiction. I love seeing that shit in other people because I can see mine.

Today, I look back and ask how did I become so fucked up? It just happened. It wasn't one moment or event, I cooked over time into an expectation-setting asshole. Layer by layer, I added to my complex internal manifesto of shit-talking, judgment, and expectation-setting. Before I wanted to change, I was proud of who I was. It took a lot of time and energy to become such a selfish prick. I was proud of myself. I had to be hard, a savage, in the game. There wasn't another choice if I wanted to live.

This next part might be hard for some people to swallow. I found that when I really told myself the truth, with the help of people who cared more about my life than my feelings, and when I was able to shed the fear or judgment from others and get brutally honest with myself, I was able to acknowledge that I like doing this. It's a really cool thing that I feel no pain about it, that I have no remorse in fucking people over. I had to remove all pretenses about this idea and understand that I must like it because I keep doing it and don't try to change it. I noticed that I have a big part of me that says everyone is going to fuck me over, so they deserve it. Get them before they get me, or get them in retaliation for getting me, whichever fit the bill. I never thought anything would work out. That's the place I put it and let it rest and acted based on this belief for my entire life.

When I tell people this, the typical response is shock and aversion. People don't want to admit this to themselves, let alone another person. I try to help people see that it isn't about judging myself or anyone else, it's about recognizing what is the truth and moving forward. I have found when people admit that they sometimes like hurting others, it's a newfound freedom. The cool part of this is the ability to change.

I can be so consumed with being right that it feels natural. I'm a really, really good con. I tell people whatever they need to hear for them to agree with me, even though I am probably full of shit. The best part is that part of me knows I'm full of shit and part of me believes the con, too. I would have to for it to work that well.

Mike would ask me: How is this shit working for you? My answer was almost always the same: Not at all. Everyone is gone, I'm dying, and I'm finding out that it's not so much the meth as it is me. It's my behavior that drives people away, hurts others, and leaves me fucked up and alone. I couldn't even blame the drugs anymore.

Once I stopped using, I didn't change. I made conscious decisions to hurt people every single day, but wanted to pretend that I had no control over it. Little by little, though, I was able to break down and break through these expectations which gave me the ability to breathe a little easier. I was also kinder to the people in my life. But remember—this wasn't the objective from the beginning. The goal was to not hate myself and my life and to have a better life for me. I wasn't trying to be altruistic, but this work did end up helping others because I wasn't such a shit anymore.

Inventory

How this affects my...
Self-esteem - I expect people to do most of the things that I won't do
Pride - it's not important to me to meet anyone's expectations, it's just not the fuck important
Security - I need to be right about everything or I lose my mind
Ambition - I set the bar very high for others as far as what I expect them to do; I expect everything for free
Men - I expect men to read my mind and never disagree; I expect more from men
Women - I expect women to serve me, agree with me, and to want to sleep with me no matter what
Pocketbook - if I could, I would pay people to agree with me

My Part

How Am I...
Dishonest - I lie about what I expect from people and I con people into doing the things I won't do
Selfish - I do as little as possible for people and I'm really ok with that
Self-seeking - I'm truly a con always looking for easy ways to get over on people
Afraid - to be humble and honest; to not force people to do things without me lying to them

5 Fears:

1. Fear of changing everything
2. Fear of not getting to be right and get things my way
3. Fear of standing down and being humble
4. Fear of letting other people be right
5. Fear of being told no

Resentment to God

For not allowing me to fix and control my life

Corrective Measures

1. Make amends to two people I control each day, find a way to make it right

Amend (example)

The amend is for thinking that John is a piece of shit, judging him, and thinking that everything he says and thinks is stupid. I talk about him behind his back and stare him down in a room while pretending there is no problem.

John,
As part of my recovery, I made a list of people that I harmed, lied to, or stole from. You are on this list. I would like to make my amends to you for hating on you, thinking I'm better than you, for talking about you and undermining anything you say or do. I owe you an amend for the disrespect I show you, for lying to your face about these behaviors, and thinking that it's ok for me to do this to you.

I can do better than this and you deserve better from me. (I don't really mean it, but I'm going to pretend because this is what Spirit tells me to do and it has gotten me far.)

Is there anything you want to say to me about this? I promise to not speak. (Then just listen.)

Is there anything I can do to make this right?

Hypocrite

You're only a hypocrite if I say you are. I base this on something you haven't done for me, but against me. It's the old saying, 'do as I say, not as I do'. Hypocrite is a big word and a big accusation that I like to throw around at opportune times. If I say you have done something against my version of the agreement of our relationship, I will throw this word at you in an act of war. Sometimes I think I sit around waiting for you to do something so I can blame you for all the problems in my life. I respect that shallow part of me. Then, I cry about everyone running out of my life.

I instantly deny when people say I'm a hypocrite and immediately blame them for how I treat them. I can't stand arrogant people, but I act like a pompous ass and never admit it. I can't stand when people cancel plans with me, but I give no reason when I do, and I do it frequently. I can't stand when I am being blamed for behavior that I know I engage in.

Come to find out, all the crappy things I accuse people of doing to me, I do to myself and others. I know I do them and have done them with no guilt whatsoever. When I got sober and came into spiritual behavior, it was made very clear that I get what I gave in these relationships. The harsh reality was within me that if I wanted a new experience, that my behavior could only be changed when activated through these principles. Principles like integrity, the kind I never had, and humility, the kind where it was never important to be right. Everything inside of me detested this, but I knew that I had made a choice to go on this path and was sticking to it. So, with my nose turned upward at the stench of self-effacement, I moved forward.

The worst part was hearing the only requirement was that I was the only one who required change. No one else was required to change at all. This is going to have to be an inside job only. The Spirit of God dude was going to require me to go to people and let them know I harmed them and find what can be done to make it right. This has changed my life.

Inventory

How this affects my...
Self-esteem - Gave me a grateful sense of control and power to judge people and make this judgment real
Pride - No one could ever really know who I was; I liked lying and hiding my dark side and only showing as little as I needed to
Security - My security is grounded in my ability to be safe but not need others to feel safe; I was really just a predator
Ambition - Being a hypocrite was necessary to being and acting better than people around me

Men - In my mind I categorize all men as hypocrites, myself included, when I really look at my behavior over the years
Women - I pigeonhole women into saying what they will do for me physically or sexually; if they don't, I have to ruin their reputation; they never see me coming because I am a hypocrite
Pocketbook - I xpect you to be loyal to me but I'm not really loyal to anyone; I'm always looking for a better deal; people seem to honor this

My Part

How Am I...
Dishonest - I do the exact things to other people, then I call them out for their being hypocritical and argue to the death why I'm right
Selfish - I'm much easier on myself for being a hypocrite than I could ever be on others I judge
Self-seeking - I minimize the damage I do to others to make myself feel better; a part of me is dying when I act this way, but I think I'm too far gone and can't stop
Afraid - That I will continue to like being a hypocrite too much change; that I won't like the consequences of changing this about myself

5 Fears

1. Fear of not caring
2. Fear of never having deep relationships or being able to be loved
3. Fear of becoming humble
4. Fear of having no spirit or spirit of God within myself
5. Fear of people hurting me on purpose like I do to them

Resentment to God

For teaching me how to be this way and not making it cool to stop

Corrective Measures

1. List three areas or relationships in your life where you are a condescending, controlling hypocrite
2. Make amends to these three people

Judgements

My judgments are a big loop. They keep coming from me and for me repeatedly. I lose it when people, especially my family or friends, judge me, but I will judge anyone and anything like it's a hobby. I believe it is my right to judge others, but they cannot possibly understand where I come from, and their opinion of me is therefore invalid. I am the definition of a hypocrite, but I'm really ok with it. I will deny it to my dying breath to you, and even to myself, but I know that I'm the most special, unique flower in this universe that I, and only I, am entitled to judge. I blame my judgments on God for not allowing me to have them freely, like I should somehow be shameful of this right. I am appalled at thinking that I'm not supposed to judge. It's a stupid idea that I shouldn't because I think I'm so smart. (Ha!)

I really don't know where they come from inside of me, but they are a constant army of thoughts fighting against everyone and everything in my life. I asked Mike what to do. He told me that we needed to begin to grind into the core in what I think and what I feel. He didn't mean just to log my thoughts and emotions as if they were fact—he meant we needed to dissect each and every one and find out where the motive is behind it and how they are full of shit. Then, we could start cutting them out through direct amends to some of the people I do this to. My dark side said that I could never pull this off. Therein started the war with my judgments, and it continues through today.

My big justification for judgments was that everyone else does it. Why did I have to be different? Besides, it was fun. Mike would say that they aren't killing everybody else with their hate, you are. He never let me use this excuse. The God piece says that I'm not like everyone else, and He expects better from me. We wrote a Covenant to God to address this. God tells me that there isn't anything fair about any of this—it's about changing perspectives and viewpoints. Fairness isn't the point. I could live a mundane life of judging and living in defects of character or do something more meaningful than that. It isn't meant to be easy or fun, it's meant to be work. But with this work comes fulfillment and being decent. I never thought I could have anything like that in my life, and I probably just wanted it in the beginning because everyone said I couldn't have it. But it's now become mine. I actually kind of dig it.

I found myself fighting myself to be the same person I've always been and not wanting to or it being feasible to change. Welcome to the loop. Then came the final prayer: God, could you make it cool for me to fall in love with not being like anyone else? And could you do something about this crybaby shit?

Judgments are cool because they're so flippant. I don't have to care about you or me to have them. They just ring true for me in the moment. Sometimes I make them up to just feel better about myself. They are entertaining, and cheap entertainment is the best. For me, judgments are conclusions that I don't have to bother to destroy. They keep working for me and I don't have to put in any additional effort. It's the hardcore knowing that I bring from years before and that I continue to make up now. I fight for some to stay true today even though I know they aren't really accurate.

Everyone seems to have judgments about everything. Mine were killing me, and that's why I had to take a hard look at them. I get so stuck in things that I can't breathe, i.e., life sucks always, I will never do anything towards any kind of purpose, I'm lazy and I can't change, and I'm offended by so much shit. All of this had to be true because there was no way I could take a knee and start living through the Spirit of God or my Spirit. I've never seen anyone be able to move about this world with no judgments. The God piece had me create the Covenant that says that we take a knee for everything, we no longer need to be right, you either work for God or not, and each day I must choose to go first.

Going first means that I must be the first person in any situation to walk in principles whether other people do or not. I am going to let other people be right and not have to argue. Me going first isn't waiting around for someone else to change, because they probably never will to my standards. Me going first isn't using other people's bad behavior as an excuse to be a piece of shit myself. It's me being God's soldier and treating everyone else with grace. For one day, I will not be right and everyone else can be, I will not be offended, and I will do what anyone asks of me. Then, I wake up and do it again. This is a day of you serving your Spirit that answers to God. Welcome to being a spiritual warrior and leave your crybaby shit at home.

My judgments are secrets. I keep these deep inside where they can be toxic, no one can ever see how fucked up I think or how normal I feel about these things.

Inventory

How this affects my...
Self-esteem - This is how I prop myself up to the world; this makes me feel equal; I stay mad hearing how people judge me, and I think I like it (cause I'm always mad about shit)
Pride - I have no need for pride; I react to the things people do to me and say about me
Security - I have to defend myself even though what most people say about me is true
Ambition - I'm like a sniper; I have to watch constantly for what people do and say that I don't agree with and then I want to destroy them; the judgment I live in is constant
Men - My judgments about men are always true; even though I know they're bullshit
Women - I don't really take women too seriously; I was like this for a long time and I don't know where it comes from (probably from my dad, whose motto was 'fuck me, feed me, and shut the fuck up'; I took it very to heart)
Pocketbook - I make more money when I keep my judgments to myself; there's a time and place for me to vomit my shit up and it probably isn't in the workplace

My Part

How Am I...
Dishonest - I lie my ass off; I make judgments where there are no judgments to be made; everything I see, I have an opinion about, especially when other people are judgmental and opinionated; I lie when I say I think I don't do this, it's the gift that keeps on giving
Selfish - I don't really care what people think and feel about me, and if I do, it's fake and self-seeking
Self-seeking - I find it mandatory to judge everyone else (but not me)
Afraid - I'll never stop taking shit personally

5 Fears

1. Fear of being judged
2. Fear of being told how to change
3. Fear of humility
4. Fear of this dark voice never leaving me and wanting my life
5. Fear of abandoning my own importance to the Spirit of the God piece and living in principles

Resentment to God

For not caring enough about me to change these things inside me for me

Corrective Measures

1. Make amends to someone I've judged
2. Letter to God asking why it's so hard not to do this

Patience Warrior

My Dark Side and Why I Pretend to be Ashamed (when I'm really not)

It took a very wise man, deep in his 20 years of sobriety, to sit me down and talk about this topic. It is not for everyone; this is just my journey. When I came into recovery, it was mandatory to take a very long, dark look at the things that happened to me. This included events in the meth world and my sexual past to my childhood and sexual and physical abuse. Like so many people, I had packaged these memories in my head and categorized them into a neat little box that these were dark, horrible, times that I never wanted to talk about and should feel pain and shame over. People, like my shrinks, counselors, etc., convinced me that it was all bad, that I had to feel shame and pain. People had hurt me, and I should be upset, offended, and defeated. They told me that these experiences forever traumatized me as a person. I was a victim, but that I could work through it all with hard work and dedication to myself as a person. They told me I could come out the other side as a survivor and put myself back together.

I guess I never bought the fact I was Humpty Dumpty to begin with. Yeah, bad shit happened, but I also grew up and kept doing all the same shit and loved it. I didn't feel broken, I didn't feel that I needed to be empowered. If anything, I needed to be disempowered. I was a predator. Although that began with me being the prey when I was a child, I had taken it, run with it, and sculpted my own masterpiece of predation all on my own, with only my volition. I had used them to build me into a powerful force of darkness. I admired myself for that. I was already a survivor, but of the evil-Batman-villain variety.

I don't expect anyone to understand what I'm about to write about. I understand this topic is controversial. When I sat with addicts like me who had been through wringer after wringer, this is how it broke down. This may surprise you, as it did me and other people I talk to. I request that you take a moment to put aside your previous beliefs and open your mind to something radically different.

Mike said, what if you're actually not ashamed of your meth life and even what happened before? Between me and you, maybe you loved it. You did these things for so many years and kept doing them way past their expiration date. Looking back at the lifestyle you chose, maybe the sexual stuff didn't offend you. You spent the following 25 years after being abused doing the same sexual behavior, both physically and when consuming bounteous amounts of porn. How can you be ashamed of something that you probably loved and would do it over again if you had to?

Since that day, this proved to be one of the most truthful and impactful ideas in my life. It rocked me, and although at first, I was offended and thought he was wrong. Upon further review and with a lot of thought, I decided that he could be right. He uncovered this truth in me and gave me the gift of freedom that I had never accessed before. Having no remorse and not being ashamed of the past has allowed me to become such a better person in my soul and in anything I could ever imagine. This only happens when one junkie tells another junkie that it's ok and gives them permission to be completely vulnerable and genuine and open up to this unpopular opinion. I have experienced both sides of this conversation, and I have seen relief flood people's faces when it clicks that these past situations have fueled their behavior in the present and therefore, they weren't the big victims they thought they were.

Even in the rooms of recovery, we're told that we're supposed to be wounded. The truth is that all of that shit happened years ago. I don't have to be wounded, especially if I don't feel like I am. I have seen people have experiences that didn't bother them, but when a counselor or sponsor tells them it was bad or abusive, they suddenly become fucked up and ashamed. Why is this? What if it's just ideas and a series of constructs, that it isn't an absolute?

From that day until now, my dark side has changed, too. It has become an integral part of my spiritual path. Instead of fighting this part of me, I have embraced it and thanked it for all it did in keeping me safe throughout my addiction. It is the part of me, which Mike pointed out, that had to have more courage, more drive, and more endurance than any other part of my life. I was dedicated to the dark side. This concept suddenly worked its way into all kinds of corners in my mind: thoughts, feelings, opinions, behaviors, judgments, etc. This was something that I could dismiss with the help of my Spirit and start closing doors and burning down memories of anything except for today. I never saw that coming.

I found out that I'm not capable of being ashamed or having remorse. I was just really good at trying to be. The game doesn't allow either of these things. This was a depressing part of my past that I had to make peace with.. Most heavy drug addicts have gone through this early in the game, too. I hate to say it, but it's a normal thing that happens in the drug world. This shift of being unashamed, not having remorse, is a right of passage into serious drug addiction. It is an initiation into being able to behave in radically degrading ways which feed the cycle. Most things that I couldn't explain that happened in the game, Mike would call the wrong place, wrong time. I had a part, and he always made me find my part. It disturbed me, but it was there nonetheless. It turn out that all this stuff was really the right place, and the right time because it was ingrained in the lifestyle. I exposed myself to these situations constantly when I was in this world. Shit happens, then I did another bump and moved on. That always made things better, helped my negative emotions to fade, and the party continued.

If I had to do it all over again, I would. It was better than getting beat to death at home. I had a choice at 15, and I made it. I would make it again. It really wasn't that big of a deal when I look back at it without prejudice, unemotionally recounting the events of my life. Removing societal assumptions, innuendos, and insinuations, the acts themselves really weren't that bad on their own. I survived and it wasn't that painful. I'm not bleeding or dying today. I have survived the incidents and have come out the other side. The point isn't to be dismissive of what happened to me, but to be pragmatic in seeing how it actually effects my day-to-day life. My dark side no longer has a place when I take out the trash or wash my car. It doesn't have to, at least. I can choose to carry this around on my sleeve and use it when convenient, or not. I'm glad that I have the choice now, whereas before I didn't think I did.

I worked with addicts that have had similar experiences in their lives both before and during their addiction. It's completely normal for people who have lived this life. I could say that I could not have made other decisions, but I didn't. I even ended up trading my ass for dope. It really wasn't that bad. It was worth it.

By the time I got with Mike and we started writing my deepest inventories, it went like this: The Spirit of God was sitting right there, giving me a path out from this insane place. It included one-on-one service with someone and understanding what other people went through with no judgment or comparison. I had to put aside how I thought my shit was different from their shit and pretend to care what happened to them more than myself. These people, like I did, stuck in guilt and shame, had no clue whatsoever what to do with this emotional baggage they were clinging to. I just said that my sex parts did heal, and I have no lasting effect today. Physically I was fine, and I could be emotionally and spiritually, too. I had to want to be better, had to want to stop using this as an excuse for bad behavior and the way I treated others and myself. My Spirit revealed that my part in all of it was that I stayed. I chose to continue placing myself in the same vulnerable situations instead of running away. In all honesty, I had motives of my own. In that sense, I wasn't raped or molested, I was a willing participant. To look at it positively, I saw that it taught me how to fuck. Silver lining and all that.

Remember, Mike said, you had the same behavior all through the years later with women—being a predator, thief, and liar—on some level than was done with or to me. Couldn't have been that bad, then, huh?

Inventory

How this affects my...

Self-esteem - I convinced myself that I am supposed to be so angry towards people forever that I thought abused me

Pride - Blame is very comforting; I visit these memories constantly and refuse to believe I'm healed, but I'm starting to find that I have been for a long time through the Spirit of God

Security - I have to continue to be a victim to myself and others to be ok, it's what I do best and it's all I know

Ambition - I swim around people in recovery that had the same things happen to them because it allows me to dwell in my misery from the past; I get something out of that

Men - I don't talk to men about this unless they bring theirs up first, and they do

Women - This shit is a great conversation piece with women who have had similar

experiences; we are instantly bonded in the shock value of it all and I use this to my advantage
Pocketbook - I was always for sale over the years; I bartered myself for the right price, no one stole me; I paid good money to the people I abused

My Part

How Am I...
Dishonest - I don't talk about what I did to women and others: my abuse to them, pushing myself on them, buying them; I only talk about what was done to me
Selfish - I don't really care about what others have gone through; I don't even want to hear about it, they need to shut up and listen to my stories about my horrible past
Self-seeking - I probably don't really feel bad about any of this, but I think I should
Afraid - To let my Spirit intervene and push me into the part of my life that is purposeful and to get me to shut up (a lot), no one really needs to hear the stuff I think

5 Fears

1. Fear of being haunted by my made-up and/or dramatized past
2. Fear of not finding my part in any of this and having the courage to amend anyone
3. Fear of my love affair with being a victim
4. Fear of taking responsibility for doing the same behavior now
5. Fear of letting God use me to bless anyone in my past (anyone)

Resentment to God

For letting me believe I'm a victim and making me look at my own voluntary participation; for not letting me blame the drugs as the cause to what I became

Corrective Measures

1. Make a list of the people that harmed me the most and write out my part in each relationship
2. When someone brings up their dark past, just listen and validate instead of competing

Needing to be Right

First, let's kick off this chapter with an important distinction. Being right is one thing. The need to be right is the powerful force that drives me to do or say what I need to so that I will win. My Spirit says that to be right or to be wrong are the same things, just a different experience. Being right is easy, but who is to say that I am? Taking the high road and allowing myself to have the experience of not being right is where the spiritual adventure lays.

I would have never believed some of the freedom I could get by doing the complete opposite of what I felt was necessary in this department. By letting someone I know be right, especially when it comes to something that I believe isn't correct, I am relieving myself of the push to control how I am viewed, among other things. Questioning that I might not be right all the time is mind blowing. It has nothing to do with whether I am right or not, just with the experience of not having to dominate people with my opinions.

Sometimes I can have the experience that my need to be right and dominate others in this moment is not here. This has changed my relationships with everyone important in my life, even employers. The relationship changed only because I did. They did not change, nor did they have to. When I treat other people with respect, and sometimes let them be right, whether or not I think they are, they aren't forced to take a defensive posture with me.

Being right has been an obsession until it wasn't. I constantly had to ask Spirit, every minute of every day, to grant me the courage to sacrifice my opinions and demands to the force of grace that I knew. Being right is especially intoxicating. The need to be right is the closest thing that I know to a drug addiction. The allure of being correct, being able to hold that over others' heads, is an aphrodisiac. Why does being not right seem so horrible?

I found some of the answers in principles. Principles don't need an explanation, they just exist. I can choose to live by them, or not. I either stand down in principle or stand up in my character defect. I don't have to fight or clash with anyone to not be right, I just have to tumble with the part of me that thinks there is a problem. When I'm focused on needing to be right, I'm always looking to change someone's words, behavior, or thought processes. I find it impossible to not beat someone else down that I think is wrong. I almost take it as a duty to help them because I know better. You can't get much more self-involved than that.

Why do I think there is a problem when I am not right? Why do I fight? These are questions for which I have no reasonable answer. The answer is because I can, and I want to. Spirit asks me, what if in one moment you don't? This is where it begins.

Inventory

How this affects my...
Self-esteem - I think I'm better and smarter than other people
Pride - I really believe this in my heart of hearts, people are stupid if they don't ask my opinion
Security - I know I'm fake when I do this, but I have no desire to want to ask the changes through principles
Ambition - I will hide this part of me to the death
Men - Truly I think very little of men; I only let men be right occasionally, and only when they pay for my stuff
Women - Women are weak, and I really don't value their opinions
Pocketbook - I feel justified and demanding being taken care of financially; I would tolerate so much less if I was paying

My Part

How Am I...
Dishonest - I talk people down in my circle to make me feel better, it shows me how shallow I really can be and I will only tell people when they're making mistakes
Selfish - I don't really plan on changing a thing so please spare me your opinions
Self-seeking - I love to criticize people when they're down
Afraid - That everyone else is writing a part of me that doesn't need to be

5 Fears

1. Fear of not being justified
2. Fear of not being right
3. Fear of not being wrong
4. Fear of getting honest with this stuff and changing it
5. Fear of making amends to the people I do this to

Resentment to God

For not making it easier for me to not be this way

Corrective Measures

1. Let someone else be right two times tomorrow (even if you know they aren't)
2. Do something another person's way, especially if you disagree with how they do things

Obsession

This entire book is about how I came to say no to obsessions, to the devil on my shoulder that really lived inside of my head. This is a brief look at some of my obsessions: meth, weed, sex, porn, people doing what I want, getting what I want, the intensity of how I will not do without any of these, deep-seated opinions, control, and defiance. My path to sobriety, sanity, and spirituality was going to depend on finding a power that could help me kill these things within me and assist me in detaching from what I think, know, and feel.

Everything I write is only about my dark past. The addiction belief system that I held onto for so long is what I need to dissect, millimeter by excruciating millimeter. I did this in the hope of stumbling onto to a path of pretending to change.

I had always refused to change but found I can pretend my way out. Pretending wasn't hard—I have always been a liar. I found that once I pretended it was easy to be a decent person, I became more decent. If I pretend that I don't hate people as much, it ends up being true. A watered down version of this is in a slogan found in the rooms of 12-step fellowships—"act your way into right thinking". That was close, but too corny and A = B??? for me. If I pretended, I was taking an asset of mine, which was being a con, and using it for good rather than evil. That was way more attractive then actually being decent. Being decent in and of itself was downright unfathomable.

I'm nothing special. Just an average junkie. There's no truth in anything I say. If anything rings true for you, it's yours. If not, throw it out.

So, what are obsessions? Defining it using a dictionary or common rhetoric isn't what I'm going for here. I'm speaking of the kind of obsession that grips your heart, drives you to push on the people around you and stand on their throats, people you say you love, and hurt them without remorse. The darkness that tells you that your behavior is more than acceptable and that has no conscience. We all have it, just no one speaks about it, pretending we're too righteous for this human trait. We sweep it under the rug and then act confused when relationships fail. It's time to start talking about it instead of working hard to hide it. Obsessions and the power they have over me is where the entire journey started to finding out the truth about what I really do.

Obsession is a knowing entity; me knowing that I will always be a slave to my obsession. I can't get out, can't outsmart this constant gnawing even though I think I have tried my best. Obsessions are overwhelming. They are so big that I justify them because it's all that I am. Acting on, believing in, and thinking about these obsessions are really the only things I'm incredibly good at. I have made myself an expert at pushing for these obsessions to come to fruition because of the intense draw and power they hold over me. The dark obsessions have the most power.

What are contracts?

Contracts are belief systems fortified from past experiences. Some examples of my personal contracts include: relationships suck, everything is hard, things will never change because they have always been this way. I never stop to think about these contracts because they lie under the surface, dictating every move I make and every thought that drives me. These are ingrained in me, sometimes since childhood, and I don't recognize that they are optional. Yes, I may have begun believing in a contract because of my mother, father, or preschool teacher. But I bought into these contracts and made them my own a long time ago. Think of everything that you were exposed to that you don't believe in. It could be based on religion, politics, child-rearing; it doesn't matter. What does matter is that I have bought into them and still do. No matter what I was taught, I made a decision somewhere along the line that made them a hard fact of how I operate.

The point is that we discard some contracts and keep others—this is our responsibility. I couldn't keep blaming my life or my past for my actions and decisions. I loved hurting people, doing what I wanted, and being a victim to my obsessions. Only I wasn't a victim—I was an active participant. Once I realized this, I knew I could do something about my life because I had control of myself. Breaking it down to the simplest parts, though, seem impossible. Why am I so attracted to these belief systems? Why is it so hard to move them?

I can't get away from these contracts about obsessions because I don't want to. Most of the time, they're still doing something for me; performing an unknowable task in the background. It might be a distraction from responsibility, avoidance of personal relationships, the list can continue ad infinitum. It is in this space that the thought of being a good, principled, helpful person disgusts me. I believe there is no way I can change and become someone good. My entire existence has shown me that it's impossible, so why try? Plus, the dark obsessions eat my lunch, but they can be very, very fun.

Mike D. is the most influential man in my life, and his role has been that of my sponsor. From the first day we met, he said that he was going to tell me exactly what I do when we write out inventory. He explained that he and I were the same, and that when we would "write a piece" of inventory. He relayed that he was really talking about himself, but that it would relate to me because we were so similar. It was more easily digestible when he put it this way—that my dark obsessions and inner asshole was really normal and that he had one, too ???. I did everything he said, things I said I would never do, just in the principle of trying to get something out of life that was different. I wasn't even sure I wanted it, but I knew that I was tired of living how I had been. When I met Mike, I made a decision to put all of my chips in the center of the table. I was going to bet, and bet big. It wasn't like I hadn't bet my life before. This time, though, I was betting on something incomprehensible. The challenge enthralled me.

Mike introduced me to my Father, who I call "G"—God, Father, Spirit Dude. I acknowledge Mike D throughout this book, and everything he has taught me. I have immense gratitude that he came into my life, and I love him dearly to this day.

Obsessions are the gifts that keep giving. When I came into recovery, I was in shock at the force and intensity of how these obsessions presented themselves. They were so crushing, it felt like they would never change. Mike told me that we were literally going to war with what I think, what I know, and what I feel. This was going to kill me or be the most amazing thing I'd ever done. Something about this man gave me the confidence to go places I'd never been before. Looking at him made me brave. Mike showed me how to be just fearless enough to do these things that, at face value, were impossible. What the hell, I figured, I had nowhere to go but up.

I found that my obsessions live because I say they do. I was brought to a place where I was told to be willing to be willing to believe that these obsessions weren't half as big as I thought they were. Going to war with everything I think I know has been an incredible experience. There is a fierce spiritual force behind this that I found out was already alive and well, living inside of me already. I had no idea it was lurking there, waiting for its moment. Honestly, it felt creepy at first. I've gotten used to it.

Mike knew exactly what to tell me to do. He was brutal and abrasive and would not bend to my complaining and refusal to move into the most uncomfortable things. The magic formula for getting down to the core of my shit was a four-column piece of inventory. It wasn't optional. I still do pieces of inventory to this day when I get stuck in some character defect, like defiance (i.e., shit that I don't think I should have to do). I wrote a four-column piece on everything with Mike. Some examples of pieces I wrote were related to fear, hate, defiance, self-righteousness, self-pity, jealousy, and being a predator.

I started to see things I really didn't want to see, but I knew they were already true. This was a type of honesty I had never met before. For example, fear is made up and I really don't have it. After being a junkie who went through traumatic events for years, what could I really be afraid of? I cried behind fear and let it run my life with excuses. As far as defiance, I really did not care for what other people needed or how my actions affected them, but they better not be defiant towards me. I was certain that if this happened, I would lose my mind. I found out that I was a massive hypocrite and loved putting myself over other people with no remorse for what I did. I hid by lying that I did care, but I really didn't give a shit but said that I did to look better and justify my actions. I didn't want consequences for what I did, but I was hellbent on doling them out generously. I was sure as shit never going to admit all these things. The only reason I did begin to acknowledge these beliefs and behaviors within myself, admitted to them, and began to change them was because I was told to. That was my choice—or keep it moving.

I really thought I'd rather die than makes these changes and live by principles. I thought it was incredibly painful. This was the way I was brought up in the game. Like most of us, I found out that I really suck at killing myself. The suicide thing was always out there, always an option. I understand the suicide option. Some people aren't going to make it out and want to go home. I don't judge or pity these people—I understand their pain.

It is important to illustrate components of this spiritual path. A piece of inventory, corrective measures, and a letter to God are all integral parts that work together to create change. I live in these daily and it keeps me living in principles. Being able to call out my most twisted thoughts and identify two ways I can change them in real time gives me concrete actions instead of frilly ideas that I can ignore. Also, it's much more difficult to ignore them when they're written down, in black and white.

What follows is my inventory on obsession. Remember, this comes from the meth addict, piece-of-shit side of me.

Inventory

How this affects my...
Self-esteem - Obsessions are what I can control, good or bad
Pride - I have to do these things to feel important and to have power
Ambition - I have to have power from these things in order to breathe
Security - I cannot let other people control me or act like they are better than me
Personal relations with men - I have no use for men, they stand in the way of everything I need
Sex relations with Women - Women are my greatest obsession; I have motives to get them in bed so I can dominate them
Pocketbook - I will do anything to get the resources to feed my obsession; I will steal, lie and whatever it takes (and I don't feel bad about it)

My Part

How Am I...
Dishonest - I refuse to believe I ever do anything wrong, it's always the other person
Selfish - I don't care about what other people think or need
Self-seeking - I take everything because I've decided it is all mine anyway
Afraid - Of not having power; afraid of caring; afraid of being honest and how hard I think change will be

5 Fears:

1. Fear of getting hurt
2. Fear of being used
3. Fear of not being good enough
4. Fear of obeying rules
5. Fear of living in principles

Resentment to God

I resent having to change when others don't; for making me stand up with a purpose, I resent purpose when I haven't given it to myself; for God letting me get so fucked up and not allowing me to die

Corrective Measures

1. Two times today, when I am about to lie, walk away and then come back to make the amend
2. Write a letter to God about obsessions

Two examples of letters to God are below. These is the corrective measure stated above. I write a question to God and allow Him to speak through me.

Dear God, why do I love my obsessions so much?

Because you do and because you can. You have spent your whole life perfecting survival in the game. The dark side in you has been your master and protector. He wants your life. Sometimes you want to give it to him, but we are now speaking to the part of you that doesn't. You are in love with the idea of obsessions. Maybe, you are not half as obsessed as you think you are. Maybe it would be half as hard as you think it is and believe it is to pretend to fall out of love with these contracts and beliefs within yourself. Maybe you just have not remembered that you are not obsessed at all, and instead you are just stuck in old ways of judging things.

Dear God, why is it so fucking hard to change?

Because you say it is. You say you want to change but keep doing the same things and then complaining nothing is changing. If you say it sucks, pretend for a minute is not half as bad as you think.

Inner Battle Warrior

Resentments

I don't even know where to begin with resentments. They're a combination of so many factors. They seem to begin early in life, and many of these have come to be the same today as they were then. They are great conversation pieces at church parties or when hanging out at my dealer's house. Very versatile. Resentments are a combination of belief systems of how I say things are, my issue with control, hurt feelings, expectations of how things should be or should have been, hatred from holding onto things that have happened to me, and defiance of how I will act if this same situation comes about.

My life is a choose your own adventure book where all the pages are preset, and the choice depends on which resentment is most active. I believe I have freedom to live life in free will, but in actuality my resentments predetermine my fate. I have no control because my belief systems have made it so.

Mike said that there was no other place to start but here. The first three steps in 12-step work were merely statements. Getting free of even a minute amount of resentment is where Spirit shows up. Spirit reveals to me my true self and how I act in my part of the situation. What I love about my resentments is keeping them, one at a time. I treat them like fledgling plants that need love, water, and sunshine to grow. I nurture these resentments and then question why they eat my lunch and consume my headspace. I can blame everyone else for my stuff and never have to hang onto a thing. Mike always asked, "how is that dark space working for you?"

In the end, some spiritual force of grace, some Spirit of God, had to be invited into my cold, black heart to give me the courage to ask to start blessing all the people I hated and judged in secret. Over 14 years I've had to do this four-column inventory on just about everything and everyone. I always find my part, one issue at a time.

The resentments were mostly the same. They centered on whichever person did whatever to me, my dad that beat me, the institutions that fucked me over (law enforcement, Jesuit prep school, people that stole from me and I stole from, my wife and kids, etc.). Most importantly, resentments were about principles. I had major issues here. Honesty, brotherly love, integrity, forgiveness (fuck forgiveness but people damn sure need to forgive me for my actions, fairness, the list goes on), etc. All my resentments were just categories. Death, justice, disappointments… I could go on for days. I was mad at everybody and everything and felt great about it. But inside, I was dying. I wanted to kill myself because of the pain I was putting myself through.

I wrote my resentments for people to show that the courage we use to see ourselves lies within the resentments themselves.

Inventory

How this affects my...
Self-esteem - I should not have to do anything to be respected and trusted; being a liar is totally acceptable to me
Pride - Everything I think and feel about life should be true; no one should question my judgment of them; I can do whatever I want up to this point
Security - People should be standing in line to get my forgiveness; everyone should have to pay their dues for what I think they did to me
Ambition - I demand to get anything I want and I don't need to give a thing back; I really believe this should be true
Men - Other men's resentments are unwarranted; I did what I did to them and it was on purpose and they deserved it and should shut up about it
Women - Most of my resentments to women are sexual, like turning me down or laughing at my approaches or not sleeping with me; they're lucky I put up with them when I do
Pocketbook - I should get reparations for what people have done to me; I blame all my problems on not having money, when I get it I can't keep it which is everyone else's fault

My Part

How Am I...
Dishonest - I will never admit how much of this stuff I caused; especially resentments towards me or other people's problems because I did nothing wrong
Selfish - I don't really owe anyone an apology or explanation for the lifetime of resentments I caused; I have to believe this to live
Self-seeking - It always has been and will be about me; no one has ever helped me change this about me, maybe someone will
Afraid - Of being resentful forever on some level; of starting a principled life within myself with my Spirit Dude

5 Fears

1. Fear of being humble
2. Fear of admitting things I have done to cause resentment
3. Fear of not being afraid
4. Fear of what making things right with people from the past
5. Fear of not having so many resentments
6. Fear of trying and finding a way

Resentment to God

For breathing me into this world and not take care of me like I think I should be taken care of

Corrective Measures

1. Find two people or institutions you are resentful towards and write what your part is in the issue you have (ex. My part is judgment of them, I expect they treat me better than I would ever treat them)
2. Letter to God asking why do you think you have to resent people and think you love it

Betrayal Warrior

Relationships

Relationships is where all my bad belief systems and behavior play. It's like an everlasting recess for each defect that I love. This part of me says that my principled behavior is how I'm supposed to act, but I don't really buy into that. I never get good marks for acting well and not controlling. And of course, praise and acceptance are really what I'm after. If I don't get it, fuck the rules.

My relationships change overtime, just like anyone else's. Year one in sobriety, I acted well and was on my best behavior with my wife, kids, friends, and at work. As the years progressed, and suddenly I was at 5 or 10 years after my sobriety date, I began to expect people to start listening more, showing up in the manner my demands dictated, and honor my personality and belief systems. The longer I was sober, the more I realized that I think my opinion has more credibility, and I'm more right than other people.

I'm only talking about myself, having been married 32 years. I have two children, 41 and 35 years old. I was always taught that the man is the head of the household, like my father. The difference is that today I can't hit the wife and kids when they talk back. My dad and the nuns at school could do that, but I can't. I feel overwhelmed at times because nothing I knew growing up is the same as today. I just can't relate.

When talking about the last 14 years of being clean and sober and control being taken away, I've had to change my viewpoint of how I relate to life and where I stand. None of the privileges of being a heavy handed, controlling, angry father were passed down to me. I've also helped raise my two granddaughters with my son in the house my wife and I have shared for the past ten years. This adds an entirely different layer to my marriage and life, plus the grandkids are girls. It's all new to me.

My lifelong belief systems and how I could act, speak, argue, and hurt people in my relationships were burned down. Spirit and the principles told me that my bullshit wouldn't do anymore.

I always had anger issues. My reactions were quick and verbal with a raised angry voice. Deep within myself I had no tolerance for talking back. Basically, anything but "yes, sir" was labeled as talking back, and therefore disrespectful. If I ask someone in the household to do dishes or take out trash, I would sit there and stare until they did it. I would get angry when people wouldn't jump when I asked them to or wouldn't obey me immediately.

I found was that I was losing my mind 100% sober. Years later, after going through self-imposed pain, I realized I could hook the two strings on the trash with my fingers and take it out in 30 seconds. I had never realized how deep my need was to not have to take out the trash. This had turned into a belief system that raged. It dictated that I was entitled to have people do what I demanded and always, especially in the household. I still do things like this in relationships today, but I'm a lot quicker to recognize it.

My Spirit says that I cannot be humble until I do something today and that I don't get to berate anyone. If I do, my Spirit says I have to make amends. The time has passed for making someone else to do my bidding.

Inventory

How this affects my...
Self-esteem - I would like people in my life more if I could dominate or control them; I need to practice being grateful to not have to
Pride - People in my relationships should behave, let me be better, and have the last word
Security - Seems my security is less important than the others involved in my relationship
Ambition - My need to go first and be right when I'm not is not going well; relationships suck
Men - I avoid relationships with men unless I need something from them or have motives; I'm dishonest on some level in any relationship with a man
Women - I need something from these relationships so I hide as much as possible so they will stay in my life; make myself out to be more honest and kind than I actually am willing to be as time goes on
Pocketbook - I tend to be more greedy with what I think I should pay for as time goes on; I want the control with any money and income

My Part

How Am I...
Dishonest - I try to hide my control of people in relationships; this looks very different with women versus men; I had my insecurity and have little mercy or understanding when it comes to other people
Selfish - I get selfish with my time and money; I like to talk over people; I don't really have any intention to listen like a good friend would because I don't really care
Self-seeking - I think and act like relationships should be more about me; you should think about what is best for me over yourself
Afraid - Of losing the ability to make people want to be in relationships with me; of people walking away and having to start over with new people

5 Fears

1. Fear of being authentic and honest
2. Fear of letting people grow in their own way and time
3. Fear of needing to not be alone
4. Fear of adding to the quality of people's lives
5. Fear of giving second chances when people fail me

Resentment to God

For having to count on people, for creating principles I have to live by now

Corrective Measures

1. Make amends to someone I act better than in relationships
2. Notice when I have the urge to dominate and call myself out in real time

Willingness Warrior

The Push

The push is the place where my defiance originates. It's my hall pass to get shit done, for me, with as little interference as possible. I'm a perpetual adolescent, a Peter Pan who never had the boyish charm with the bonus of an impulsivity problem. The push shows itself when something isn't going right. It's a voice that slides in to my conscious and tells me how me and the dark dude are going to manipulate the situation to get the outcome I wanted to begin with. Sometimes I instigate the push, sometimes it's a response. Either way, it's always in play.

When I decide I've had enough, I start to push back. I can only take so much before I tell myself that I have to push back on what people say and do—this is where my anger resides. I want to do battle with people including kids, partners, parents, bosses, friends, etc., just for the fun of it. I look forward to people giving me excuses to be a dick. It's like debating with someone you actually agree with just because playing devil's advocate and making them mad for no reason is pure, unadulterated entertainment.

The push in me says I have to control what I do for you. The push is the energy within me, good or bad, that pushes back and pushes forward. It's been my protector in a lot of ways. That's why it took a period of time for me to identify it as something that I didn't want running the show anymore. The push got me what I wanted and kept me safe. Without it, I couldn't have kept my schemes going for as long as I did, both in and out of sobriety.

The push is dark energy within me that I've noticed my whole life. It is greatly associated with reaction. When I get angry, I push out to survive, to be ok. I feel this energy brewing when I'm told "no" or when something isn't happening the way I want it to. I feel this dominating momentum rise in my chest to make things "right" or to create change as I see fit. Any obstacle is an annoyance, and I will somehow overcome it—I just don't want to have to waste the energy. Getting people to agree with me is a whole lot easier than trying to convince them. Either way, I know I'm going to get the outcome I want, it just depends on how hard I want to work for it.

The push is the divide between my defects versus my Spiritual Dude in principles in the moment. It really shows up when big things are not going my way, or worse.

I had a set of principles I used to live by that were directly opposite of how I live today. There was an epic battle between them when I started to shift into the Spirit from the dark. The part of me that has to be right, has to win, or will not be disrespected or hurt, rampaged to keep living and fighting to disrupt my spiritual turn. Day after day, the God piece started pushing back on those parts of me. It's a defense mechanism that allows me to make it through the hundreds of low spots that are coming my way.

I never processed much of anything, and no matter what I always had a chip on my shoulder. I thought I earned it and displayed it with pride. The push I had thrust on others was waiting to come back to me in folds after I was willing to do something different after decades of addiction, anger, defiance, and judgment. I had always been the person forcing others to stand down, bullying them into fear and submission. Now, I was the one taking a knee. My dark dude didn't like that much, and he fought hard. He fights to this day, but he's now one weak son of a bitch.

Mike made some things clear to me. He told me that I would serve principles in real time and that I would notice that no other person will do or have to do what I'm expected to do in the Spirit of principles. He explained that here were some principles that I could use that would allow me to pretend not to hate so much in the Spirit of the Spirit Dude. Thank God we agreed on the Spirit Dude. That's the part of me that woke up that I could deal with. He said that I was probably going to want to bitch about it, and that I had an option to either to shut the fuck up and do something significant for another person today, or not. No one would care if I quit. I really liked how he talked to me; it has carried me into spiritual submission for over a decade.

Inventory

How this affects my...

Self-esteem - I believe that I can push or control anything; I think have a right to do this, even when I'm in the middle of huge failures in my life; I'm going to push back, surrender isn't an option

Pride - I believe I control all my belief systems for a reason because they work for me; I already know what I'm going to do long before I do it

Security - if I didn't do selfish, judgmental things, I would do nothing at all; I only do what I know, good or bad, I believe in myself

Ambition - I believe that listening to myself works, even though when I look around in my life, it's clear that it isn't working; I refuse to wave the white flag

Men - I have to push my thoughts and belief systems on men so that they can hear from me and believe I'm important, I make men feel better about themselves with a subtle dominance

Women - I push because I have nothing but fucking agenda, it gives me an excuse to talk to them; even when it's pushy, I have a hard-on even being a dick to you just cause you're a woman and you smell good

Pocketbook - I'm going to have to talk to get money; I push on people to give me what I want and what I think I'm worth; I have to push on people to notice me because I think I can change people's minds even though I do the minimum and am a piece of shit; I'm less pushy when I get what I want

My Part

How Am I...

Dishonest - I don't ask for permission to push people and myself in what I call the right

direction they need to go; them being in my life is my permission slip
Selfish - I give as little as possible; every good idea is my idea; I love being a con and a manipulator
Self-seeking - I really only think about being right and being demanding but I need more
Afraid - of people seeing through my dishonest shit

5 Fears

1. Fear of people pushing back with their thoughts and belief systems on me
2. Fear of not being able to stand down and let in the God piece come and save my life
3. Fear of thinking this is all there is and being seen as fake
4. Fear of being exposed, yet I won't stop doing it
5. Fear of people pushing back to hurt me and take my ideas and have better ones

Resentment to God

For not allowing me to be better and stronger than His other kids; for not allowing me to stay the same and be ok

Corrective Measures

1. Prayer to God asking for the push to be half as big as I think it is and to show me that I haven't remembered that this is the truth
2. Make amends to someone I push on and put down

PART II:
Chief Concerns

Submission Warrior

Amends vs. Forgiveness

It is a misnomer that these two words are interchangeable or even related. Amends has nothing to do with forgiveness. The process of amends pertains to an exercise of reaching deep within myself to find what I have done to harm others and admit this to them. Then, I must find a way to let them know this and make my actions right. The point is to pay it forward to the people I harm in the same way or make it right in some way to the people I have harmed.

Amends seem to be one of the worst things I have had to do. The same time, one of the greatest things I have done. This process was the only way I have reached the level of awakening my humility and honesty in my soul that I now try to maintain. This was namely because of the courage it took to show myself I was not a product of the dishonest life I've led.

My parents might have been horrible, but I have been more horrible to my wife and children. I did not beat my kids, but I abused them mentally and emotionally. My dad cheated on my mom, and I also cheated on my wife. I will not cave into the excuse that my childhood traumas have formed me and driven me to be who I was. However badly I was treated and how much people did to me, I found I did worse. The difference was I justified what I did while working from my dark side. Something had to equalize all this. I had to get honest and hold myself accountable, focusing on my part only.

The following is an example of an amend I made to my father. I wrote every amend out and read it verbatim.

Dad, I made a list of people I lied to, stole from, and hated. You were on my list. I owe you an amends for the following: all the lies I said to you, for hating you for everything you did to us, for the disrespect, for thinking I'm better than you, for blaming you for everything bad in my life, for all the things I stole from you.

Is there something you need to say to me about this, I promise to just listen?

His response: I did the best I could with you. I did not understand the drugs with you, it scared me, so I had to stop you from using. I would do it all over again, that's how I was raised, we had no money, so I tried to give you all you wanted.

What can I do to make it right?

His response: Just do better than me, raise your kids different. Stop blaming me, good God. Be a better man.

We then said goodbye and never saw each other again.

Inventory

How this affects my...
Self-esteem - Amends break down the false esteem in me and show me a spiritual side and dignity I never saw myself
Pride - My pride was not going to cooperate, so me and my sponsor had to find the courage to kill and illuminate my pride when I made these amends
Security - My security is best based on lies and what it can get, it has always worked before now
Ambition - I don't change unless change beats me up, pain is the mother of all change; the 12 steps worked on me in a way nothing had; I was beat down and stopped persisting in real time
Men - Amends to men was never going to happen until it did; timing is everything to me, the timing was finally right
Women - Making amends to women seemed harder because the harm I did was more personal; I had nothing to lose but my soul
Pocketbook - The hardest piece of amends was not wanting to pay back money, but I paid back $26,000 in seven years

My Part

How Am I...
Dishonest - I really did not mean the amends I made, I just made them to get my sponsor off my back
Selfish - I expected the people I made amends to so give me an amends I felt they owed to me in return; this rarely happens
Self-seeking - I wanted the benefits of spiritual living and the God thing to be real in my life, but there would be no payout if I did not change my behavior
Afraid - I was afraid I would be honest with people; I was shocked at the thought of not needing to steal and was afraid other people would keep doing the same shit to me that I am no longer allowed to do in pirit

5 Fears

1. Fear of people telling me more I had done to them that I wasn't aware of
2. Fear of feeling a badly about what I have done when I talk about it face to face
3. Fear of not making amends as I go day by day today
4. Fear of finding a way quickly to change behavior
5. Fear of not having the courage to find to make things right

Resentment to God

For allowing me to do all the fucked up things in the first place

Corrective Measures

1. Make a list of whom I have harmed and write out amends with a sponsor
2. Make amends to all of them honestly

Anger Warrior

Anger

Everything that comes with anger is tied up in belief system I have carried with me for as long as I can remember. When I get angry, it is understood that it is justified. There is never a time I questioned this. I blame something or someone for making me get angry, always. It's my go-to, my feeling above all feelings. It's the first emotion that comes up in my marriage, with my children, with my business, and with people that get in the way of what I think I deserve and am entitled to get.

I have taught the people around me that when I get angry they should agree with me and run. My anger commands power over others. I like the control that the threat of anger provides me. I don't have to use it as often as I used to—the thought of my anger arising scares people into submission. It's one of the laziest control techniques I have in my arsenal.

When anger surfaces, I think I'm defenseless. People and their opinions should just run because I am at anger's mercy. On some level, I love to get angry and I don't try to control it. I reason with myself that I can always make my amends to people later, after the consequences of my anger appear and the emotion dissipates. The cycle continues because I rationalize my behavior with amends but then change nothing.

When the Spirit of God and my Spirit entered my life in recovery, they told me that this behavior and cycle will not do anymore. It was no longer acceptable. I am on a path, moment by moment, where I to go to war with this angry part of me as it comes up with God by my side.

I made a covenant with the Spirit of God to serve for two years. I committed to the idea that no matter how justified the anger is, I was going to have to prepare for it before it even gets here. I figured I had nothing better to do. I was out of my own hare-brained solutions and was up for a challenge.

A big question in one of my letters to God was: why is it so easy to get so angry and why does it seem so hard to get unangry? God said: anger or no anger, these were positioning statements when my motives are not met.

I thought once I got to anger, there was nothing I could do to shut it down. I thought there was no stopping the momentum behind the rage, the years of pent-up anger, that fueled my current behavior. Mike would tell me, in Spirit, what if you're not half as angry as you think you are? Could you be willing to be willing to believe that's true?

I thought, what the hell? Let's give it a try. I had an instant epiphany with the concept of being half as angry as I thought I was. The other part is, what if I just haven't remembered and I might not be angry at all? This blew my mind and it caught me off guard. This is almost automatic today. The part of me that wants to be angry comes along for the ride, too. But I don't have to buy in to being a victim of anger. I can disarm this emotion by questioning if it's even real, or if I just think it is.

What if I was just used to believing the anger is always so and real? The entity of anger—what if I haven't remembered it isn't as big as I thought it was? What if your inner angry dude just wants you to think you have to be angry because you still serve him as a master? Could you be willing to be willing to believe you might not be in love with your angry dude?

What if I changed the word anger to a little pissed? What would it look like if a little humility could process right in the middle of a little pissed? I might have some gratitude for not being a lot pissed anymore. A little pissed is so much smaller and manageable deep within me than full-on anger. The anger is every shitty thing that's ever happened balled into one, and I bring it into everything that's about to happen.

This is about pretending that this shift is really going on within me, a transformation for just one minute, in real time. That change means that now is like never before. All my shit is in the "God's got it garage", until I decide to take it out again and rift through it.

What if I just haven't remembered that it's already done? I'm not angry, I'm just used to allowing myself to tell people that I am. Anger is almost like a good conversation piece. What if I'm not? What if I haven't remembered that I'm probably not, that it's an automated response? What if I could pretend that this is true for a minute, just like everybody else is? Welcome to changing one time in real time and then I'm allowed to go back to being really angry. Come to find out, the motive behind that is that I just really like it. Maybe I can learn to like it less, and to like the principled part of me more.

Inventory

How this affects my...

Self-esteem - I have to get angry with people first before they get angry with me, I fight their anger with my anger

Pride - If people would just do what I need them to do, I would not have to get angry towards them

Security - When people don't agree or go my way with what I believe is true or with what I deserve, this is a great time to be angry

Ambition - I like to believe that my anger is the only way to react because I say I've always been this way; Spirit says, 'but what if you're not? You're only angry because you say you are'

Men - When angry, I'm just being like every other man that I come across that is taught to be angry; this is an excuse I use because I was taught it's part of my DNA

Women - I get angry with women because I thought they were weak and didn't really have anything to say that I needed to hear; when women tell me no, I lose my mind

Pocketbook - Not having enough resources to support my household makes me crazy, depressed, and suicidal at times; I was always taught to work as little as possible and expect the most money possible for it

My Part

How Am I...
Dishonest - I believe I have justified anger because I have to; I taught myself well and I blame my dad and teachers for making this ok and just a way to be
Selfish - I did not care how my anger hurts or affects people
Self-seeking - I love to pick fights with my opinions and show people that they're wrong, it's a fucking hobby
Afraid - I won't ever find the courage to internalize the belief system of justified anger

5 Fears

1. Fear of looking weak/wrong
2. Fear of not having justified anger (what would I do without it?)
3. Fear of finding peace in my heart and Spirit
4. Fear of not fighting with people
5. Fear of not taking other people's anger so personally

Resentment to God

For allowing people and myself to become this way; for making my path to change seem so difficult

Corrective Measures

1. When anger comes up, walk away and write a prayer to God instead of blowing up
2. Write a letter to God about making it easy to let go of justified anger

Integrity Warrior

Betrayal

The deepest wound I could think I have is betrayal. I am the best victim. I convince myself that I have been wronged in an unimaginable way and then play that up until I have no responsibility left in the situation. I have a standard of the people in my life. It says that they are not allowed to ever change their mind when they say they will be there for me. If this happens and they do, I have predetermined they are betraying me and their intentions originate from a bad, spiteful, selfish place. I have a contract that dictates these people need to stay positioned to be able to do what I need when I must have it. If this does not come to fruition, it is their fault I feel betrayed. This was very real for me for a long time.

Betrayal is aheavy word or expression of how deeply I am wounded by people. Friends, family, kids, spouses—they can all betray me. This is not a word I ever used lightly. Betrayal is a vicious act that will cause pain and suffering to someone, and it is usually on purpose. There is never notice given in betrayal and it cuts to the core.

I betray people mentally and emotionally with intent. I do this because I can. There came a time in my recovery when my Spirit said that it was time to inventory when I have betrayed people. I also made an inventory of why I blamed them for my actions. This was a revelation. At that moment, I was tired of living in my past and was ready to look at how I was involved and invested in this belief system. It was a moment when my sponsor became a spiritual guide into the inner workings of what I have thought and felt about my past actions. We were able to find a spiritual path out of who I acted like into who I wanted to be.

One of the ways I found out I've betrayed people was by holding old behaviors against them. My need to blame people for my hard life was categorized as a betrayal in my head because I did this to people in my life at the time. Usually, they had not harmed me today or even in recent history. I had to start making amends to my wife and children for all my dishonesty, disrespect, and the horrible ways I have treated and talked to them. In order to move closer to a spiritual path, my recognition and acknowledgment of my betrayal behaviors had to be exposed voluntarily. I found I was given the courage to begin to live outside disrespect and betrayal. First I began to go down this path.

Inventory

How this affects my...
Self-esteem - I expect people to ask me if they can betray me before they do, it's just common courtesy
Pride - I don't tolerate being betrayed; I convinced myself it is painful when usually my feelings get hurt but I really don't have feelings
Security - I don't feel bad when I ruthlessly take from people, my conscience is clean

Ambition - When anyone takes something or receives what I should have I conveniently feel betrayed
Men - Men don't betray me until they do
Women - I expect more from women, I get very possessive but only with women; I feel justified betraying women, relationships are only supposed to last so long as women obey me
Pocketbook - I have a false sense of thinking I deserve more because of my life and being betrayed; I should not be expected to do as much as everyone else, I should have privilege

My Part

How Am I...
Dishonest - I prefer to be the best betrayer rather than be betrayed; I don't feel bad about betraying people even though I act like I do
Selfish - I don't need people to have or share opinions about what I do to them
Self-seeking - Betrayal to me needs to be punished on some level
Afraid - Of the things I do to hurt people will come back to harm me; of not growing up and continuing to obey the dark behavior

5 Fears

1. Fear of being betrayed in some way
2. Fear of being loyal
3. Fear of not falling out of love with betrayal
4. Fear of forgiveness
5. Fear of giving people a second, third, or fourth chance

Resentment to God

For betraying me during the times I needed his courage to not do harm

Corrective Measures

1. List three examples that say how I am betrayed and how I have betrayed the same way
2. Make amends to someone who you have betrayed with your actions or thoughts

Blame

I have a love affair with blaming. There is nothing like a beautiful, calm afternoon of blaming everything on everyone else. I blame for what I don't have, everything I can't do or control, what I can't get from other people, the list goes on. It's my favorite to blame God. It's so easy. Everyone does it. Right?

When I came into the rooms of recovery after being committed to addiction for thirty years, I had nothing. No money, no food, and the mortgage was six months late. I was about to lose the house, too. I could not stop blaming everything that was wrong on the people that did not help or give us assistance. I never knew how to take responsibility until my sponsor told me to stop and just shut up. Being jarred back into reality did not come instantaneously. I thought it was in my nature to blame and that it was my birthright.

Even today, 14 years sober, I find myself blaming something on somebody at times. I blame people for not understanding me, for not feeling sorry for me, for that big pay cut I just got, the kids for putting me in a bad mood, whatever it may be.

Now, let's talk about what I do when I get blamed for things. Sometimes, I throw a fit and argue. That's when I'm not being very spiritual. Other times, I go to work and tell everyone that if someone needs to get mad, blame someone for something, or if they're having a bad day and want to yell at someone, bring it to me. I love to think that I can be that guy people can take it out on instead of someone else. I think I can handle it. I get it, I took out my frustration, anger, etc. on people for decades. I'm spiritually awake and I won't take it personally. It's exhilarating to be bitched at knowing that it isn't my responsibility to do anything but listen.

Blame was one of the most crucial things on this path that the Spirit of God pushed back onto me. He told me that school was in session and that this blame shit won't do. I tell myself that anything I blamed God for is a lie. I feed myself bad information and blame people for things that they did when it was really me. I spread lies and blame God for what he did not do for me. There's a part of me that shines here—it is the lying little bastard I like to entertain. This part of me keeps me going in all the wrong directions.

One day, I wrote a piece of inventory asking my Spirit about why I need people to not blame me for things I did or did not do? What is the opposite of not being willing to blame? Can I wake up to the point where anyone can blame me for anything, and I say OK without argument? What can I do to make it be this way forever?

Inventory

How this affects my...

Self-esteem - Blame makes me feel better when the world feels like it's caving in; it's

how I hit people back that harm me and talk about me, they do the same thing as me so it's OK
Pride - My pride gets better when I can blame people for things that they do not even do; it feeds my deviousness
Security - I really only think about myself; I will lie, cheat, and steal on some level by blaming people for my shortcomings
Ambition - Blame helps me get people out of the way of things I might or do want
Men - Men lie and blame me for things, I just get even; blame is a perfect weapon to use
Women - I blame women for everything I don't get from them; I always give women a chance to change if they don't do right (how nice of me)
Pocketbook - Money, jobs, and coworkers are always to blame for my problems; I feel sorry for myself first and then I start to blame like clockwork, it just kicks in

My Part

How Am I...
Dishonest - Most of the things I blame people for are not true; I make stuff up to hurt people or to make myself feel better
Selfish - I rage on people that blame me for what I say and do; most of what they say about me must be true or I would not have so much anger
Self-seeking - I use blame blindly to hurt people or better my reputation, I really don't care about how I hurt people, deep inside I am shallow and really don't have a problem with it
Afraid - Of being blamed for things in public that I did but cannot get honest about; I blamed stuff quietly so no one will know it's true

5 Fears

1. Fear of being brutally honest
2. Fear of not gossiping and blaming others
3. Fear of not making blame my business
4. Fear of judging people that judge me (half of it is true, I do some shady stuff)
5. Fear of being blamed for anything I do

Resentment to God

For not allowing me to fix or control my life; for making me need to blame when I think I need to

Corrective Measures

1. Take responsibility for something I would usually blame on someone else
2. Agree with someone when they blame me for something I did do (don't defend myself)

Caring

I only care about people that care for me and have proved it. When I say care for me, I mean my controlling, selfish, judgmental nature. I expect people to overlook these behaviors and aspects of my personality. However, if they are controlling, selfish, or judgmental in their nature, I decide I don't have to care about them. Caring is a sick subject between me and Spirit.

I say that I've always been this way, but Spirit says that I am only this way today because caring means I have to go first. I think about if I really care for anything, and the answer is I don't. Where I come from, it isn't really cool unless it's a manipulative tactic and I need something from someone. Then, it's acceptable to pretend to care. I almost feel like I should have a warning label that says don't care about me, I will hurt you or use you only when it is convenient.

I had to pray about this, and my first prayer to Spirit was to ask for it to be easy for me to feel like what it is like to not need to not enter this part of me today. I found a belief system that I can't care about anyone because they would one day betray me. I only think of life experiences that back this up and conveniently forget the ones that don't. Spirit pointed out that I am the one that betrays people. I judge them and don't show up to commitments, punish them for my own behavior. Me and Spirit decided that I would take a knee when this appeared in my behavior. At least two times a day I would pretend to care about two people as if my life depended on it. Because it did. Spirit said that even thinking about pretending to care about someone's best interest is a huge step on the path to spiritually caring or blessing someone on their journey.

The worst part for me is that unspoken caring in my head has never connected. My favorite way for me to keep pretending is I go to someone two times a day and say, "I see you". Once I see some of the good things in someone, and let them know about it, I feel a change in myself and see a change in them. I especially do this with people I like to hate and judge. Caring in me only happens when I tell someone and I have to care out loud.

Inventory

How this affects my...
Self-esteem - I really expect people to care more for me than I do for them, I rate this on how they show up for me and what they do for me
Pride - My caring is mostly for show, I try not to mean it because then you will expect more caring from me
Security - I need guarantees that people will care about me the way I want to be cared for, otherwise I'm not that interested
Ambition - I'm a shallow guy in the inside; I will care about you and your company if I get that raise, if not, I don't so much

Men - I don't really care about men, they're always trying to get something I want, mainly attention

Women - Women need to show me they care with their bodies being submissive to my self-righteous guy; I don't care about women, but I think I want to—this is a very deep defect

Pocketbook - If do you care about me, pay me, but I don't think that applies to me with other people

My Part

How Am I...

Dishonest - I lie about how much I do and don't care, depending on what people need to hear

Selfish - I need you to care more about me than I do for other people

Self-seeking - I prey on people that care for me because I don't want them to care about me because it comes with expectations

Afraid - Of caring about people being too much work; that people will always expect more; I can't just tell people I care without showing it

5 Fears

1. Fear of not being cared about
2. Fear of being taken advantage of if I care
3. Fear of brotherly love
4. Fear of not having expectations
5. Fear of my Spirit abandoning me if I don't begin to care about some of His children

Resentment to God

For caring being overrated and usually one sided, not letting me care about people until I don't, caring should be a mood that I can change

Corrective Measures

1. Treat two people I care about the way I want to be treated in two situations with each
2. Tell two people "I see you" tomorrow

Confusion/Thinking I'm Confused

I am confused when my old ways of thinking seem to no longer be working. This shows up when I can't lie, I can't tell the truth, or my conning no longer works on people. I feel stuck. This type of confusion is always related to big things. No one letting me control them wants to translate into confusion in my head. It really turns out that I'm never confused, I just like the options in front of me when I think I'm confused. I doubled down on pushing my old belief systems with relationships that won't allow me to control the outcome as I see fit.

The truth is, I was told that I'm never confused. It is a moment where I decide my next move, when I think using the idea of being confused gives me options, that's when I decide I'm confused. Usually, thinking I'm confused means I'm about to start getting angry on some level and blaming other people for my confusion. My thoughts and feelings always tell me that they have the answer when these storms come into my life, even though I don't want to admit it.

Confusion is an outburst about to happen. My belief system about confusion tells me that I must know exactly what is happening and what will happen from every angle, or else. I will deny this to the death when asked. I'm clear that my Spirit dude and principle, through me, cut through confusion when I adopt honesty, integrity, humility, and gratitude in any crisis.

My core confusion lies in the space in my head where I constantly ask why I was treated the way I was. I believe I have always been treated unfairly, and I then ask why people don't give me what I want or favor me. The work environment is the perfect setup for acting like I'm confused. There are opinions bouncing around in and outside of me constantly. My confusion is really my mind asking the question: why do I have to put up with inferior people in my life? Why can't I punish people without having to be punished for my behavior? Or is it rooted in intolerance and refusal and trying to understand others?

This is from living in the drug addict life and expecting to have leverage. If I don't have any, I use the word confusion. I'm just a lazy asshole that wants shit for free.

Inventory

How this affects my...
Self-esteem - I act confused while I look for the best, easiest way to do things
Pride - I don't need pride, I just have demands; I think I'm better even when I know I'm not, and I'm not really confused, I'm just in between what is right and wrong
Security - I like to have time and space to consider my actions when it comes to doing what is right or wrong; I expect guarantees that my choices are safe
Ambition - Without the Spirit dude I always doubt myself; old belief systems rule my judgment

Men - I give men mixed signals so they can't figure out my next move
Women - Women cannot see me confused; men cannot see me confused where women are concerned
Pocketbook - I can't figure out how to get more but I'll keep trying; I'm not willing to truly be loyal and dependable to earn more

My Part

How Am I..
Dishonest - I ask people about my confusion knowing they will give me answers I want and cosign what I think
Selfish - I know the answers of what to do in my so-called confusion, I just have no intention of doing things where I can't control the outcome
Self-seeking - I feed on other people's confusion because this is where I can be important
Afraid - Of admitting I'm not confused; I'm just terrified of honesty, integrity, and purpose today; in the form of confusing principles and behavior

5 Fears

1. Fear of not being confused
2. Fear of not being selfish and lazy
3. Fear of being asked to do too much
4. Fear of doing the next right thing when I don't want to
5. Fear of doing the opposite of what I'm scared and confused about

Resentment to God

For not saving me for myself, for not giving me clarity, for not giving me safe passage in the direction I should go today

Corrective Measures

1. When I think I'm confused, do what principle dictates instead of my motives
2. Don't say that you are confused to anyone regarding your opinion, instead ask how I can be supportive

Crybaby Shit

I was taught that I should feel bad when bad things happen. The question to God is, why? God says, "what if there are no bad or good things by spiritual standards? These are just events. Your love of complaining is a separate entity altogether."

My daughter committed suicide. We showed up to the funeral, took care of her daughters, celebrated her life, blessed her on her journey, and then we got on with our lives and raised our grandchildren, dealing with life as it came. They were 4 and 8 and here we are, ten years later. I could have whined and complained, and sometimes I did, but it didn't change the fact of what I had to do to step up. it was either step up, or don't. Do or die. My opinions on everything that had happened didn't change the fact that I had decisions to make.

Mike gave me an option of how to translate the Spirit as far as the constructs of good and bad. He said they were the same thing, just two different paths with two different outcomes. "At least for addicts", he specified. Good and bad are plainly just a different experience. I came into recovery with a deep memory of all the things I called bad that I didn't get, that I couldn't control, that made me angry beyond words. These are the things that were killing me and drove me to try suicide a couple times. I almost got it right once. There's nothing more depressing than not being able to kill yourself right. Most addicts, though, suck at killing themselves. I used to be jealous of the ones that were good at it, that got it right. Hell, sometimes I still am.

I found all these judgments, belief systems, self-pity, and anger always go back and blame something or someone for why I am so fucking unhappy and depressed. This is where my Spirit said that I might be half as angry or depressed as I think I am. Could you be willing to be willing to believe that for a moment?

I loved to be a crybaby and throw a tantrum whenever something wasn't going how I wanted it to, whatever that looked like. I felt better when I screamed and shouted and cried. What was that? Why did that expression of emotion cure everything? It didn't change shit. I love to be a crybaby because it's all I've ever known (ask my wife). For some reason, it makes me feel better when I speak my unhappiness into existence. Most of the time I'm not that upset about it but the sound of my own voice, with all the added drama from tone and cadence, riles me up further.

The question was presented by Spirit: "why do you think you need to be a cry baby about things? Could you be willing to be willing to believe that you only love being and acting this way half as much as you think you do? Just a concept to consider. Could you also consider pretending to believe that, on some level, you like not having to automatically have the anger or deep need to control everything that you can't? Imagine not needing to make people digest all your complaining. Pretend to seek a moment of not needing to think you are unsatisfied, especially with needing to control others. Imagine, in Spirit, not needing to be or do all these things that you can't stand, especially the ones that others do. Imagine a willingness to do or not do the things you crucify others for doing. Imagine for a moment your Spirit gifting you the grace and ease to change and shift all the belief systems that keep you from becoming a spiritual warrior or agent within yourself today.

Inventory

How this affects my...
Self-esteem - People need to listen to me when I'm complaining like it's the most important complaint they received that day
Pride - I can always justify my complaints and bullshit; don't know where it comes from, but I'm my own biggest fan
Security - I have to suffer more than anyone else to be ok; people need to know I suffer and feel bad for me
Ambition - I have to be the only right person in the room; people only come to feel bad for me
Men - I will take no criticism from men; no one puts me down except for me
Women - Women should want to console me and not question my motives; I expect women to always agree with me and understand and tell me how charming I am
Pocketbook - I should be able to buy people, then all would be good; things should be given to me because my life is so hard, and I shouldn't have to do anything extra to earn them but live

My Part

How Am I...
Dishonest - I cannot stand listening to people's complaints, but I expect people to be riveted by mine and give me their undivided attention when I spew negative shit
Selfish - I really only think about myself and how alone I am; my motives are for others to approve everything I do and force them to agree with me
Self-seeking - I love to listen to the sound of my own voice, especially when it's complaining
Afraid - of being quiet, to care about people that I'm not sleeping with

5 Fears

1. Fear of being humble
2. Fear of not being cared about
3. Fear of being sincere
4. Fear of acting in principle
5. Fear of not complaining

Resentment to God

For making me become this way and not giving me the desire to change and be a good person

Corrective Measures

1. Two times tomorrow, for ten minutes, shut my mouth and don't complain about anything when I want to—there has to be other people there (it's going to be horrible)
2. Let someone else complain and don't argue, say nothing but "I understand" or "That sucks, I'm sorry"

Honesty Warrior

Demanding Attention

What if I took the word demanding away and just looked at my belief system I acquired in life and my motives for acting this way? Demanding is a pushback behavior that came from abuse in my life. I subsequently decided that I would push back to the people that I thought were strong enough to take it. I especially made demands in all the traditional relationships in my life: friends, wife, kids, parents. My thought process is that they are demanding to me, so that opens the door for me to be me to be demanding to them. That brings me to my motives or reasons why I justify my demands. I prefer to call them my requests. It sounds nicer.

My motives for this topic are encompassed by my supposition that the world and its people make incredible demands of me. I rationalize my behavior by telling myself that no one should be able to tell me what to do or criticize me. There isn't one person that should be able to tell me that I need to do better when they accuse me of doing something wrong or substandard. I never admit it to them and defend myself to the death, but they are usually right. My motives are typically vindictive. When demands are made, I instantly go into defiance mode and only see it as unfairness to me.

I don't know why I freak out when people demand things of me. Maybe there is something about that word that triggers me. I would like to find out why I need to be so demanding. I know that part of it is that I get in these moods when my demanding belief system gets the green light and I have warranted it to go off. I'm not sure how that happens, I just know that it does. I get clearance from some tower in my brain to lose control and argue with anyone who challenges me.

My path has brought some internal direction. All my change must take place outside of what I think, beyond my feelings, and has to get ready to set up change in spiritual principles. This is a new arrangement being requested by me to be formed. I can only do this with the Spirit of God's help. Being demanding and shifting into not being demanding is a massive inside job. I have to request the realignment from the Spirit for the way I hope to become. My Spirit says that this is not at all about learning about being or not being demanding, this is about remembering that you are not until you choose to be again.

I will do anything for the attention I think I need. Good attention or bad attention, it does not matter. When I'm alone, I can get very depressed. The attention I find myself needing counters is sadness when I'm by myself. I get much attention with my dark opinions in crowds. Fighting is another great way to get negative attention. When I'm in jail, I have a captive audience with people just like me or even worse. When I'm condescending and feel like being hurtful with my words, I will get attention. It's guaranteed.

A lot of the attention I try to attract is full of self-pity and feels unbearable to be in. It became apparent in talks with spirit that there is nowhere I can go with this need for the attention when I'm only focused on myself. My sponsor always asked me, "how is that working for you?" The dark need for attention when it's your only option in running from what you have to offer yourself it doesn't go very well.

I came into sobriety, out of addiction, wanting so badly to have something I could no longer create for myself. Everyone around has grown tired of my frantic need for attention. I was denied at every turn, even with the ugly words and behaviors I exhibited in an increasingly desperate attempt to get attention. What now? I only had Mike and my Spirit to go to, and there were only going to talk about my part dealing with this matter. They asked, "what are you willing to be willing to pretend to do to ask for reigning in your need for attention?"

In other words, let's go down a road that is the complete opposite of everything you think and know. Starting today, let's do that two times a day. They would ask me when I needed to give someone else attention, like the kids, grandkids, or my wife, to put myself under the radar and attend to their wants or needs. When I became willing to disgustingly do something that draws attention, I was directed to go to someone else who needed something. They asked… "are you bleeding, is there a needle in your arm, are you in jail, are you in pain?" The answer was no, and then it was my job to pretend that this is not a problem for me.

Inventory

How this affects my...
Self-esteem - I love to demand attention and talking over people; I think I've earned it
Pride - I need people to see how much better I am than they are and what I do
Security - There's a part of me that must have attention or conversation from another person that makes me feel special or better
Ambition - I believe it is painful and wrong for people to not acknowledge everything I do
Men - I expect men to stroke me and make me feel important or there's a big fucking problem
Women - There is no way that I can be average or feel less than when it comes to what I do around women
Pocketbook - I think money means status and I'll be goddamned if I don't have it

My Part

How Am I...
Dishonest - I don't tolerate this behavior in anyone else and I put these people in their place
Selfish - I will be the only bitch demanding attention at any given event and the events called my life
Self-seeking - I don't allow other people to do the same stuff that I pull off when it comes to attention

Afraid - of not being mean spirited and to really be exactly how I am without hurting people and comparing and making people serve me

5 Fears

1. Fear of not being able to demand that people make me important
2. Fear of not pointing my finger at people for what I think is wrong about them
3. Fear of not becoming genuine in Spirit terms
4. Fear of not being understood and interpreted the way I think I should be
5. Fear of being an average person without recognition
6. Fear of not believing what people have told me about me that is negative

Resentment to God

For not giving me the power to not command the attention I want' for making me see my part in the behavior I can't stand in other people

Corrective Measures

1. Make amends to someone I demand attention from
2. Pay attention to someone else without strings attached

Purpose Warrior

Defiance

Defiance is a drug in and of itself. It should be FDA regulated on the highest level. It's one of my favorite words and sides of my personality. It means that I can't let you control me or tell me what to do. However, I have a contract that reads that no one can be defiant towards me. I like to tell myself that it's because I am more important, have more power, and am superior. In reality, it's because I am a big baby and I can't handle it.

With the myriad of issues I picked up throughout my life, I have to be defiant. I know so, because supposedly I know me better than anyone else. Turns out, I'm just a slave to my behavior. I like to believe that how I act is who I am, but actually it is how I justify my behavior when I don't like what you do or say to me.

My specific breed of defiance mandates that people will not have their way with me. Even worse for my dark dude self, I believe that the way I see things is the truth. Always, no matter what. I am the superstar right-fighter and will provide you with the lowest of blows until you get off my back and submit. I know this can't be true, but I don't care. I exaggerate things to the death and blatantly lie and twist things to suit me. I have a love affair with this set of conduct.

I took a deep look over the past few years at why I am so internally defiant. Why do I push back so hard at surrendering anything? It doesn't matter where it comes from, I discovered. I feel a strong urge within me to push back in defiance. It's like a survival instinct, a reflex of mass proportions. At the same time, I know what I think and feel cannot be right in any way. It's funny when I can see my own bullshit. This is nothing new for me. I've been defiant for so long, just for the love of the sport of defiance. I believe it is just how I was designed. Turns out, it's just how I behave.

I made a wish to go down a path with Spirit and began to be different. Even if it seems like it hurts, it never really hurt at all, it just feels like it should. Not reacting on people and being defiant happens, one person and one situation at a time. My Spirit tells me it does not matter if I am defiant or not. Each way is a different way and a different experience. I'm told I have to have the courage to be defiant, otherwise I would not know when I was not defiant. My defiance is arrogance, condescension, manipulation, judgment, and mean-spiritedness.

Inventory

How this affects my...
Self-esteem - I need to win, I need to be right, because I think I have to be; what if this is not true, says Spirit
Pride - I like to push my way of thinking and my opinions on people, mostly because I've done it for so long

Security - Defiance or being defiant is so easy to do; I like to take hearts, minds, money, and women; I was taught that this is what being a real man is about, that's my excuse anyway
Ambition - When I'm defiant, I'm going to win at something, if I can't win, it seems like I can't breathe
Men - I am defiant to men before they can be to me, better if I go first, I've convinced myself this is true
Women - Women are not supposed to be defiant towards me, I'm a hypocrite here
Pocketbook - I'm defiant when I don't think I get enough or too much is expected for what I do; I'm a great thief when I have to have something; at the end of the day, I really just take and don't give

My Part

How Am I...
Dishonest - I cannot tell people all the ways I'm defiant, it's all in the little things I do
Selfish - I really have no problem loving the dark side of what I do and don't do; people don't deserve what I can do, I'm selfish to the core until I'm not
Self-seeking - I always question people on why they won't measure up to me, why don't you? Why did you? What are you thinking? This is a great part of my defiance
Afraid - Of my defiance haunting me in every relationship I might have in life; I'm afraid people won't want me around

5 Fears

1. Fear of not allowing myself to be a good, principled man
2. Fear of not allowing the spirit of God to enter me and my defiance
3. Fear of integrity
4. Fear of living in the present without remembering the past and using it to push back
5. Fear of pretending to be tolerant, humble, and kind, what could it hurt?

Resentment to God

For making me unchangeable, unteachable, and unattached to everything I think I know

Corrective Measures

1. Find two small ways I am defiant every day at work or at home and take a knee
2. Write a letter to God asking this to be half as big as I think it is

Dominate

Dominating is easy to do, but not as easy to pull off. I have the gift of being able to push my ideas and belief systems on select people that will be willing to submit to my thoughts and ideas. There will always be someone to dominate, the goal is to find the right person. I choose when it is time to move on, to spin my fantasy world in another arena. In the game, I always had to dominate my space, my drugs, and my women. Everyone else was trying to do the same thing. Dominating others is required to survive and get what is needed to continue that journey. I was my own alpha dog in a very limited pack; I would only accept new members if they played by my rules. For me, it was four or five days of being up at a time, always on. Dominating is awesome, it feels like power; until it doesn't.

I was taught to try to dominate women and it showed in my relationships with my wife. The funny thing is, I have found that just because someone lets me be dominating, that doesn't mean that it will continue forever. t some point, they will put an end to my antics. This occurs especially in sobriety. The reason this shift takes place is because they wake up and no longer want the experience of being dominated. This change is shocking and jarring for a dominating person like me. I feel like my world is shattered when I'm still in that dominant belief system of entitlement, thirst for power, and control and I'm left with no one to take it out on.

When I don't have the domination aspect, the thought of leaving the relationship comes out swinging. I think I can find someone else to put up with my shit. On the other hand, I also consider if I am willing to walk away from all of this. But then, I have to identify, what is the this part? What brings me the hesitation in going after my wants like I always have before?

When I came into the 12-step process, I had a man propose we could walk down the road of thinking I needed to be dominant together. He suggested that we try to see if I could find a path with Spirit to examine how easy or hard it might be to wish to no longer need to be in love with thinking I had to dominate anything or anyone. He said it might be the easiest thing I ever did, even though it felt like I was dying.

Inventory

How this affects my...
Self-esteem - I fulfill a need I think I have to have power in areas of my life that I think I do not; I think I suffer in these areas, so I seek to dominate to relieve some kind of suffering
Pride - My pride inserts power;. I am in love with what my pride drives me to do; my pride is what I call God; it's always dangerous and I think I love danger
Security - The security is in the hunt to have the power to dominate, whether it is real or not doesn't matter, it is in the existence of the possibility, the fun is in thinking I can within myself; it can get ugly

Ambition - To make sure I am beneath no one, that I am above someone on some level, I seek satisfaction and this path gets it for me immediately
Men - It's more like don't let men dominate; I really don't mess with men too much, they're bullies
Women - I can't just ask for what I want, they might say no, so I think I need to position myself to ambush or take advantage of women; I found out there was a problem within myself about being told no; I think I must dominate at all costs
Pocketbook - I would pay anything to dominate people without pushback

My Part

How Am I...
Dishonest - I have to deny that I am doing anything wrong; I deny telling myself this is wrong to be this way, but my dark side says shut up and be a man
Selfish - I think I don't need to care about anyone when I do; I have a belief system that says I should take what I want from people, they don't know what they need till I deliver it to them
Self-seeking - I'm in love with the idea of overpowering people because I can; I don't feel depressed when I act this way, so it must be good for me
Afraid - To be taken advantage of, of receiving all the things I like to do to other people

5 Fears

1. Fear of the unknown when it comes to acting on principles
2. Fear of getting caught
3. Fear of telling on myself
4. Fear of being dominated
5. Fear of killing belief systems

Resentment to God

For not finding me an alternative way to not feel so powerless, and feeling sorry for myself; now I am reaching to be open to the God piece

Corrective Measures

1. Make amends to someone who I'd like to dominate
2. Write a prayer to God asking to fall out of love, just a little bit, with dominating other people

Expectations of the Family

It was so easy to beat my family to death shortly after I got sober. I thought they should treat me like nothing happened for 25 years. I truly believed that since I wasn't doing drugs anymore, that all should be forgiven and forgotten. I thought I should have been off the hook. I did the unthinkable—getting sober—and should be rewarded by permission to do whatever I wanted.

My delusional thinking about my family tells me that if I act better, I expect no one to hold the old behavior against me. The truth is that I really don't want to hear about how I hurt you. The kicker was that I was still doing the same shit, just not high. I thought that because I was sober and an asshole, it was much better, so I was therefore exempt from criticism. I would tell them that I wasn't a liar anymore, that I wanted all my old privileges back (including being welcomed by my wife into the bedroom again), and I expected everyone in the family to do what I tell you to do so I can rightfully return to the head of the table. If I could snap back, why couldn't they? I decided they were self-righteous and vindictive and felt justified in this conviction.

Even though they were sick of the sound of my voice and of seeing me, I expected them to push aside their experiences, disappointments, and anger around who I had been for the last two decades. This was my new hustle; I had just moved the con into my home.

The result? Shocker… they told me to fuck off, shut up, follow their rules, spare them my opinion, and to be a passive member of the household. Explaining they had done just fine without me, they gave me the option of staying and keeping myself in line or of promptly getting out. I was shocked by this ultimatum. Being self-righteous and strongly attached to being right, I felt wronged. I felt rejected. I was in self-pity and angry. I also knew that I didn't want to be kicked out of my home.

For the past 14 years, I decided to stand down. I have made it acceptable to take care of everything for my extended family. Those orders came through Spirit—I knew if I didn't do it all, I wouldn't survive. When I say everything, I mean taking care of the house, doing the chores, being the financial support, and going to get a candy bar at 11pm because my wife asked me to. And I mean all of it. Or at least pretend to.

When I want to get irritated by the fact that no one has taken the trash out for the last eight years, and I see the full trash bin, I take a breath and invite Spirit in. I realized that it takes 30 seconds to tie up the bag, walk it out to the trash can, and put in a new bag. I could choose to make it a big deal, but why? Instead, I spend thirty seconds of taking care of the issue instead of giving myself a coronary. It's an easy choice once I take out my expectations.

Inventory

How this affects my...
Self-esteem - I really don't care about anything I did to the family, and I really have no remorse
Pride - People don't see the family disrespecting me, I expect better
Security - I need them to believe anything I say, the lies and the truth are the same thing
Ambition - I believe I own these people; I do not suffer consequences for what I did to them
Men - Men don't see my family treating me with anything but respect
Women - Do as I say or suffer the consequences; women don't tell me no
Pocketbook - What is theirs is mine, these people work for me but don't know it

My Part

How Am I...
Dishonest - I put expectations on every breath they take but don't dare put an expectation on me; I act like I care, but I'm not capable
Selfish - I'm really just out for myself and don't give a damn about them
Self-seeking - I want to take credit for everything that's good and blame for everything that isn't
Afraid - of serving my family unconditionally like a principled person would; afraid of caring without expectations

5 Fears

1. Fear of having to do too much for people
2. Fear of humility
3. Fear of caring more about other people than about myself
4. Fear of not being recognized as the most important
5. Fear of having to earn respect

Resentment to God

For letting things get to this

Corrective Measures

1. Open amend to family members
2. Shut my mouth and not criticize or control for a day

Fairness

Fairness is merely a judgment I make. I'm happy and everything seems great when I'm treated fairly, but when I think I'm not being treated this way, I demand to set things straight. I make this demand immediately and expect it to carry weight. It's never an option for me to not speak up. I gauge fairness using my mind and feelings, which is very dangerous. I recognize that I can be crazy and a little unstable at times, and I'm really not the best judge of what is fair for me. My inherent selfishness gets in the way. I realize that only my rules apply here.

I like to think I treat people well when I'm treated fairly. That is a lie, because I only do this when my motives come into play. I have a chip on my shoulder and inherently believe that life is mostly unfair unless I get my way. When that happens, I act better until something happens that doesn't go my way; then when I realize that I haven't gotten what I want. Usually this is because someone else got it. I suck myself into a vicious cycle where my actions are dictated by what I'm getting and what I want, not by possessing character.

The only way I have been able to change this is to live and act in some principles when I don't want to. If someone gets something that I want, like a job or raise, humility tells me I have enough and I should be happy for them. I don't always believe that, but every time this happens, it's practice to it becoming second nature.

I've had a big issue over the years about believing that the Spirit of God is unfair. I felt I got the short end of the stick with how I looked, when I was rejected by people or women, that I had depression, I had shitty parents, I had to work to get ahead, how people judged me, and how people avoided me. Even though I treated people unfairly and with disrespect, I never wanted to look at that piece of the puzzle. I loved to play the victim and used that to my advantage for as long as I possibly could. Sometimes, I still do.

In sobriety, I dreaded writing inventory on all this to seek my part in the concept of fairness. The fairest part my Spirit ever gave me was the courage to change, see, and be open minded. What I began to see is that fairness is something that can only be given by me. I was granted the ability to see that fairness really has a different light when the Spirit of God in me recognizes it.

I've been unfair in my judgment and behavior throughout my life, even now. I've been offered a life where I have the opportunity to give fairness. I take this option because my life today is much worse when I decide what is fair and unfair instead of letting God decide.

Inventory

How this affects my...
Self-esteem - I could be a good guy when all is fair for me; when I think things are unfair, I give myself permission to push back until I get the treatment I think I am owed
Pride - Pride says I am always fair, especially when I'm not; I say I'm unaware when I treat people unfairly, but I know exactly what I do
Security - People need to play by my set of rules when it comes to being fair; I have to be a victim and people have to know
Ambition - I think everything in my relationship should be fair to me; I don't care about my behavior and when things are unfair or fair to others as long as I get mine
Men - Men treat me unfairly, they are just like me; I treat men unfairly because I think they owe me something and they deserve to be treated this way because they're liars and thieves
Women - Women leave me and they don't care about my desires; I treat women unfairly for the harms they are going to do to me; they deserve how I treat them because they will treat me unfairly soon and I need to get them first
Pocketbook - I make up what I think is fair; I have a belief system that I do more than others and deserve more; I have constant resentments about what I deserve and why it's unfair that I'm not getting it

My Part

How Am I...
Dishonest - My judgments and how I blame others is really not fair; I know this, but cannot be treated unfairly because I don't know how to change the reaction I think I have to have
Selfish - I demand to be treated better than others treat themselves
Self-seeking - My motives are for people to want and need to please me; people are expected to not accuse me of things I do to them; true, objective fairness does not exist in my belief systems
Afraid - Of being falsely accused, even though most of the time I have done what I've been accused of

5 Fears

1. Fear of being truly alone
2. Fear of treating people fairly
3. Fear of not being treated fairly
4. Fear of getting what I deserve
5. Fear of caring outside of myself

Resentment to God

For making me hurt people; for people treating me unfairly; for making it so hard to want to be caring and honest

Corrective Measures

1. When I think something is unfair, let it slide
2. Advocate for fairness for someone else instead of myself

Obsessions Warrior

Fake

When was I not fake? To all others, I appear to just be what I am. Being fake is just something to do when I get bored with what I'm doing or being. Sometimes I'm not fake because I forget to be. Being fake is how I made it out alive from the years of abuse in my childhood and in the using world. It saved my life over and over. Even now, I struggle to see it as negative at times. I am grateful for what this ability has done for me. It's a weird word and can be played out in many ways. When the time comes to impress people, like a woman, or just to fit in, this is my default. And it works.

I spent a lifetime trying to fit in to gain some level of access. When I'm fake, I am usually trying to be like someone else that has something I want. Most women can see it a mile away. I was always scheming. What do I have to be like to get the kind of woman I choose?

When I think I have to be fake, it's both depressing and irritating. I think and feel that I have no other choice, which I know isn't true once I'm out of it. But when I'm in that situation, I'm paralyzed and do what I've always done. When I go into fake mode, I realize I could not get the job done being genuine. So, I start being fake all the time because it has started to work better than being me. I looked at the results and learned that me wasn't working and being fake was. Easy decision all things considered.

At 44, when I came to the 12-step rooms, I was a fully loaded, fake ass, dishonest, self-righteous, defiant, condescending punk. There was nothing fake about that. One day, my Spirit let me know that when I was feeling sorry for myself, I was right on course. He said, "you actually have to have the courage to become and live like all those things you want to be and to stop being the things you don't. How do you know when you are not being self-righteous, defiant, condescending, etc., if you had not become those things first? How could you learn to be tolerant of people being these things if you did not know the experience of being intolerant for years? Tolerance is a contact sport. You and I can only gauge your tolerance in Spirit. By allowing people to do to you what you have a history of doing to them, hurting others, now you have the opportunity, with Spirit, to take a knee to these people and say 'I get it'."

Inventory

How this affects my...
Self-esteem - I deny being fake in any way; I tell myself I love myself just the way I am, it is not up for discussion or I might crumble
Pride - Pride knows the ways I'm fake and what is real; whether I'm fake or not cannot really be determined by my belief systems; I never see anything wrong with myself, it's always someone else

Security - I believe I need to say, do, and be anything I need to for my security, but I really feel that for no more than a moment
Ambition - I believe I have to be fake at times to get where I want to go in this world; I find for me it is a setback that can bite me in the ass; in the world of being an honest, good dude, it's a hard habit to break sometimes
Men - Fitting in by being fake is better than not fitting it at all; I have a belief system when I think most men are fake I conclude that I'm just feeling insecure
Women - Women probably have to be fake to tolerate me; I have acted like a predator all those years; I judge women the most for being fake out of my own self-pity
Pocketbook - If I'm not fake, I'm not conning people to pay me; being myself makes me less money

My Part

How Am I...
Dishonest - I only call out other people's fakeness publicly, but I won't call out my own
Selfish - I have to become someone that I think I'm not to get things I deserve that are not freely given; truth is, I am the person I think I am—a fake and a con
Self-seeking - I try to convince people that I'm honest and have integrity so they won't find out I'm fake
Afraid - Of waiting to receive things on my own merit; I'm afraid of people being fake to me and taking advantage of me

5 Fears

1. Fear of being humble and honest
2. Fear of I not wanting to be fake
3. Fear of old belief systems being changed
4. Fear of being exposed as a con and fake
5. Fear of letting others be fake and not judging them

Resentment to God

For pushing on me to be authentic or just go back to drugs; for pressuring me to become honest and humble

Corrective Measures

1. Choose a situation where I would usually be fake and just be myself
2. Call myself out for being fake in real time

Gratitude

Gratitude is a spiritual action that I find difficult to see or put into words. This has saved my soul. It stems from grace in action that I can choose to bring into the presence of my anger, depression, control, self-pity, jealousy, etc.

It is when I need gratitude the most when I abhor the thought of it. I pray for the Spirit of God to direct my Spirit to stand up in me completely and to have me stand down. It sounds like a wonderful experience, but it's a downright brawl sometimes. I know I have done this when I can take a knee so someone else can be right, no matter what I know or what I think. It's unbelievable to watch within myself, especially because I did not think I was capable of this Spiritual magnitude. It still makes me puke in my mouth a little bit, but it's a necessity.

When my daughter overdosed and died, gratitude did not come naturally. At first, gratitude is a performance that I might mean someday, but not now. It is not necessary to mean gratitude when I'm in it. It is the storm of shit that brews in my head. When I stew in it, pretending and moving forward with the right thing to do is really the only option that's left. I've done the other way so much that I became exhausted from the fight. In other words, gratitude within me is an intention, action, and decency that comes up and that I do without my own permission.

I don't like a lot about living in principles or being sober. I am very grateful when I don't have to sit in all my hate and misery, though. This requires me to do something and soon or decide not to and keep on truckin'. My choice, and I know the outcome either way. I'm grateful for the moments I am not in this stuff I have created in my own mind.

The part that I don't like is that I have to do something to move to the gratitude from the hate. It ain't free. It is mandatory for some of us to be ungrateful and full of extraordinary self-pity first in order to identify when gratitude shows up in a particular moment.

I have to be dishonest to know when I'm being honest. I had to quit things in order to know when I'm not quitting. I have to be controlling to know when I'm not being controlling. I could be my worst self in so many ways coming out of the addiction game and find gratitude for the courage for me to be willing to wake up again and have the Spirit rule me in my breath and heartbeat.

I'm incredibly grateful for my Spirit Dude and its ability to rouse within me and keep me from and/or threatening me to running back to that life in the game. I always had to pretend that gratitude did not suck as much as I thought it did. I had to recognize it as the greatest gift I could have ever received in this waking up process.

Inventory

How this affects my...
Self-esteem - I don't really do gratitude; I'm not wired to be grateful but I'm able to at times
Pride - Other people need to be grateful to have me around
Security - I don't need to be told what to appreciate and be grateful for, my security lies in being right and controlling people
Ambition - I'm grateful for the people and situations that go my way; I need people to get with me no matter what (I am broken in this area and I know it)
Men - I feel no gratitude for men, especially the ones that come with bullshit and opinions on how to do things
Women - I'm grateful for the ability to con and woo women to like me and do things for me
Pocketbook - I expect what I get and I don't have gratitude for it; I think I deserve everything and am grateful only when I get what I want; I blame God when I don't and sit in self-pity; I can't believe I have to work to get paid

My Part

How Am I...
Dishonest - I pull out the grateful card when I have to look a little spiritual, it hides dissatisfactions and pulls the wool over people's eyes quickly and easily
Selfish - I don't believe people when they say they are grateful in rough times, I think they make it up (because I do)
Self-seeking - I only believe the things I believe, I'm not grateful for that
Afraid - To allow myself to have gratitude; I wonder when will I see that the gift is in the give from my Spirit and not something else

5 Fears

1. Fear of not depending on myself
2. Fear of the Spirit of God moving through me
3. Fear of not letting go of old religious bullshit that blocks me from God
4. Fear of listening inside and letting someone guide me to something I can't see
5. Fear of change

Resentment to God

For never having shown up when shit hit the fan; I needed the Spirit of God to help me, although I would have never had listened anyway

Corrective Measures

1. Write a gratitude list everyday with ten things on it (and they can't repeat)
2. Tell someone you dislike you are grateful for them (for a real reason you come up with before you tell them)

Justice Warrior

Happiness

Happiness is a ball of shit mindfuck. It's an illusion and a hyped expectation. What does it even mean?

When I came into the 12-step rooms, I was very angry to be there. I thought the people talking about happiness were full of shit. Nothing made me happy, and it never really has. There are things that have made me unhappy and maybe not so unhappy, but I've never been the all-out-smiling-because-it-hurts-so-good happy. Maybe that's just me, but it is my reality.

People talk about happiness like it's something that shows up one day and makes life perfect. There's an image of everything going smoothly, of a fresh scent in the air, sounds of laughter, and no conflict. It is the most unrealistic thing I can imagine; I don't even have dreams like that. Aspiring to this is setting myself up for a big, massive failure. Plus, then I get to act like a victim when it doesn't come to fruition.

I see a lot of addicts that say they're happy. Until something comes along, all the right circumstances, to take away their happiness. Then suddenly, there's a relapse or an outburst and everything goes to hell. Happiness is an extreme that begets the other extreme.

I decided that my version of happiness was to ascend to being less unhappy. That's my path. Screw happiness. Less unhappy was so much easier to comprehend and make possible. I could make myself less unhappy almost instantly, and that was a hell of a change for me.

I've been able to live with less unhappiness through anything. My Spirit always reminds me by saying, 'what if you are only half as angry and unhappy as you think you are?' I can then follow up with other questions: what if I'm only half as offended as I think I am? What if I'm only half as sad as I think I am, in this moment alone? What if your self-pity is only half as big as you think it is? What if you're regret is half as big as it tells you, and your attachment to it is the issue at hand? What if I'm only half as dishonest as I think I am? What if I'm only half as alone as I think I am, and what do I do to cause myself to be alone? Maybe, alone is where your Spirit can dissolve old belief systems and experiences that hold you down and are killing you from the inside out. I make these challenges to each negative thought. Maybe it's invalidating, but it has saved me from insanity.

My dark side says that the answers to all these questions must be a complete and resounding 'not applicable'. He reminds me with all the voices in my head as often as I'll let him. I get stuck down in that trap and swirl around the toilet bowl of self-pity until something inside of me (or someone who tells me the truth about myself) pulls me out. I'm still wet, dirty, and miserable, but then I have a chance.

Happiness is something I'm supposed to make important, but every part of me says I'm not capable of achieving this on my own. I have found that there are moments of not finding unhappiness, and in that space, I believe happiness is a moment or moments of no pain minus bad memories. I've never done that on my own, without my Spirit.

My belief systems sit next to my Spirit. They must, to be able to move through the fights I have in my head. Spirit allows me to remember that I have all my needs met or that my needs can be forgotten to be needed. The next moments come, and there I am: happy or less unhappy. My Spirit says, 'now take this moment of no pain, bring it to consciousness, into a moment of distress and judgment. Then see what happens.

I choose to believe that happiness and unhappiness are really the same thing in Spirit world. Same path, different experience. Bringing happiness into unhappiness is a monumental experiment. I always find my part in unhappiness is my expectations being larger than life. My laziness and **Resentment to God** for letting me stay in my fake and refusal to being giving place also contribute. This is where I learned everything.

Inventory

How this affects my...
Self-esteem - I always think something is wrong if I'm not happy; as a lifelong drug addict, I mindfuck myself into trying to do something that comes in time when it comes to shifting
Pride - If I let people think I'm not happy, they will start asking deeper questions that I do not want to answer; many times I'm not happy until I remember I'm not suffering for a minute
Security - I get depressed trying to be happy instead of just being where I am and moving through it
Ambition - I think if I hang around people that look happy it will rub off on me, and maybe it does until I get alone and there I am
Men - I avoid happy men, I know sadness is coming for them; I like to watch for their meltdown; my dark dude tells me men suck and have nothing that I want
Women - Happy women drive me crazy; women don't push their happy horseshit on me
Pocketbook - I make more resources and money when I pretend to be happy; people like it when I put on a good show

My Part

How Am I...
Dishonest - I lie about being happy when people ask just to shut them up; I crave being less unhappy—that is a big world for me
Selfish - I don't like to add to the quality of people's lives unless I have motives to get something out of it
Self-seeking - I only believe half of what people say on this subject, period

Afraid - To stop searching and believe that my Spirit is here to serve the Spirit of God which will bring me to big moments of being who I'm supposed to be

5 Fears

1. Fear of walking through unhappy shit to see the experience on the other side
2. Fear of not acquiring some kind of respect and empathy to the people around me
3. Fear of constantly living in fear of the outcome of things
4. Fear of not respecting other peoples' path to happiness
5. Fear of staying and living in old, dead belief systems

Resentment to God

For leaving me alone in my unhappiness; for not resetting my mind and emotions to allow happier, easier ways to be

Corrective Measures

1. When someone is happy, let them have it and don't rain on their parade
2. Find two things that make you unhappy (small things) and pretend for a minute and see that you are half as unhappy as you think you might be

Service Warrior

Hesitation

Hesitation is a ten-cent word for a slew of behaviors that boil down to 'I don't want to right now'. I lie and promise to do all kinds of things when people are with me. My main motivation is to get them to shut up—I don't care what I commit to, I just do it to be able to exit the situation. When these people are no longer in my presence, I choose to make them insignificant to justify the fact that I'm not going to do what they want me to do. I think I like people being mad at me, and it seems to be another branch of my control tree.

There are a few types of hesitation. The uncertainty kind of hesitation leaves the door open for me to decide later. It's a flimsy commitment that leads to backing out more often than not. There is hesitation where the underlying motive is to agree with little intent of follow-through. Another avenue of hesitation comes from self-doubt and/or paranoia. I think I might not have all the information and think more scrutiny of the situation is necessary to make an informed decision. The ironic part is that I tend to not think critically and fly by the seat of my pants when it's my idea; when it's yours, I must analyze the situation and my thoughts and final decision originate from a deviant place.

I love to promise things. Getting the attention of being the "yes" guy is awesome. When the time comes, though, a big voice inside of me tells me to not do whatever I agreed to, to not show up, and that I don't want to anymore. It seems that I love disappointing people. I must—all signs point to my behavior signifies that I do. I don't even let anyone know; they always figure out I won't be there. I always did this whenever I just decided to, simple as that. It's a big part of my defiance.

However, I get mad when people say I'm inconsistent and undependable. I get in the head space where I truly believe that they should just stop asking me for anything and be happy whenever I do show up. When I decide to grace people with my presence, they should be happy with what they get. I'm like a celebrity in my own mind. My self-importance is the cornerstone of these behaviors.

I can't let this slide and just pretend it never happened. My ego won't let me. I end up going to great lengths and creating a web of detailed lies to explain why I didn't show up instead of being honest and telling people that it wasn't worth it to me. For some reason, I can't say that wasn't worth my time, my energy, so I changed my mind. Although my words do not express this, my behavior is clear. My actions show you that you are not important to me.

In the deep recesses of my thoughts, I find it acceptable for people to be let down or hurt by my not showing up, not caring enough to do so, or when I don't even let them know I can't make it. I love to cancel at the last minute; I must because I've done it for so long and will do it again gladly. These actions are quiet acts of defiance and egotism.

There's a huge piece of me in this that cannot seem to care about what other people need and how I affect that. I like to downplay what they say they need and dismiss it for what they want and reason to myself that my wants are more important than theirs. I never want to put myself out for anyone else and justify this because I say no one does this for me. This is also a lie that I conveniently use to dismiss all doubt within myself.

Coming out of addiction, I had to look at changing my mind and how it has everything to do with how I feel about no loyalty and obligations. I carry resentments, which I see as facts, that people were never there for me and have done the same things to me. It's very distorted. I'm a punisher. I pay people in the present back for what people did to me before, even people that were not in my life when these awful events happened.

I ask God, why do I do this? His response: because you can, because you have the amazing ability to be lazy and fall back on grudges on a whim. If you weren't good at this, what else could you be good at? I chuckled with God on that one. What if this isn't a bad thing? We could call hesitation being cautious, not doing what you're guided to do in the moment, or not being impulsive.

I don't really sacrifice and show up to add to the quality of people's days, but I'd like to. I say I don't know how, but I really do. I still get something out of letting people down, which taps into my motives. Mike always told me that I do what I do because I'm getting something out of it still; that I always have an agenda always running in the background. This applies to hesitation and changing my mind.

I'll always have an agenda. If it wasn't still working for me, I probably wouldn't do this. I like the control and freedom I get when I can change my mind whenever I want and feel beholden to no one.

I found this stone cold contract that says this is just who I am. My Spirit says that this is bullshit. No one has really been given a chance to hurt me because I just won't let my guard down. That adds to a big portion of my so-called insanity. I keep covering myself up with the same shit blanket hoping it'll smell nicer.

Inventory

How this affects my...
Self-esteem - I'm not committed to doing anything for anyone unless it serves me; I'm only devoted to what I want to do at any given moment
Pride - People need to take pride in the fact that I have none and expect no more from me; not coming through for people is real power
Security - I demand people to think only about me first; I should not have to do anything to earn their trust
Ambition - I push hard on people to change their mind which makes them hesitate on what they want to make me important even though I do nothing for them
Men - Men that hesitate are weak and I'm sure I let them know about it

Women - I manipulate women into not changing their minds when I need them; women should want to please me but I'm a liar and a con
Pocketbook - My time is very valuable and I get resentful when people waste my time but wasting other people's time is my favorite hobby

My Part

How Am I...
Dishonest - I reserve the right to be dishonest and feel good when I do; I pretend that I'm definitive and exacting when I am fickle
Selfish - I expect others to do the things I won't do in the time frames that I won't do them in
Self-seeking - I'm famous for only thinking of myself and what's best for me; I'm condescending and judgmental when others do this
Afraid - To be a good man and do what I say, but what if I'm not?

5 Fears

1. Fear of not being a coward
2. Fear of letting my Spirit Dude tell me what we will do in principle
3. Fear of loyalty
4. Fear of not being disgusted with myself
5. Fear of the Spirit of God molding me and relieving me of what I've done in the past
6. Fear of integrity

Resentment to God

For asking me to burn down some of the self-righteous and humble myself to a purpose that He would have me be; for asking me to do too fucking much

Corrective Measures

1. Two times this week commit to doing something you don't want to do and actually show up
2. Spontaneously say "yes" to two things in real time you usually wouldn't do

Conscience Warrior

Hurt

This chapter is about weaponizing the emotion of hurt. I get hurt over the stupidest things. I do this because the small things that aren't important help me to practice for the big things that are. Spirit tells me that they are both the same experience, the difference is how angry I get, how I justify that anger, and how long I'm angry for. I'm such a victim or have been when I think I'm hurt or when I get hurt. In reality, I'm not injured, I'm not bleeding, my ego has just been put in check. And that's usually a good thing.

I think about the experiences that set my hurt guy off. I get hurt for some of the following reasons: when people are condescending, when others try to control something I am doing, when I am criticized, when people embarrass me, when someone else takes something that I want, when people avoid me, when people don't want to hear my story (especially my wife). With all these things, I think I want or need to get hurt so I can push back on people. I do this by telling people what I think (usually not in the nicest way) and how wrong they are to do these things to me. Keep in mind, I'm the guy doing all these things to people first, justifying it, and not acknowledging it. I tell myself that they hurt me first, but that's usually not the case.

The dark side of me just loves to hurt people. I do this regularly with how I talk to and about them. I like to tally all the times I got hurt and by whom. Parents, pedophiles, priests, bad relationships, cops, dealers, the list continues. I bring all this up in my consciousness to help me wind myself up and justify the hurt I dish out to people freely. I also like to remember how God hurt me in so many ways by not granting me the people and things I think I should have gotten.

I manufacture hurt from the things that happened and the things that did not happen that I make up. I fabricate this feeling out of convenience, usually when I have ulterior motives. Whether it is outward or inward, I weaponize hurt to allow myself to treat others poorly or take revenge. I had to have someone that could make me sort through my attachment to being hurt. I could not do this by myself.

I love to live in the dichotomy of either being incredibly hurt to justify my behavior or not being hurt at all because I'm a tough guy. I claim to be either/or one minute to the next, depending on what I'm thinking about or who I'm talking to. I have a love affair with weaponizing this emotion and I don't really feel bad about it. It works for me in ways other things won't. If I tell someone my feelings were hurt, the typical response is an apology. That is a swift power change in the dynamic and I feel on top again.

Inventory

How this affects my...
Self-esteem - I don't get hurt; I hurt people
Pride - I will not be embarrassed
Security - I need to hurt you before you hurt me
Ambition - I'm never going to tell you I'm hurt, but I'll do something for you to know
Men - I manipulate men by blaming them so I can get mine
Women - I need women to know I'm hurt the worst so they shut the fuck up about what hurts them
Pocketbook - when I get hurt, I get paid

My Part

How Am I...
Dishonest - I lie about being hurt to get what I want and justify my own actions
Selfish - I have no mores for hurting others
Self-seeking - I seek to be hurt so I can tell someone about it
Afraid - To let go of what being hurt looks like

5 Fears

1. Fear of not manipulating
2. Fear of not having control
3. Fear of not having an excuse for my behavior
4. Fear of putting others first
5. Fear of not reacting

Resentment to God

That I like doing this sometimes

Corrective Measures

1. Prayer to God about beliefs regarding getting hurt
2. Two times tomorrow when I feel hurt, don't say anything

Jealousy

Why do I think I need to get jealous today? The answer usually lies in the idea I sell myself that I believe completely: I'm not getting something I am entitled to. I tell myself that I don't know how to not be jealous. The truth is, I had not found anyone I could be honest with that knew how to walk through jealousy. I had not met anyone, until Mike, that would show me my part in being jealous. He did this without wounding me with his opinions about my behavior and how bad it was.

Spirit told me that jealousy would work until it wouldn't. I have to remember that jealousy is never free. It is entitlement wrapped in control and self-pity. The perfect combination for my dark side to fall in love with and in turn justify my jealousy.

The Spirit of God told me to bless other people more than me. This was the opposite of what I've done my entire life. It was uncomfortable and I hated it. I asked for people to be smarter and more attractive than me, for them to get bonuses and raises, for them to be in the relationships they wanted and maintain the happiness I craved. I even laughed at their jokes when I didn't think they were funny.

I trained myself that I could be jealous over anything I did not get, and everything everyone else got. The truth is, I do not deserve what I had in the first place. Spirit told me that if I don't get something, it's not a punishment, it was just not meant for me. The selfish, entitled part of me came and raged at this idea.

When I came into recovery the first year, I was not at a place where I was open-minded to this idea. Even though it rang true on some level, I refused to even acknowledge how this pertained to me. What I was willing to do was to write to the Spirit dude. I wrote a letter to God about this major piece of me. Why do I think I need to be jealous? Because on some level, it fills the void of not needing to be jealous.

This belief system of my jealousy has been of great service to me. What would I have filled the jealous space with otherwise? I would have found some gratitude in all the experience I have around this and self-pity. I had to be jealous to know when I am not. I needed to focus more on where I am going instead of the burden I carry from being stuck. Pretending was not as hard as I thought by at least half.

Inventory

How this affects my...
Self-esteem - I think I'm entitled to anything I want; I don't want other people to get what I want and they can't have what I do have
Pride - The only reason I want it is because you have it, so give it to me
Security - I need to have more than you to be OK and I need you to know about it
Ambition - I want what would you have and I shouldn't have to ask for it
Men - I refuse to show other men I'm jealous and require their jealousy of me

Women - You are my property and you will thank me for it
Pocketbook - What's yours is mine and what's mine is mine

My Part

How Am I...
Dishonest - I judge others for being jealous but I'm a jealous fuck
Selfish - I compare myself to others and isolate myself as a result and to create my own suffering
Self-seeking - I do whatever is necessary to get what I want and think I need
Afraid - Of not getting out the measuring stick in every aspect of my life

5 Fears

1. Fear of gratitude
2. Fear of letting other people win
3. Fear of being equal
4. Fear of being average
5. Fear of not controlling

Resentment to God

That I believe that what other people have or do has anything to do with me

Corrective Measures

1. Congratulate someone on something you're jealous of tomorrow
2. When comparing in the moment, write a gratitude list

Justice/Fairness

Things I think should be fair: relationships, work, money. Of course, that list isn't all inclusive, but it's a start. When I say fair, what I actually mean is that these things are fair if they go my way. I see things as fair until they aren't. I love to think they aren't and that I'm not getting what I deserve. My favorite thing ever is to deem something fair or not fair, to judge whatever is happening just so I can mindfuck myself and have an opinion. Which then, of course, I am determined to share with almost everyone. Then I try to convince them. This is a con I play to myself and others as a pastime.

I have programmed myself to only think of me. I want to believe something in my childhood or my past caused it—there's no way I could have done this to myself. I have spent a lot of energy in convincing myself and others of this "fact". Every waking minute I look to blame others and past experiences for my fucked up-ness. The weird part is that I think me being obsessed with me and not feeling life is fair and having opinions about deservedness is really great. I enjoy having these disagreements and feeling unjust. The truth is, I don't feel guilty or ashamed, I feel gipped. I'm self-righteous and entitled and I like being that way.

I don't care about what other people get or deserve with justice; I only seem to care if it involves me. I care about work hours and how it affects everyone else if (and only if) it affects me either directly or indirectly. No one else may see it. I may appear to be altruistic and helpful, but I'm really not. I'm out for me, always. This is an internalized, deep part of who I am.

Before I got into the work of the 12 steps, I didn't even know what justice was. I never wanted or had the courage to see it. Justice (outward from me) is like an outcry that it shows a huge weakness that keeps me from any kind of peace or spiritual life of any kind. It consumes me and eats my lunch.

What is justice, really? It's a belief system that I fight for that may not even be real. The belief system is that I should not suffer in any way, that I've suffered enough, and that I deserve better. I do whatever it takes not to have to suffer, though I have found that isn't even the point. What others do to me, or I do to them, is suffering and I believe that it is fundamentally wrong, even if there's a point to it or it has a purpose. None of that matters if I feel wronged, though.

Another side of it is that I think I should never be questioned or shown up, even though I know my actions are off and should be confronted. I tell myself that I will not be threatened or doubted. Is any of this real or just how I thought I had to act? Is this just something I have convinced myself of?

There is only one way that justice should go for me—my way. It is always unfair if it doesn't, and I gladly deem it so. At the same time, I'm a huge liar, thief, and predator in any relationship I'm in. I say I deserve to be treated fairly, but I don't treat others with the same respect. I'm full of all kinds of beliefs that people don't deserve me to be understanding or empathetic, that they get what they deserve. However, I'm different. This hypocrisy runs deep within me.

I've been declaring that I get stuck in this harsh belief system called justice. What if I'm not? What if I just act like it?

There was all the justice stuff going on in my past. I had to write about it, inventory it, let my Spirit delete what had happened. I began to see how much of that stuff isn't present or happening presently. It was unbelievable when I saw how my old constructs of justice ruled my life and how I acted every day.

I was ordered to give and believe in the present for three minutes at a time. That was all I could handle. Only then could I see what was real and what wasn't, what was carry over from before and what lives today independent of the past. The present, the now, doesn't look at all as it did then, but I still question it regardless. Mike told me to stop that shit, too. It was because it was, is because it is. Simple as that. Me thinking whatever it is that I think just puts a spin on truth that distorts it and then gives me the green light to justify how I want to act.

These spiritual shifts concerning justice and how I view it don't accidentally happen. My Spirit within is the demolition crew when it comes to these haunting belief systems of justice and fairness. Why does what I think I need or want seem so important? It does because I have a belief system that says it does. Clear as day, it exists because I say it does. What if nothing I say, do, or believe is true in this moment? Going with that, I started writing more deeply and getting things on paper I couldn't get to with just my thoughts.

Inventory

How this affects my...
Self-esteem - I think I'm entitled to be right and get my way
Pride - I am not interested in people's excuses to not let me be right or better
Security - I know how to be arrogant and condescending, it comes naturally to me; I don't feel right having to be tolerant or humble, matter of fact it makes me angry
Ambition - I really don't care about justice for all; I expect to be favored, I think I am better than most people, most of the time
Men - I don't owe men justice at all; they are the ones pissing me off and laughing at me
Women - I hold women to a different form of justice; I expect them to know how to look at me, talk to me, and give into me; justice is sleeping with me and doing what I want no matter what
Pocketbook - I constantly feel like I should get more; I'm always a little angry and full of self-pity; I get angry at the spirit of God when it comes to money; I have no gratitude, but I hope it will come

My Part

How Am I...

Dishonest - I don't give justice unless I need something; my motive is to give as little as possible and to take everything I can

Selfish - I hold what I know about people against them, but I don't tolerate this behavior in anyone else

Self-seeking - I pretend justice is important and part of my life; I can't really see what I do honestly

Afraid - of going against everything I believe by changing everything I do

5 Fears

1. Fear of not being treated fairly
2. Fear of not hurting people
3. Fear of consequences for what I do
4. Fear of being a positive and fair person
5. Fear of changing everything I do to harm people on purpose

Resentment to God

For making it hard to give and live more with justice in my heart

Corrective Measures

1. Make amends to two people I treat unfairly, for disrespecting, judging, and harming them
2. Tell two people "I see you"

Inner Rage Warrior

Loneliness

Loneliness is yet another area of my life where I paint myself into a corner. I have the visceral need to do anything to not be alone with myself mentally, emotionally, or physically. However, I don't want to be with other people most of the time. People tend to annoy and bother me and all I do is complain when I'm with them. At the same time, I feel awful when I'm by myself. It's a lose/lose situation, and it's my favorite topic to get into self-pity about.

I believe I've always suffered from perpetual loneliness. By not having something present, like a person, I fall into a deep depression and believe I'm alone. I have a great need to not be by myself, but when I'm with groups of people outside drugs, I still feel hopelessly alone. Even in a group of people, this feeling persists.

As an only child of an only child, I was always isolated. I had some interesting family dynamics that also contributed to the situation. My father never wore clothes in the house when it was just me and my mother. I was never allowed to have friends at the house because of this, among other reasons. It wasn't an issue anyway, because I never felt comfortable having friends because of my father's strange behavior. I learned that my family was different and that this was a fact of my life.

Loneliness has continually brought on deep feelings of despair. I didn't ever think this was going to change, that I would feel this way forever. Sobriety taught me, along with Spirit, the question: what if I'm not really alone, I just assume that I am? Spirit asked me, could it be true that you have just been practicing this whole time, in loneliness, to be open to God becoming present and real in your space? What if you have been training your whole life to demonstrate instant companionship with a part of you that can only be revealed through the illusion of loneliness? What if loneliness is a rite of passage to not being alone, what if you can only see, feel, and touch? What if you have to have the courage to experience loneliness first? To be able to move into loneliness you must have great courage, you must be open to the ability to be lost in feeling and being alone.

I see those things now, having been guided to not feel loneliness. Loneliness meant that Spirit directed me to be selective with who was around me. Maybe I was spared all the talk and chatter that comes with not being alone. Loneliness may have been a gift I didn't realize the nature of until today.

Inventory

How this affects my...
Self-esteem - I push people away and blame them for my loneliness
Pride - I use this as a con to make you do what I want and get away with things
Security - I need you to know you've caused me pain
Ambition - I want to control everyone in my life and then to shut up about it

Men - I don't do without someone to cling to
Women - I control the narrative of my loneliness with women
Pocketbook - Money cures my loneliness

My Part

How Am I...
Dishonest - I only want people around when they do what I want and don't care otherwise
Selfish - I don't care if other people are lonely because I'm more important
Self-seeking - I tell people I'm lonely to get them to jump through hoops for me, but I won't do that for them
Afraid - That I don't really need other people

5 Fears

1. Fear of being alone
2. Fear of having to meet my own needs
3. Fear of relying on God
4. Fear of finding out I'm not really lonely
5. Fear of not having to con people to stay in my life

Resentment to God

For me thinking loneliness is so painful

Corrective Measures

1. When feeling lonely, write a prayer to God
2. Respect other's space and don't be pushy

Pain Points

Where I think I suffer in my life, real or not—these are categorized as pain points. I am awesome at suffering. I claim that I always suffer on some level. The reason changes like the weather: someone is getting what is mine, I'm constantly jealous, I'm being disrespected or talked down to, people won't do what I need them to do. My self-pity or my demands are like a constant high-grade fever of 103. No amount of meds or remedies from old wives' tales will make the temperature drop or treat the illness inside my mind.

These pain points are buttons that I believe are installed in me since birth. People in my life, usually those close to me, push them today. What I never realized was that I allowed them to be installed, have surveyed them routinely, and kept them current with updates and bug fixes to verify their function. I truly believe that I cannot do anything about these most of the time. Then I realized that I was wrong yet again.

My expectations are constant, and my pain is real. Expectations and demands have fed my pain points as long as I can remember. Spirit came in and said that erasing old and recent memories will now be part of the path and we will create new possibilities in principles. Will I pretend to let my pain points die? Will I really step into Spirit world? I had to get busy, writing notebooks full of four-column style inventories. After I was done with a piece, I burned it to signify that it is over, done with, and real no more. I had to at least start with pretending that those pain points, one by one, were not mine anymore.

Pain points are pain and suffering that I hold and don't even know it. The pain got comfortable because I never saw how I caused it. I thought it was always someone else's fault. I used my past experiences as excuses for my actions and to justify why these pain points still existed. Saying "I was molested" became a trump card—the most powerful in my arsenal. Anytime I really needed to get out of trouble, it worked. These pain points came in handy.

Parents, teachers, and counselors could tell me very little about pain points. They didn't know much but shared what they could. They tried to help, but it didn't touch me. 12-step programs revealed that it must be my doing and I needed to take responsibility for my role pertaining to the issue in the present. Although the situation may not have been my fault, I should search for my contribution. Whether that was in the original situation or how I mistreat people today based on experiences from the past, I had a role to play somewhere. I was never the perpetual victim of circumstance, even though I had operated under that belief system for years.

Pain points are typically bad memories of things that took place in the past. The issue becomes that I use them to guide my behavior and my reactions to what I think are the same things today. I use these experiences as ammunition by pretending to be wounded by them. This is a manipulation tool that is like a Swiss Army knife—remedies most situations when used appropriately.

I bring my pain points into every relationship. I believe I know how people should treat me and what they should do for me. When something gets said or done, and it is a familiar type of hurt, I let people know these pain points will never change. In fact, the four-column writing has to be done by me, seated with my Spiritual Master and sponsor to translate what was is not what is anymore. I am the person who must insert spiritual principles, not them. Even though the situation looks, smells, and feels like the same as in the past, it isn't. I had to stop referencing anything that happened previously. I couldn't move forward unless I burned all of that down.

In the present, my pain points have nothing to do with the situation now or then. This loop of acting out the past with judgments, dishonesty, and even cruelty to the people in my life today are throwbacks to the past. Relying on my judgment and memory of how to act when past painful situations come up won't ever work for me in real time. I keep living the same stuff over and over and blaming people for not stepping up for me and my belief systems. It's been a painful and lonely way to live. People will never meet my expectations this way. I set myself up for failure if I continue to live from the pain points in my life. I actually create new ones on top of the old ones, which is one hell of a clusterfuck.

Inventory

How this affects my...
Self-esteem - I should be able to live past pain points and should be above having the experiences in my life; I refuse to see the good in pain points; life is hard because of what happened to me
Pride - Other people should suffer based on the judgments I have set down of regret and wrong they do to themselves and to me; I'm convinced that I have to get my way when I'm not getting my way
Security - I need to not have to suffer as much as possible for me to think life is ok; all my excuses come from my needing to not suffer, which means everyone else has to change what they do to accommodate; OR I have to be wounded to be ok—there has to be something wrong so I can not be ok and blame my actions on this
Ambition - If I did not have to spend so much time with pain points, I would get to the things I want that pain points are a block to the things I deserve to get; I really blame my woundedness on the past and I refuse to not keep using it as a weapon to not do things now
Men - I expect men to stay out of my way with their complaints and self-righteous ways; I blame most bad things on men; I find it gratifying to punish men for harming me in the past
Women - Women are expected to not tell me no; when women do not serve me and take a knee to my demands, they suddenly become my enemy as a species

Pocketbook - If I don't have the money and things that I expect, I instantly think I'm in pain and life is unfair

My Part

How Am I...
Dishonest - I blame everything I don't like on somebody else; I have no intention on changing, it's got to be you
Selfish - I use being wounded as a way to get people to change now
Self-seeking - I have no intention of changing my wounded behavior; it gives me something to do
Afraid - Of not being wounded and not comparing everything to something in the past, I blame how I act today on the past as a whole

5 Fears

1. Fear of not projecting my wounded shit onto other people
2. Fear of letting people be difficult with me
3. Fear of not conning people into acting differently
4. Fear of being ready for the force of this change to come
5. Fear of exposing my wounded child

Resentment to God

For letting me know that it is my time to make this shift to really have a life

Corrective Measures

1. Don't share stories having to do with being wounded when someone else is sharing (no one-upping)
2. Make amends without blaming anyone but self for crappy behavior

Respect Warrior

People have to like me

I have a belief system set in place that people must to like me no matter what I do. If I act poorly, I expect everyone to look the other way and not hold it against me. It is a blind expectation that I like to keep. I treat this as truth.

I have found out the hard way that I have to be somewhat likable for people to be able to like me. Who would've thought? My pattern in my life has been that I judge quickly whether I like people or not. I make snap decisions about what my opinion is about someone and I stick to it. It is very hard to change my mind. However, I strongly believe that people should not do this to me.

I have a deep voice within that says I have to go into total insecurity if I'm not accepted. Loneliness that is brought about from this reaction feels like abandonment, self-pity, and anger. It is always directed to these people that keep me from being accepted instead of myself. I have always been alone because I acted like someone who cannot be accepted. My solution for my own reactions. I always seem to be able to make problems about other people instead of taking responsibility for what is mine. This massive insecurity was the reason that I sold weed to all my clients. The weed guy is always loved and accepted.

At 44, I came into this path with Spirit and principles. There are horrible rules that I have to follow that no one else does. These included the commitment to begin respecting people. It doesn't matter if they like me or not. Everyone is deserving of respect and good treatment, even if this causes me to shrink humbly. This path also asked me to have the courage to have the experience of not being liked and to not react poorly. Spirit gave me this blessing prayer to these people (especially in traffic), the people I really get angry at. I pray, "God, bless this asshole that judges me and lets me know they don't like me. Give this person all the blessings you have for me. Bless his family and everyone he cares for. Bring your grace and ease into this moment."

The last few years, between years 12 and 14 of my sobriety, my prayer became that I had a wish to not be a slave to people loving me. Also, to sex and all that's about and fear. I wanted to allow my Spirit to let good things and bad things being true equally and remembering all that stuff might be half as big as I make it. The path is to be more principled, honest, and at least pretend to care until I actually do. If I work on taking care of the things within me that I judge other people for, a shift takes place. Every day seems to be a new lifetime. Nothing from yesterday applies today in my life.

Inventory

How this affects my...

Self-esteem - People have to meet my level of happiness

Pride - I have to control people temperament with a big smile and an expectation; if they don't match it, something is wrong with them

Security - People have to show me that they like me in order for me to not get full of self-doubt
Ambition - I will torture people into acting a way that I can see that they like me and want to do things for me
Men - I expect men to prove themselves to me by making up shit for them to do and I want them to know I'll throw a fit if they don't
Women - It is my fucked up belief that women have to like me for me to be OK and if not, I talk shit about them
Pocketbook - This has nothing to do with money

My Part

How Am I...
Dishonest - I deny this shit all day long; I would never look at this perfect part of me, I love this behavior
Selfish - I shouldn't have to change a thing about my personality for people to think highly of me; I really don't give a shit anyway, I just think I do
Self-seeking - I really only want to think and do what's best for me and what I want
Afraid - Of growing up and letting people be exactly where they are without having to change who they are and what they do

5 Fears

1. Fear of change being easy
2. Fear of getting comfortable with people not liking me so much
3. Fear of being average
4. Fear of being myself and calming down
5. Fear of not controlling people with my mood

Resentment to God

For not giving me the power to control and affect people to meet my needs

Corrective Measures

1. Amends to someone who you think should like you but doesn't
2. Amends to someone you try to control with your mood

Pride

Pride is how I tell people my way is the best way. If you don't do things the way I believe is best, I turn into an arrogant dick. If you are not like me, it follows that you are not good enough. After making this determination, I will then take it upon myself to let each and every person I know that this is the case. All the shit that I have inside of me falls under a dark cloud disguised as pride. I really think this is me. And most of the time, I really think this works well.

A lot of people look at their pride differently. I hurt you or do not show up for you because my pride made that decision. Truthfully, I did not show up because I found a better place to be.

There is good pride, too. For example, pride in work ethic or pride in being honest. This is not the topic of this chapter. What I'm talking about here is the pride that comes with me from where I come from, not from what I hope to be.

My pride is formed from the lowest level of my own expectation of how I need to be. I claim to be working from a place of positive pride, but what I do and how I treat people comes from a selfish, self-pity, controlling place. My pride is built on the foundation that I do what is best for me, no matter what. And I think I'm great at disguising this, so no one knows.

The problem is, I like it this way. I've convinced myself it's best. I get angry and resentful, and I can't seem to make people accommodate my picture of reality. My picture of reality is that people and God need to owe me a certain way of being treated. My pride is my minimum standard of how people need to let me operate. People talk about my pride being hurt, but my secret is no one can see that I hurt back.

My question for Spirit is, why do I need to hurt people back when it feels like someone hurts my pride? The answer is, because I think I need to. People hurt my pride and that might just be an illusion that I create to get attention that I give yourself. It must bring me some joy, or else I would not keep needing to participate in this cycle.

Moving through pride is a path. People have to keep stepping on my pride for me to have the opportunity to see that its origin is false. This is the natural order of things so I can find a spiritual path to facing it and understand that principles that are a substitute.

Inventory

How this affects my...
Self-esteem - Pride makes me feel more powerful on command then the people I view as less than me
Pride - This is the one thing that keeps me from wanting to commit suicide sometimes; this is my path to help and a future of some kind

Security - Pride is always accessible to do the heavy pushing I need to be OK, or at least pretend to need to be; it is my life force field in the middle of a big world
Ambition - This gives me false hope that I'm better than others when I need to be
Men - My pride makes me feel equal around men; whether this is good or bad, it allows me to breathe
Women - My pride kills me around women, it makes me feel like they owe me something; that they need to like me and it's my job to force them somehow
Pocketbook - I have a set standard of what I think I should get with money or resources

My Part

How Am I...
Dishonest - With myself about the value of my dark side pride; working to create good spiritual pride seems like a chore, but it really isn't
Selfish - I think other people's pride is just an excuse for how they want to control me or rate me
Self-seeking - It is just set in my ways of behavior that I need to have better resentment than those of anyone else; I should be the most important, even when I'm not
Afraid - That my pride is too deep to change; that I'm a fraud if I'm humble

5 Fears

1. Fear of letting go of the pride I know
2. Fear of believing I could be wrong
3. Fear of humility
4. Fear of respecting what anyone else says or thinks because I disagree
5. Fear of pretending to not buy into my curated pride

Resentment to God

For making me believe my ways are fake and cannot serve me the way I've created them

Corrective Measures

1. Do two acts of anonymous kindness and don't tell anyone about it
2. Don't take credit for something you usually would

Procrastination

I love to procrastinate. Whenever I'm in the middle of procrastinating, it never feels bad. I do it today because I still get power out of it. I love to put off stuff or decide I won't do it. I do this mostly because someone's told me to. It's one of those samurai defects, the giant defiant part of me that won't quit. He's a big motherfucker who won't back down and is super pushy. I think procrastination should be a professional sport. Whoever lies or hurts people the most is the winner today!

I have a contract that says people don't tell me what to do and really should not expect me to do the things I say I will when I say I'm going to do them. Expecting consistency is pointless from me. I reserve the right to be on the inside, undependable when I want. I don't think I have a problem with that—my actions dictate that.

Procrastination is me saying I really don't fucking want to, and I'll put it off as long as possible to see if that will make it go away. If, at that point, I have to do whatever I've been putting off (or else some serious shit will happen), then I'll half ass it to keep the cycle going.

Almost always, I already know what I will or won't do when I've been asked. I say I will no matter the decision. As an addict, I justified how I show up a long time ago. Why stop now? I take no one's feelings into consideration. I base these decisions on grudges and anger about people from years ago that still fuels my internal fire. I punish people today because of my history and decide that it isn't important that they don't know they're doing the punishment for other people's crimes. It makes me feel better, so who cares?

I prefer to only see where people let me down and blow me off. Why would I ever look at my part and how I do the same stuff everyday? It's scary to look at my behavior and think about changing it. Looking through the lens of being a victim makes my life easier and allows me to be irresponsible with the added bonus of getting away with it.

Somewhere in the drug life over 30 years, I decided whatever people did to hurt or lie to me this was not going to be the way I lived my life pushing out. I had to be almost reincarnated in the journey of sobriety. I had no clue how to change, nor could I find the desire to. This is the shit I thought about every night, deep in the dark when no one could reach me or even cared to.

When I came into the 12-step program of my choice, the drug rooms, I could not breathe. My hate and intolerance were eating me alive. They were all that kept me going. This woke when it was black outside and the rest of the world was asleep. My dark dude was up and dancing, manipulating me into being a piece of shit who would make him proud.

The phrases and the fluffy bullshit talk in recovery and in the rooms had no real truth or weight for me. I couldn't find a way out with their words. I rarely saw anyone go past 6 months of continuous sobriety. Mike was the opposite. He said that my nature, as is, will devour my spiritual self as I knew it. We have to fortify your spiritual nature, he told me, by breaking down your daily worship of being dark. We have to find a way to fall out of love with some of that. It's ok to finally admit that I really serve, have always served, and love my dark side because of everything it's done for me. I couldn't change who I was until I embraced every part of me that I had tried to hide from other people. After this, I had to set upon a path where I created a spiritual nature that was capable of doing battle with my old belief systems.

I talked about Spirit stuff, but in the middle of the night I couldn't bring it up. When I was alone and afraid, the dark dude was all I had. I had to make a covenant with a spiritual path because otherwise it wouldn't stick when the sun went down.

Inventory

How this affects my...
Self-esteem - I like to procrastinate the things people tell me to do; I love this defiant part of me
Pride - I have no pride in this; the issue is when people put off the things I want to control them to do
Security - I need people to do the things they say they will in my time frame to be ok
Ambition - People do not blow me off, they don't procrastinate on what I think is important
Men - I put heavy expectations on men to perform; I'm consumed with control
Women - I'm only demanding with women when it has to do with what I want or sleeping with them
Pocketbook - I don't really procrastinate when I'm getting paid or stealing money

My Part

How Am I...
Dishonest - I procrastinate all day when it comes to doing what other people want me to or things I have no intention of doing
Selfish - I really only care about when I want to get, not give
Self-seeking - I expect way more from other people than I do myself; I can always justify what I do
Afraid - Of finding it in me and my Spirit to value other people's time and needs

5 Fears

1. Fear of getting out of my bullshit and being there for people
2. Fear of getting honest about this part openly
3. Fear of people telling me what to do
4. Fear of not expecting people to do what I want
5. Fear of not having expectations

Resentment to God

For not allowing my procrastination and hypocrisy to do anymore

Corrective Measures

1. Find two people to make amends to when it comes to procrastinating what they want
2. Make a list of five things I'm procrastinating on and ask someone to oversee my doing them and hold me accountable on a timeframe

Internal Warrior

Promises

For many years there was never a promise I intended to keep. Of course, this was unless it was for drugs, sex, or money. When someone else promises to do something for me, I'm making you sign a contract that you will be where you say, when you say, no matter what comes up in your life. You usually don't know this, though. If and when you don't keep your promise to me, I will hate you forever and I will let everyone know you can't be trusted. I was that kind of insecure, shallow guy my entire life. A promise is a fancy word for a set up.

On the other hand, if I make a promise, It is a big deal if I even write it down in my calendar. I will let you know if I can't hold up to the promise, but here comes my defensiveness and anger to and for you. For some reason, I can't make the promise. This almost always happens, and it's usually because the promise I made wasn't as important as what I want to do in the moment. I expect you not to hold it against me or be angry at me. I also expect you to still treat me well. I should lose nothing with you for not being able to fulfill my promise.

Today, my Spirit commands me to honor all promises. He tells me to act as if I am making the promise to God Himself. I do this or I don't make them at all. Honor and integrity are now to come into this sacred thing called a promise. It does not matter either way in the Spirit world, make it or don't make it, it's the same thing. It is a lesson and the way of this path, but with different consequences today. My Spirit makes it very clear that I made a covenant to Spirit to take a knee and to brutally bring all principles in all of today's affairs. Spirit tells me to get dishonest and then see how bringing honesty into that same situation and space changes things. If I'm being controlling, Spirit says to then bring in integrity. If defiant, then I must ask Spirit for the willingness to be willing to be humble. My Spirit says often, if someone breaks a promise to you, pretend it was God. What would you say to Him?

Promises are funny for me. I was brought up with other people's belief systems about promises. I used to condemn people that I saw making and breaking promises. When I came into Spirit world principles, I started to see a different path through the intention of promises. It wasn't really the physical or mental part, but the intent of a promise. I'm in a place, that took me years to get to, where I can see that promises are made with the best intentions of caring through and by a person. Today, I am asking to allow anyone making promises to me to be able to change that or break that because life happens. It needs to be cool. It does not matter if they tell the truth or lie, I can and must allow it as a spiritual warrior. Some of the times I'm at least aware of how I project my shit on them for not being there for me. I don't have to be so personal in my reactions. When I go to my Spirit dude, He asks that if I enjoy the experience of having someone break a promise. He says to take this lesson, and if I don't like how it feels, then I need to stop making promises and breaking them myself.

There is a dark part of me that makes promises I have no intention of keeping in a moment to get people to do things for me now. I say anything in a moment to get a promise of sex or money. If I am moving, for instance, and I need a friends help for free, I promise my ass to be there to help them move. It's called a con to friends. When the time comes to fulfill my promise, I am nowhere to be found. I'm probably hiding for a couple of days, so I don't have to listen to them to tell me the truth and hear their criticisms. I'm not capable of caring or feeling bad. There is a new Spirit part of me that might like to begin to care a little. It is demanded of me to find a way to do what I say. I have to be on time to the event and to even bring some drinks. Why? Because I don't want to. The path to God today is to find two things I have no intention of doing and do them. This is a relatively simple task. Then, God directs me that doing these intolerable things is the only place that I will find Him. It's not for everyone, but it gives me something to do. I always see the Spirit in me when I finish completing something I never intended to do to begin with. I also see Spirit when I show up as a person I never intended to be. It's just something that I will do until I finish walking this earth. I dedicate this to my wife of 34 years and who she has become to me: today I'm most grateful to being awake and willing to move toward what my Spirit would have me be.

Inventory

How this affects my...
Self-esteem - I want guarantees from people, but I will not have to honor mine
Pride - I really have no pride with promises; I pride myself and my selfishness and abuse other people's time, but never mine
Security - My security is based on what I should not have to do, yet it is also based on what I expect other people to do; don't criticize me no matter how I behave
Ambition - I'm usually only out to get what is best for me
Men - Men don't need to expect me to follow through on commitments; I lie when I make promises; you will figure it out eventually
Women - I break promises to women because I can always find another woman; I expect women to keep their word no matter what
Pocketbook - I don't make promises with money, but I expect promises to be kept with money especially when I don't earn it or perform for it

My Part

How Am I...
Dishonest - I'm never really honest; I tell people what they want to hear; I love the game of the con, it's exhilarating
Selfish - I have no real intent to get out of myself; I blame all this on old belief systems and excuses

Self-seeking - I have and keep the right to change my mind; even if I make a promise, I really have no loyalty to anyone but myself, even that does not work most of the time
Afraid - Of getting caught in my lies and having to face people about why my promises mean nothing; of people not wasting their time on me; afraid of my own arrogance

5 Fears

1. Fear of not being able to make excuses
2. Fear of caring less about myself and more for others
3. Fear of not lying and doing what I say in integrity
4. Fear of being honorable in the future
5. Fear of understanding when people break promises to me

Resentment to God

For caring too much in making me change without my permission; for not making me better at killing myself; us addicts suck at killing ourselves

Corrective Measures

1. Commit to yourself to prompts to do or help someone you don't want to, then let them know what it is so they can hold you accountable
2. Let someone important break or promise to you and do what they said they would do for you and do it yourself, find a way

Resistance Warrior

Resistance

I am world-class at resisting. As an addict, you are always pushing back with resistance. In sobriety, resistance is part of so many daily things. I actually have to plan on how I will react to people, places, and things. I resist getting angry when people say hurtful things or when people disrespect me. I resist getting my feelings hurt, like I did yesterday. I was just having to tell people exactly what I think and feel. I resist or don't resist. It isn't always positive, but it's not always negative, either. I resist the ways expected of me by my Spirit. I resist my sex drives. I was just telling the truth, my love affair with being dishonest. Sometimes, I really think I'm just in love with being the embodiment of resistance.

I have to ask the Spirit of God to give me the courage to not really resist. The deep mandate spiritually not to have to resist so much is what I'm going for here. I asked God to find a way to help me to not need to resist, because it seems like it's in my DNA. I've been working for 14 years, especially the last five, to find out from Spirit what it would look like if we adopted a code of spiritual ethics and took a knee whenever Spirit would have me stand down.

Because I can't ever see this in my first thought, I need rules. This is where principles come in. God said, "you will only see me when doing the opposite of what you would normally do. This is radical. You will probably never like this path, but it will give you something to do that looks nothing like where you have been." Spirit asks me every morning, "who will you be working for today?" Either way, I know that it's my decision, but if I work for God, he makes all the decisions. All I have to do is chop wood and carry water. God will take care of his kids today through me.

When I do this, my insanity and depression is less. If I surrender my resistance, I find hope from obsession.

Inventory

How this affects my...
Self-esteem - I resist when people want too much for me or ask too much; my resistance gives me control and allows me to be defiant
Pride - My security lives in my control to be resistant; I have a belief system that I have and need power here; I must call the shots
Security - I have been taught by people in my life that security comes with winning or being right; my obsession that I need to be respected is like putting a bullet to my head, I want to not do anything for it
Ambition - I think I control my own destiny here; my resistance is a battle I choose to fight, I fight what I don't get, in relationships and all other areas of life

Men - Men are too much like me; I really can't get over on them without wounding myself in some way in principle; I resent this most of the time
Women - I never seem to resist an attraction to women; I've been a predator to women and probably still am; I still undress them with my eyes before I even say hello, but at least I don't touch them and have changed for the better in that way
Pocketbook - People will not take anything from me; I will give as little as possible and do as little as possible to get the things I want

My Part

How Am I...
Dishonest - I lie about anything I don't intend to do; seems like my resistance is a forcefield around me
Selfish - I really don't play well with others; I really only focus on and think about not giving; I think I like it more than not
Self-seeking - When I look inside, I'm a greedy, selfish, immature guy because I act like one; sometimes I pretend I'm not
Afraid - My soul is dying and I know my resistance has a belief system that says I'm afraid not to die; I'm afraid to change and I know I can't do it with my dark side; I have to have a powerful person that teaches me to surrender to my Spirit; I have to give permission for this to happen

5 Fears

1. Fear of not resisting principles
2. Fear of not being full of shit
3. Fear of doing things I don't want to
4. Fear of surrendering
5. Fear of people resisting me as a consequence to how I lie and treat them
6. Fear of consequences

Resentment to God

For putting me in a position to make choices each day; of letting my guard down and taking big chances for God

Corrective Measures

1. Let two people be right and let them know they're right
2. Let in two things you usually resist with people that are close to you

Quitting

The art of quitting should be a spectator sport and I'd be a professional, top ranked! Quitting comes down to the honest statement that I don't really care about people until they have something I want. Following the dictate of a principle like honesty or integrity is one of the reasons I don't quit things that I don't want to do. I stick with things I have every intention of quitting just because I know that if I want to quit, it's probably a bad idea and against Spirit.

My mind and my emotions make quitting an emotional up or down thing, so I thought. I always feel like I'm on the edge. It's a rush knowing that I could walk away from anything at any moment, no bluffing necessary. It gives me relentless power in my own mind.

It always seems ironic to me the timing of my quitting. I don't quit things like relationships or jobs when I'm getting what I want from them. Then there's the world of what I don't get with these things, which is where I do what I do best: quit.

I quit things because I have no loyalty until I acquire loyalty, and it usually does not happen on my own. It's all behavioral, and I'm seeking new behavior in my Spirit and my spiritual world. I have 50,000 reasons to quit or leave, it seems. I can make them up in my head simple as snapping my fingers. I have had little attachment to staying and finishing things. I had to find the worst in my behavior before I could seek better behavior. To do this, I had to ask my Spirit to reveal my part in why I quit giving, caring, or participating.

When I do quit, it is always convenient. At least, it is for me. I don't consider what my quitting does to those around me because not only do I not care, but I'm also too self-centered to even give it a thought. I quit when I quit, that's all I need to know. I don't owe anyone an explanation. There came a time, for two years, that I would go to battle with one defect a day and bring one principle, like humility, integrity, or honesty, into wanting to quit something.

My quitting dude is the same as my I'm-not-doing-that dude. "I won't show up for that, I'm not doing that, I'm not up to doing that, I'm better than that, I shouldn't have to do that." My internal dialogue was full of this shit. The things I write about myself in inventory are not subtle. They are about something I won't do or quit because I don't like this or that, not getting anything out of it—it's just a very dark place and I never have been able to handle letting that come up. This is where Mike guided me to the principles and the Spirit Dude that could do it for me. It's the gray cloud that I've lived with. I was never able to quit quitting. I quit because I can, yet I expect others to never quit or give up on me. I'm a hypocrite by nature and I usually can't even see it. Fucking hilarious.

Inventory

How this affects my...

Self-esteem - I'm stuck in the mindset of I don't answer to anyone, it isn't a good space; no one tells me what to do

Pride - I tell when people can quit; no one should quit until I'm done using them or getting what I need from them

Security - I align with only myself unless I have managed to get a woman to please me; I know I have to do something to keep her

Ambition - I expect to be respected no matter what I do, but I have no need to respect anyone else except when I have motives and things I need

Men - I don't owe men an explanation for what I do or don't do

Women - I quit relationships with women that won't give me what I want; women should not expect me to be honest and decent

Pocketbook - Follow the money; I have no loyalty to employers, even if you pay me well it won't be enough

My Part

How Am I...

Dishonest - I believe that my reaction to quit or stop is always valid; I tell no one when I quit

Selfish - I convince myself I can always be better or get more but I will not do more to get it; I have this mindset that people owe me

Self-seeking - I never criticize myself, just other people; I have the same shitty attitude for men and women

Afraid - Of being treated equal in work or personal life; of doing my share without telling anyone

5 Fears

1. Fear of not quitting
2. Fear of people not looking up to me
3. Fear of doing more than I'm asked
4. Fear of commitment
5. Fear of finding more value in others than myself

Resentment to God

For quitting on me and not making me more special, for making it too hard to leave my dark side

Corrective Measures

1. Find two small things that I can do for two people and find a way not to quit and follow through and not tell anyone
2. Find one thing you've quit today. List it as a priority to finish or do tomorrow. Tell someone what you are doing so they can hold you accountable.

Listening Warrior

Respect

I don't need respect. The Spirit of God tells me to take a knee to anything and represent the spirit of humanity. I need no respect other than my own Spirit.

My ideas about respect change based on my approval or disapproval in and of the moment. Respect for what other people do and say is heavily based on what I'm thinking, especially when I have opinions regarding what other people should believe.

I expect respect on the same level, but this changes based on the circumstance, my mood, and the person. I have a delusion that I respect other people all the time, but when I look at my actions, this is the farthest thing from the truth. This whole idea is really a joke because I really don't respect anybody or anything. I don't respect rules of the country, institutions, or the Police Department.

I found out that respect comes with a price. I tell myself that I must use it as a gauge of how I see myself over people or how I believe they're over me. I complain and judge anything I don't like and then wonder why no one respects me. Then I take a moment, listen to the shit I spew, and it becomes clear. I weaponize respect into a comparison tool.

I asked God, could I ever be part of the solution? Could I even not need to hate the idea of being part of any solution with people?

In the writing work I have done over 14 years, I had to begin to ask my Spirit if he could help me to become willing to be willing to begin the process of laying aside everything I think I know about respect. This also included everything I think I know about needing to be right, changing, releasing belief systems, and being attached to what I think I know. The idea was that this prayer would spawn a new experience with respect, needing respect, needing to be right, instant change, releasing and letting go of belief systems, and being attached to knowing what I know about anything with my beliefs and myself and the Spirit of God dude.

When my Spirit today tells me God's kids deserve respect, at first, I laugh and disagree. Today I know it is about not needing respect, but how I serve God's kids when he asks me to. I respect the spiritual piece, and to that I've taken a knee.

Inventory

How this affects my...
Self-esteem - I was conditioned to believe I must get respect while giving as little as possible, no matter how bad my disrespect hurts and effects people
Pride - I do nothing to give respect when I don't have to; I deserve respect because I'm breathing
Security - I know I treat people and what is important to them like crap most of the time; this is exactly the best I care to do

Ambition - To take as much from people mentally and emotionally as I can and to give as little back to support them as possible in return
Men - If men can't respect me, I automatically go on the defensive; I like this part of me, because I love the battle
Women - I expect women to show respect, if not I will just go after their feelings and how they look and do my best to embarrass them; this goes both ways
Pocketbook - I would pay anything for respect

My Part

How Am I...
Dishonest - I lie up and down regarding respect, depending on who I'm talking to; what I do quietly is my best secret
Selfish - My inside standards change constantly depending on the old belief systems I am in; it will be about me no matter what, always
Self-seeking - I have no respect until I need to have some, and people need to see I have some; the respect is fake, but I play this character well
Afraid - Of taking everything personally that people do and say; of not finding someone to put me on a spiritual path where God allows life to happen not my way

5 Fears

1. Fear of taking a knee
2. Fear of not getting respect when I don't give it
3. Fear of grace
4. Fear of allowing disrespectful things to happen and react in principle
5. Fear of not allowing Spirit to make all this easier to live in

Resentment to God

For making me feel unimportant; for not saving me; for making me wake up now (when I think it would be easier to keep being the other way)

Corrective Measures

1. For one day, notice all the times I am hypocritical about respect (giving and getting)
2. Make an amends to someone I disrespect (could even be a food service worker, etc.)

Satisfaction

Satisfaction is a brutal topic. It fits in every single one of the motives I choose to keep. Satisfaction has to do with taking and pushing things around with no end in sight. The real things like girls, skydiving, cars, and other big goals seem to have an expiration date of how long I stay interested. There's an invisible alarm that blares inside of me when it's time to move on to bigger and better things. Satisfaction is about the hunt to get what pleases me.

On the dark side, I'm talking about things I can't have. I am in love with things that have to be taken. This falls under the secrets of my controlling bullshit, my defiance of the rules you have, and the deep dark need I relish in to make people look bad so I can shine. I seem to always find a way to satisfy my jealousy, whether it is jealousy over other people and what they have or in a sick relationship.

For years, me and my wife had a very sick relationship. Some of the nasty arguments fell under one's needs of satisfaction over the other's. It's astonishing I was able to grow up and change myself. In the long run, it happened for both of us separately. I was a very horrible person to her because I thought I needed to be.

The need for satisfaction is intoxicating. I was taught by so many that I'm supposed to get mine, whatever that may be in the moment. What I'm satisfied with can change in a day, a week, a second. Something I found to be acceptable yesterday is abhorrent today. I believe that my happiness is super important, that I need to find balance based on my satisfaction. I tie satisfaction to what I need, even though my needs aren't really needs at all, they are wants. I personally don't believe in balance. I celebrate being up and down, riding the rollercoaster.

Within myself, I had to ask, why does my satisfaction have to come at someone else's expense? When and why does that have to be the case? I'm always craving something from the dark side for my satisfaction to be satiated. Things that seem to really satisfy me seem to hurt others. This is true of judgment, how I make someone else wrong and show them I'm right, and stepping on the throats of others to feel better. My Spirit shows up in these moments and I start to be able to see how cool it could be to not need to judge or one-up other people. I realized that I really don't need to be out to get others, that it's pretty cool to be the humble, in the background type of guy. This is how Spirit has taught me to change my definition of satisfaction.

Inventory

How this affects my...
Self-esteem - I think and act like I'm the only one that deserves satisfaction
Pride - I believe others that are trying to get satisfaction are a threat; I am immature about getting and giving; I don't ever want it to be equal because that doesn't satisfy me

Security - I can't allow everyone to get what I want; equality is something I stay away from
Ambition - I believe and still am OK with being a taker; satisfaction is a take, not give situation except for in sex, because for me to be satisfied, she has to be satisfied too
Men - Men don't deserve me trying to satisfy them; they take me for granted (I take them for granted, too)
Women - Here is where I live by the old phrase, feed me, fuck me, and shut the fuck up; I had to have the Spirit of God rip some of this out, my dad used to say this phrase and I truly accepted this in my dark belief system
Pocketbook - Nothing satisfied me more than drugs, women, and money; I had to go deep within my Spirit and work this out because this was killing me

My Part

How Am I...
Dishonest - I lie about wanting the best for people, but I just want the best for myself; I pretend to want what's best for them because it really serves me in the end
Selfish - I say I don't know how to love and respect people, but I do know how to act like it; mostly I just choose to play the con
Self-seeking - I will go to any lengths to justify pleasing myself
Afraid - To not need or crave satisfaction; I'm afraid to handle the feelings or the voice that comes when I think I'm suffering

5 Fears

1. Fear of not needing anything when I think I should get it
2. Fear of people asking too much of me
3. Fear of being humble
4. Fear of being content
5. Fear of blessing other people and what they need

Resentment to God

For making me need to be so dependent on my own satisfaction; for not making it cool and easy to give other people the gift of satisfaction

Corrective Measures

1. Do two things for two other people that you would only normally do for yourself; pretend you want to
2. Sacrifice something that would satisfy you so someone else's satisfaction can be met

Secrets

This topic relates to the secrets I keep to myself. My behavior from the game, and after, is mostly for my eyes only. It has to be. My dark thoughts and wishes can't see the light. People can only know me by what I want them to see. My dishonesty, the true depths of it, my conning nature, and my control and obsession have to be kept secret to all. This is one of my core beliefs. This is the fake part of me. As a side note, you may be surprised, but I also have a side that is genuine. But that is for another chapter, another day.

It drives me crazy to try to keep these parts of me separated. There are so many secrets and half-truths inside of me that I can't see straight sometimes. My obsessions that people won't understand and would judge me if they knew I had these secrets loom over me everywhere I go. Then there's the worry that if people knew, they would probably spread rumors about me. Then I wonder if they would be even rumors because they would be true. The lengths I go to manifest my obsessions are bizarre, even to me sometimes. That is a pretty overwhelming standard.

One example is that I would do anything to get in a girl's pants and for her to want me to be around. The lies and dishonesty I have used to be right and to prove people wrong is limitless, even today. The rage, at times, is a byproduct of my self-pity and insecurity, and is, for the most part, a secret. You wouldn't even know it unless I let it out of the cage for a brief moment. My jealousy and my judgments are mostly kept secret until I can't keep a lid on them anymore and I lash out at someone. This includes my wife, kids, anyone important in my life, but especially people I don't care for.

I found Mike, and his role as my sponsor, was to translate my secrets and to match them together with a principle. He told me to crash the principle into the middle of my secret that I hold on to so dearly. This changes a secret into what it actually is, which is an old belief system. It downgrades the power that I think it has over me. He would bring light to the courage I had inside of myself that I wasn't aware of. This I then brought into the middle of any obsession or secret I was holding onto. He would bring humility to the middle of dishonesty in the exact moment of deception. Then, I could remember that maybe I am not as dishonest as I think I am or claim to be. This process was about my waking up to Spirit.

It isn't that I am a dishonest person through and through, I just act dishonestly sometimes. I had to separate my behavior from who I was—otherwise I could never see that it could go away. If I was an overall dishonest person, there was no way I could survive without being dishonest. I had to stop labeling myself and distinguish who I was, who God wanted me to be, from my behavior.

I was taught that I could go to a person or institution that I really hated and make my behavior and how I've behaved right without cowering down. In that moment, during the amends process, I am not dishonest. This means that there was a moment today that I was honest about something and a decent person. It may seem small, but to me it was gigantic. I had to start small—anything that changed how I operated overall was too overwhelming. I didn't know I could do it and didn't think I had the spiritual connection to make it so. I was never honest, so I didn't know how to be. In fact, I was vehemently against it. Dishonesty was one of my biggest protectors, my bodyguard to the outside world. I was terrified that if I let dishonesty go that I would be hurt repeatedly without recourse. I forgot I had to really remember that I don't give a shit about people on my best day.

My secrets are not as big as the energy and effort it takes to keep them. My belief systems and old ways of trying by myself to keep these parts of me never allow me to be able to move forward in who I hope to be. There came a day where I was willing to be willing to believe, deep in my Spirit dude's presence, that any secrets are probably half as big or complicated or as bad as I think they are.

My Spirit told me to pretend to be open to believing that you just have not remembered that your secrets are average. No better or worse than anyone else's. I had to find a man, Mike, that had all the same secrets as I did. He normalized anything I thought was unique about my secrets. He showed me how to make amends to the people I affected by the daunting secrets that I thought I had. We made a list of my five worst secrets and began to move through them, cleaning them up one by one. It was scary, but doable.

I never knew something like this path could exist for me. It only happens for moments at a time in between all my other shit. This is what's kept me coming back to the 12-step path. Turns out, nobody thinks about or cares about my secrets except for me. I found in the rooms of 12-step drug addiction recovery that everyone has done the same shit, thought the same crap, and probably was into the same dark, nasty stuff that I was. I found out that all the dark stuff I have is normal and fair to the right person like me in these rooms. My secrets are average to the right person—that's what my shame and pain turned out to be after all these years. I can't count the number of times that someone has sat across from me, ashamed and depressed about things that I have done several times over, usually worse. We all think that we are the worst, have been the worst, don't deserve shit, etc. None of that is true. We have all done equally disgusting, scumbag shit in our addiction. There was freedom in the idea that I was just an average piece of shit, nothing special.

Inventory

How this affects my...

Self-esteem - I only want to feed people the little secrets and keep the big stuff between me and God; my dark dude tells me my big secrets are so horrible that people would judge me and run from me

Pride - I want to look good in the rooms of recovery; come to find out that I'm trying to be 'normal' in the nuthouse

Security - I need people to only hear what I need them to to be ok
Ambition - I make it my hobby to judge and laugh at people's secrets; half of my secrets are made up depending on who I talk to, what I want for them, or plainly for social clout
Men - I only deal with men when I have to; it gives me something to do until I find a woman that will listen to me
Women - I don't honor what women have to say; I think it's great to brag to men about what women tell me in confidence
Pocketbook - Half the money I've made in my life was not legitimate; I do whatever it takes to make a buck; it doesn't matter

My Part

How Am I...
Dishonest - I can only tell people what I want them to know; I don't trust anyone, but I believe you can trust me
Selfish - I do what is good for me when I do something for you (or else I wouldn't do it)
Self-seeking - I use your secrets against you, I pride myself on being a con and I really don't care; it's a gift
Afraid - Of being exposed; that people won't trust me even though I lie about many things

5 Fears

1. Fear of not being trusted
2. Fear of integrity
3. Fear of being a real friend and being loyal
4. Fear of being trusted
5. Fear of being alone
6. Fear of honesty

Resentment to God

For making it so hard not to isolate myself because of my belief systems; for the paranoia that I'm dying in; for making me afraid to change things that I don't know anything about

Corrective Measures

1. Make amends to someone I held hostage with my secret of what I think of them and how I treat them
2. Expose a big secret to someone to find out that they don't care

Wisdom Warrior

Self-pity

Self-pity is a state of mind that comes very naturally to me. It's attached to every other defect of mine in some fashion. It is a convenient emotion that allows me to play the victim and give myself excuses. Self-pity is a bitch, but she's mine and I like her. There's no way out for me that I can think of. Sometimes I don't want out; I want in deeper. I can depress myself anytime I want through what I think and feel when it comes to self-pity. Sometimes I enjoy digging myself a deeper hole, until I can't breathe and can't get out. I am unable to break out from this jail alone, it must be with the help of the Spirit of God aligning with my Spirit.

I have a heavy resentment to God that rolls all the time. I've yet to lay aside everything I think I know about that entity or, really, anything else.

I cry about and dwell on what I don't have and can't get. These things are not meant for me, but I firmly believe they are. I think they must be for me, and these opinions devour my soul if I let them. Universal principles say otherwise.

Self-pity is a tight noose. What if my self-pity, at any given time, is half as big as I think it is? That would be huge to see. I never seem to have self-pity for all the things I do get, for all the horrible things that didn't happen.

My Spirit Dude, one day, told me that there's no room for God or Spirit in my self-pity. And by the way, it's a gift, just for you, when you're in it. You'll never find a better teacher.

The God piece can, upon request, give you the courage to move through any experience and to take a humble knee. Moving through self-pity and having an experience which leads to seeing Spirit within yourself is something that cannot be taught or explained on paper. To move to the next thing that you can participate in after coming through the struggle of self-pity is impossible alone. When God and my Spirit come together, it is possible to be able to add to the quality and experience when someone gets what you think had to be yours. It is an exercise in gratitude, generosity, and selflessness. I'm none of those things on my own.

It is priceless when I don't throw a fit when someone else gets what I want. I typically can get what I want, so allowing someone else to have that experience and maybe even feeling gratitude for them is amazing. It'll make you throw up in your mouth a little bit, but it gets better.

My first encounter with the shift of humility happened when I got sober, I totaled my car. A friend offered me his old Buick for $1,500 and I could pay it out. The car had no A/C (I was in Texas in the summer) and the driver's side window did not roll down. I could hear the paint on the hood chipping onto the windshield when I drove above 30 mph. I was working in the sales industry. Before an appointment, I would spend 30 minutes in a bathroom in a random building to cool off, quit sweating, and get myself together to be somewhat presentable. I had been getting thrown out of places because I looked like shit, so I learned that a little preparation goes a long way.

Being the good addict that I was, I was both pissed and embarrassed. God sat me down and began to show me what a piece of humility would look like if I wanted it. I wrote a gratitude list. The question was: how would it be if I didn't wreck my car driving for my dealer and totaling it at 90 mph? After the accident, I even was ballsy enough to have my wife pick me up and bring her to my dealer to grab some stuff. I was amazing, I can't believe that I pulled that shit off on a routine basis. I have to laugh at the audacity.

I had to imagine: no ride to the grocery store, riding the bus, no ride to the food bank, no car at all. Imagine no friend offering a car. Now concentrate on the self-pity you don't have about having no car. God couldn't give me gratitude freely. I had to pretend to have some to move into that space. There will be many times that we do this and have done this.

When I see someone in self-pity, I ask… are you in prison? Are you dying? Are you hurt? Are you bleeding? Then how painful is that shit, really? It helps bring sharp focus into the situation.

The God piece said you must have Spirit and principles on some level to get to the other side and to breathe. A four-column on my self-pity in the moment always leads me to what my part is in the situation and some variety of gratitude. I make a list of the things that are not going wrong versus my expectation or demands of what I expect to be getting from people and things.

Inventory

How this affects my...
Self-esteem - In my own worst nightmare, I don't really need anything from anybody; this does not require me to do anything for anyone else, either
Pride - I really don't put up with other people laying their self-pity on me
Security - I need people to feel sorry for me and want to help me to be ok
Ambition - My ambition likes to force my crybaby bullshit on others; I think I really need to tell other people about my self-pity; they better care and feel sorry for me how I expect them to
Men - I should not have to be there for men; men need to shut the fuck up and spare me their self-pity stories unless I'm going to get something out of it
Women - I need women to be available to hear whatever I have to say; women need to want to be there for me
Pocketbook - I should get paid for feeling sorry for myself; I would listen to people's self-pity if I got paid for it, could it be a business opportunity?

My Part

How Am I...

Dishonest - I lie and pretend to care about people's problems, I do if it makes me money
Selfish - I'm only interested in me telling you what I don't like, you can hold your thoughts and spare me your opinion, I don't care
Self-seeking - I need people to justify my self-pity as a way to feel better about my bullshit
Afraid - To be humble and have the integrity to see some of things that are right about things I think are wrong

6 Fears

1. Fear of not feeling sorry for myself
2. Fear of having some empathy for what other people go through
3. Fear of hearing what other people have to say about me and my behavior
4. Fear of becoming less important
5. Fear of asking for the courage to change spiritually in real time
6. Fear of being corrected

Resentment to God

For not changing me and making change look so hard

Corrective Measures

1. Write a short gratitude list on two horrible things that have happened and do a four-column on it to find my part
2. Answer the question in writing: Based on whast you do, why do you think self-pity is easier than finding a good reason (in Spirit) to surrender and find motives or why you love it (since you ask for self-pity to stay)

Protection Warrior

Self-righteousness

Self-righteousness is a punishment I give to myself. It's the pedestal I stand on when I get insecure, say I hate life, and all my control mechanisms are failing. This shows up when I double down to make myself more important, as important as I think I need to be. It gets ugly when I'm around people or in relationships. It's all I know and all I have ever known to be in the storms I get myself into. That isn't meant to be a justification, just a statement of fact.

I feel self-righteous when I know I'm not. I tend to act this way when I know I'm wrong around people and don't want to be. I always think people are making fun of me. I have this voice in my head, the dark dude, that says something is always wrong with something. This can be deafening when there is, in actuality, nothing wrong, and my Spirit agrees with that. There are massive fights in my head between dark dude and Spirit. They are mostly one-sided, with the dark dude arguing that things are wrong and I'm not getting what I deserve. Spirit is always calm and laid back, waiting for my dark dude to run out of steam.

I ask myself, why do I always listen to the dark voice first? The answer is simple and largely unfulfilling. Because I can and it is familiar. Self-righteousness is a lovely place when I'm in my darkness. I tell myself that I always have to react to what people say, assume they're putting me down, and bite back. Most of the time, I find that, in Spirit, none of it is really happening.

I've had people say that they don't even care about me enough to talk down to me and criticize me. I say that, too. That crushed some old belief systems about how important I think I am and how the world revolves around me.

When I met Mike, I made an agreement with him and my Spirit that my path was to only be about me and the self-righteous dude. I was only to ever look at myself and not blame other people. This included my belief systems such as self-righteousness, control, expectations, resistance, and what my intense secrets are.

Why do I think I am self -righteous? I think I am because I really don't think I am. Because I asked this defect to reveal itself to me. It had been a part of my life in addiction in every way. I had a wish that this part of me could refrain from showing up in the same way in my spiritual days. I was able to see that I am only half as self-righteous as I think I am and every bit so much in how I act. I saw that I wanted to act self-righteously, until I started asking my Spirit if it could become cool to not act this way. When I'm being self-righteous, it requires me to treat and talk to people like shit. The issue is that I really don't have a problem with how I come at people. The prayer to Spirit is: I would like to pretend to have a problem with it sometimes. Could it be easy not to be self-righteous one time today?

I burned this prayer within: I ask the Spirit dude to make it easy please to remove the need for me to believe I love to be self-righteous. Could I begin to believe the need was half as big as I think? Could I, with Spirit, begin to fall in love with not wanting to be better than anyone? Could I love being equal in Spirit and allow others to be self-righteous over me and me not retaliate? Please help me to fall in love with this positive statement and with the Spirit of God. In other words, go down the path of treating myself and others like God would. God instructed me to just put Him on and wear Him like a coat, and that He would always fit.

Inventory

How this affects my...
Self-esteem - I don't need anyone or anything to make myself feel better or more important than my own self-righteousness
Pride - This self-righteousness handles my self-pity; I can just ask myself when I'm down how I feel about myself; this is always there to take away my pain for at least two minutes
Security - My security is not so much based on what other people think than on what I am trying to make them think I am; I can always make what you believe fit into the lies I told myself
Ambition - People cannot do better or be better than I have to be to breathe
Men - Men need me to be self-righteous so they know what they can aspire to be
Women - Women need someone like me to show them how to fake self-righteous behavior; women know I'm fake, they just let me make a fool of myself and I'm grateful for that
Pocketbook - Being self-righteous costs me nothing; I do this for free

My Part

How Am I...
Dishonest - I can't stand people who are self-righteous, they're fake and annoying, but it isn't when I do it
Selfish - I love to waste people's time by imposing my belief systems and opinions
Self-seeking - I choose to be this way because I believe I don't know how it is to be OK
Afraid - Of being exposed; of people seeing my insecurity, my control, and moving away from me as a consequence

5 Fears

1. Fear of not being self-righteous, what else would I be?
2. Fear of being rejected
3. Fear of not being accepted
4. Fear of humility
5. Fear of listening instead talking

Resentment to God

For not teaching me how to feel better about myself without putting other people Down; for making me self-righteous and allowing me to use this as a coping skill to get along in this world

Corrective Measures

1. Identify a place where I exhibit this behavior, and ask people to hold me accountable to it (when they do, don't argue and say thank you)
2. Make amends with someone to whom I've been self-righteous

Control Warrior

Shame or Guilt

This might be an unpopular opinion, but it's mine and I think it's worthwhile sharing. So, here goes. I don't feel shame or guilt for anything I've done to myself or others. I think this is a gift. It came from being a ruthless drug addict and a liar. Meth addiction guides you to do all kinds of weird stuff, mostly sexual. I had days of time to think of off the wall things to do with others and myself. The things to be obsessed with are endless.

How could I feel guilty or shameful about things I chose to do? I stole from and used people because I wanted to. The same seems to be when I'm sober, even in principles. Shame and guilt are after-the-fact emotions. They usually show up because I feel like I should feel badly for doing something that someone else has judged me for. I'd rather beg for forgiveness than ask for permission, and shame and guilt are just methods I use to get that job done.

I don't practice principles all the time, but I do eventually and get back to where I need to be. I don't feel guilty when I argue with people and I don't feel shame when I talk about people at work or with family. I disrespect and harm people mostly in what I think of them and how I talk about them in my head.

I have this voice that just goes off when I talk to myself. I think if I don't say these things out loud, only think them and pretend to not have these opinions, it doesn't count as harm.

The darkness inside of me does seem to have an effect on my Spirit. My sponsor told me that a shift would occur from the dark dude voice to my true Spirit voice. I will keep cycling in the dark things and behavior and the judgmental thoughts as long as I allow the cycle to continue. In other words, my darkness has to be brought to the light. I have to call my dark dude to the carpet. But I will never figure out what to do with this on my own.

This is not about changing or adding shame and guilt in, it is already there, even if I don't access it. We are just identifying it for what it is, good or bad, and moving it into Spirit so it can become something that is not trying to kill me. My Spirit can deal with flipping it into something useful.

Inventory

How this affects my...
Self-esteem - Shame and guilt dictate how I should feel bad about what I say, do, and think about other people in bad ways
Pride - I would love to find out if there is a part of me that does not allow for shame or guilt
Security - Shame and guilt can be overwhelming, it's like prosecuting myself for things done over time; I forgive myself for these things in real time today

Ambition - It's difficult to use people and judge people with any level of shame; there has been no shame in my game and that is why inventory allows to make things right, thank God for that
Men - Men should be ashamed and guilty for all the abuse they have done to me
Women - I could feel shame for all the crazy sex things I've done to women, but I don't; everyone chose to participate, I did put a lot of needles in women's arms
Pocketbook - Shame is not profitable, so I pretend I don't feel any

My Part

How Am I...
Dishonest - I act like I care to feel good about how badly I treat people, but I don't
Selfish - I try to lay guilt and shame on people when they don't let me control them
Self-seeking - I need to shame people when they are just looking out for what is best for me; I treat most people badly except the ones I need to win over, I do whatever it takes for them
Afraid - People won't buy into what I need them to be for me; I need strong, grounded, spiritual people that I can't lay guilt or shame on in my life

5 Fears

1. Fear of having too much false pride
2. Fear of not controlling people
3. Fear of things in my past coming up
4. Fear of hearing the truth
5. Fear of having remorse which could lead to guilt and shame

Resentment to God

For making me feel shame and guilt for the dark things I love to do and feel good about

Corrective Measures

1. Put another person's feelings before my own
2. Ask someone who have harmed how it made them feel and affected them and make amends to them for that

Thinking

It is my opinion that what I think has to be right. Always. My thinking about many things has been set in stone years ago. It's like watching the same TV channel for decades. My thinking is very tied into the path of getting what I deserve and what I won't be told to do. I can clearly see that my thinking has already transitioned to what I know and what people will not be allowed to do to me again as soon as my neurons fire. My thinking constantly changes when it comes to taking, blaming, and how to find who I need to be. My thinking is always trying to figure it's way out of self-pity. I automatically search for sneakier ways to complain and planning how to manhandle my way through my day. I never have to argue with myself. I only question myself when people think I should. Even then, I only do it about half of the time.

However, my current thinking pattern tells me that it does not want me to change. It wants my life. Most of my thinking begins on the dark side. I really don't want to live coming from my past. I want to align with my awakened Spirit, which is forged out of a set of principles which came from the thinking which brought me to this moment in time. My thinking in the past will not tolerate me making amends for harms I did. My dark dude makes me believe my anger is normal and justified. He also feeds me the line that my attachment to what I think is right. It will not do.

My thinking is centered around entitlement, arguments, and so on. It is the matrix of what I think I have to be to be okay with myself. After all, I am told I have to be okay with myself and love myself as is. So, I did, and it almost killed me. My thinking had to be destroyed on many levels the way everything else about me was.

My Spirit and the Spirit of God appeared the first week I got sober. Spirit told me that my thinking had to be destroyed and violently burned down, so that Spirit, principles, and values could rise up through the dark stuff. Spirit made it clear through prayers that this shift is not about learning new things, but it was about remembering and acting my way into what I originally meant to act like.

My prayer was to ask Spirit to make it as half as hard as I think it will be to act and speak in a much cooler way. So, my prayer today is to ask Him to make it easy to remember that I already shifted a couple things in principles now. God, could you make it cool to be a spiritual warrior in action and make it possible today in the moment? That's my wish. I never thought I would say this to my thinking. The principles, when activated by the parts of my Spirit, tell me it is not completely necessary to think when I am about to do the next right thing. Principles put something in motion in me to where my thinking has happened yesterday. My thinking has proved to be dangerous throughout my life. They say in the world of Spirit that when I know something lacks attachment, there are higher possibilities. This is true for me.

Inventory

How this affects my...
Self-esteem - I need safety; I think that where things have worked in the past they will work the same today
Pride - What I think I believe has to be true; I need no feedback from anyone; why would I think differently?
Security - I think that my security is grounded in how I think about myself, but I come to Spirit broken; but I soon think I am not again, the loop I choose to live in goes on
Ambition - My thinking is always on the defensive with others; I think I know what is best for me out of survival; I guard my old belief systems to protect me
Men - I think I have to go to war with men and what they're thinking of me; I'm working on my belief system that they aren't bad and are actually decent
Women - My thinking about women has been delusional; I think they owe me something physically; I have no honor for their species and how they are designed differently, I just learned that a couple of years ago
Pocketbook - I am so stuck at times about what I deserve and how little I think I will do to get money or resources

My Part

How Am I...
Dishonest - I believe what I think is awesome, dark or light; I also think I am stuck in a belief system that doesn't work; I tell myself that I never lie to myself and I should do exactly what I think I should
Selfish - I disregard what other people think; it's hard to think and be humble at the same time
Self-seeking - I say have an open mind about what others think, but deep inside I know I don't unless I have motives to get something I think I deserve from them
Afraid - To follow other people thinking and ideas; I think I am afraid more of dishonesty and self-pity; I think there's no other side to get through it to something better; my thinking knows everything I won't do and makes it so every breath is like my last breath; God please remove this thinking

5 Fears

1. Fear of not thinking or not knowing
2. Fear of not being in self-pity
3. Fear of being inferior
4. Fear of not getting justice for what I think
5. Fear of what others think of me

Resentment to God

For making it so hard to let go of my thinking in real time; for making my thinking irrelevant to me

Corrective Measures

1. Spend 30 minutes listening to other's thoughts without judging them
2. One time in the evening, sit down and pretend you don't need to think with your Spirit; think about why you think what you think is important in this moment

PART III:
Finding and knowing the God dude

Defiance Warrior

Aligned with Spirit

Before sobriety, I worked hard to conveniently forget concepts like God that I learned in Jesuit school growing up. God never did anything for me, and I was never going to bow to any motherfucker. Then, I got sober and realized that the idea I had been fighting for so long wasn't even mine. Mike told me early on in this journey with Spirit that I had to personally find a face and a voice for God, plus a place where I could meet the Spirit of God and bang out all this stuff. I needed to make God a real image that I could speak to and hear respond. The only way that I was open to bringing my shit to the table was through an entity that I could interact with. I knew that in this process I would get cut, wounded in the interaction, and I needed a Father I could see, hear, and relate to, to help me through the pain of excising my demons.

At first, the face of my Spirit Dude looked and acted a lot like Gandalf from Lord of the Rings. The voice of my spirit was James Earl Jones (AKA Mufasa from The Lion King). Every morning, he would say "Good morning, Michael" in that deep, rich timbre and it would get me going.

Spirit and I got down into the depth of the hugest arguments and shut-the-fuck-up lessons 100 miles out in the ocean on flat water during a calm day. I imagined us sitting side by side in two Lay-Z-Boys hashing it out. We talked, yelled, and mostly I listened. But I kept showing up. I knew I hadn't given myself much of a choice.

The Spirit and alignment with principles has shown me what it is to take a knee. It was awful at first. I saw that I have a control piece that I have a part in anything and everything that goes my way or doesn't go my way or that I get or don't get. I have everything to do with relationships in the respect or disrespect that I'm willing to give and that truly nobody owes me anything. This includes honesty, respect, etc. That had everything to do with finding my purpose, which is taking a knee and letting other people be right as often as possible just for the experience. This includes purposefully doing the opposite of what I internally say I will not do.

What Spirit told me was that if I wanted to feel my Spirit in me, I had to imagine the place where my heartbeat and my breath met. That was where Spirit lived in my presence, in my soul. I hadn't realized that it was there, dormant until I was ready and willing to bring it forth. What could I do without those two things? Maybe Spirit has been running me all along, I just didn't acknowledge that.

Spirit said, 'come into the space between your heartbeat and breath. Ask me to come all the way into your house and for you to come all the way into my house, from head to toe. If you doubt this, then it isn't our time. But maybe it is.' Mike told me to ask the Spirit of God to come into my Spirit and my Spirit go into God's Spirit and repeat 'God, come into my house, all the way in, and grant me the ability to come all the way into yours.' This prayer had a profound impact on me.

When I live one day like this, it somehow created a purpose and a belief system that begins now and supersedes everything that came before. I had gotten desperate, realizing that I was crazy. I reached for anything different, and this is what came. I don't have to believe it's true, I just need to be willing to be willing to believe that it's true and always has been. That little buy-in makes the difference and started me down the path to where I am today.

No matter what bullshit is running through my head at any given time of the day, I ask myself this question: what would it look like if I threw one principle into some of my favorite defects? What's weird, is when I do that, something about that little bitty principled part of me is incredibly familiar. It's almost like these principles were always there, lying in wait for the day I would open the door to them and shed light on my true self.

When in self-pity, I inject the idea of what I think gratitude in this situation might be. It is the opposite of what I'm doing right then, including how I perceive, judge, and talk about things. I inject the gratitude not for what I can't have, but for what I can and do have. This was totally foreign to me the first year of sobriety. I understood it in concept, but in practice it seemed impossible. I could never seem to figure out what was so great about my shitty life, what the positives were when I was in so much agony. The self-pity was so deeply ingrained that I couldn't find a way out on my own.

I talked about the effect of people telling me what to do and I was never taught how to pretend it was already happening when it was not. I couldn't see gratitude if I wasn't acting on it, and I certainly wasn't. Humility is like a tidal wave. When I'm in the middle of some huge jealousy, judgment, control, or some other hateful shit, Spirit gives me the ability to pretend to have that emotion half as much as I think I do. In that moment, just for a minute, I make it true. This moment-by-moment relief has opened up a world of freedom from my ruminating thoughts.

Spirit said that an asshole like me is always getting the things an asshole deserves. Until I pretend that maybe I'm not an asshole, nothing will change. The truth was, I had been getting what I had been giving for years. I never wanted to acknowledge that so I pretended it wasn't true. I wasn't bought into the idea of changing to be better, but I could get on the change-so-my-life-could-be-better wagon. Little changes over time gave me some space and a realization: Holy shit, I could perfect not being angry (or having any other extreme negative reaction) in real time when I thought I was. I had a sponsor that hammed this shit down my throat, and for that I am eternally grateful.

Today the face of my Spirit is Morpheus from The Matrix. His voice is Bruce Willis. The Spirit voice represents the Spirit of God in me. It's the greatest thing that Mike ever led me to because this is very real in my everyday life.

Inventory

How this affects my...
Self-esteem - Drives the dark part of me to expose it to myself and demands that I take a knee and serve God's kids in principle
Pride - I will not serve anyone or anything; I know what I am, and I can't change
Security - I believe I have to be self-righteous, controlling, condescending, and angry to be ok
Ambition - Spirit gets in the way of my ambition to control that I spent my whole life trying to perfect and became numb to; I don't really care about anything but me on the inside
Men - There's not a man that I have met for quite some time that talks and lives like this when shit hits the fan
Women - Part of me is only interested in undressing women; I don't talk to many women, but it's gotten better
Pocketbook - Spiritual behavior and principles aren't necessarily profitable

My Part

How Am I...
Dishonest - I really don't believe in Spirit stuff; my behavior says I don't, but that changes from one moment to the next
Selfish - I've been taught I don't need to help people, that no one is that kind to me; why should I do anything for others; I'll just stay angry and depressed about it and will never look for my part
Self-seeking - I don't believe in Spirit or God from what I've learned in the past; I do believe in people that are good and honest; I question people's spiritual beliefs and I argue about them if they don't line up with their behaviors
Afraid - I pretend to accept; I'm really afraid to accept this spiritual stuff but I question what I have to give up and what I have to change in that realm

5 Fears

1. Fear of treating people better than myself
2. Fear of turning over my belief system to Spirit
3. Fear of talking about this to people
4. Fear of humility
5. Fear of becoming willing to be willing to believe things that I don't

Resentment to God

For making it far too hard for me to change everything and to believe a different spiritual part of me exists deep within

Corrective Measures

1. Inventory on God
2. Designate three minutes to spend with the possibility that God exists here versus not at all, twice a day

Covenant to God

About five years into my sobriety, my mind and emotions were coming undone yet again. I started to question my service to principles within myself. I went to my sponsor and asked what was happening. He said, "year five is happening." The commitment to this path and all the unrewarding things that occur take their toll. Or at least, I think they do. I had to cement who I worked for. At the time, my answer was that I was not clear. I knew I was in the middle again, fighting about what was most important to me. The turmoil within was a struggle between the pull from my dark dude and the pull from my Spirit dude. In ideals, I wanted to be the Spirit dude. But at times, the dark dude was just too strong. Mike made it clear that it might be time to make a covenant with my Spirit and the Spirit of God, the Father of the Master of my Spirit. So, I went deep within. I did this without any reservations, laying aside what my life had exposed me to. I left all my baggage and dove in, pretending I wasn't torn.

To this day, 14 years into this journey, this covenant is in place concerning anything I do. It is not important that I fail at times and sometimes miss the mark. What is important is that God is in me and my Spirit, and that I will serve Him without hesitation. I think of this covenant and the magnitude of impact it has had on my Spirit. It does not allow me to unconsciously act like a liar, predator, etc., without having consequences to my living and breathing soul.

I choose principles like honesty, integrity, and brotherly love because I really don't want to. I usually choose the principle in a situation with someone that I despise the most. Being spiritually active and awake seems insane. A different kind of insane than my usual dishonesty, control, and defiance. After a lifetime of being on the dark side and addiction, I was totally turned on by serious expectations, self-righteousness, secrets, and resistance to anything good with integrity. Resentments were everything, I had no principles, I liked being a poser, I enjoyed taking anything because I could, and viciously seeking control over everyone and everything. I also had the fun effects of depression weighing on me. My Spirit approached me one night, about two weeks into sobriety, and asked me, "how is all that working out for you?" That made me laugh. The answer was that it was not, but I couldn't see me with principles because I never have had them and I didn't know if I wanted to change. Being a good person looked very boring and unsatisfying. Spirit told me, "how would you know? Are you up to grind it out with me and see?" I said ok, and now here I am.

The covenant to God, the Father, and my Spiritual Master is for all the days I will serve. I have made a commitment that these are all the days I have left. I will take a knee to His will, I will follow the commands that He has set forth to live, breathe, and act regarding His standards. I accept the courage He breathes into me to no longer need to be what I see. I will take a knee to manifest to be in alignment as we go forth. I represent your spiritual warrior in what I say and do.

Inventory

How this affects my...
Self-esteem - My self-esteem thinks I should not make a comment so I have the option to act out on some bullshit when I want
Pride - Part of me, the dark side, believes my covenant should continue with my dark master
Security - I want to believe I am suffering in the covenant, I'm willing to believe I do not need to be
Ambition - I don't really get too attached to the future, that is the wish, not attached as often as possible
Men - Blessing men when I don't want to, like in traffic, that is where I am told to practice this covenant
Women - I can stop undressing them and I don't have to have a problem if I continue to look away; they no longer owe me anything
Pocketbook - It comes now, and when it comes, I can just take a knee and have gratitude for lack and abundance

My Part

How Am I...
Dishonest - I don't think I'm good enough and there are times I want a softer, easier way; I think I need to be afraid of commitment so I pretend I'm not
Selfish - I tell people what they need to do including shut up for a change
Self-seeking - I want to believe I'm one of a few committing to this
Afraid - Of some of the situations with people where I'm asked to stand down and surrender my opinions; of blessing people more than I wish to be blessed myself

5 Fears

1. Fear of expectations my spirit has for me
2. Fear of not needing to be satisfied
3. Fear of not needing this to be too hard
4. Fear of taking a knee
5. Fear of being chosen by the Spirit of God to serve in this capacity

Resentment to God

For having to ask Spirit to not need or wish to be resentful

Corrective Measures

1. Write a personal covenant to God
2. Everyday find two ways to come out of this covenant and not myself

Exit Wounds

Exit wounds are all the wounds my belief system thinks that I have from leaving the drug world and my childhood. These are all the things that people did to harm me, cheat me, and hurt me in my life. Included are the wounds that I inflicted on myself because I thought I had no other choice.

Coming into sobriety and the world of my Spirit and principles after methamphetamines, these issues that I claimed to have had to be addressed and dealt with in writing. I had to ask myself, were my wounds really real or are they just expectations and demands I made up because I thought I needed to? We will see.

I think I feel so incredibly wounded, but I have already survived the stuff that I think wounded me. What I feel and think is where these wounds lie and how they affect me today. Spirit says, what if you are not even wounded, what if you're just think and act like you are? You do this in relationships, you always ask if they are going to hurt you like the last few did. It hasn't even happened, but I think it might and act accordingly. I want to guarantee that I won't get hurt by someone.

I live every day waiting for disagreements like before. I know everything I don't want to happen to me again, never seeing the good things that did happen today.

I only care about others exit wounds and how I treat them around the wound when it suits me. It's amazing to me how much I throw around new wounds on people with my opinions, controlling behavior, jealousy, and self-righteousness. I like to wish I could be kinder and more considerate, but I blame where I come from and my wounds for the reasons I choose to act this way.

My wounds turned out to be in the past and kind of made up. I act like crap because I like to. I give nothing because I can. I don't respect where others have been because I need to be understood and treated specially first. I don't know who I would be if I could not act out through my exit wounds. My Spirit and God say just act appropriately and believe you can be better and are better.

Inventory

How this affects my...
Self-esteem - I live on the defensive; I harm and harass people first so they will think twice before harming me in relationships
Pride - I can never really reveal myself to others; I live within the walls of my dark secrets, pride says no one can know
Security - It is really real that I can't trust because I live in past harms, which is where my values lie; I believe nothing changes
Ambition - I never really feel free to become who I was meant to be with in my Spirit in principle because I say I can trust no one

Men - I blame men mostly for my wounds and the wounds they would not let me inflict on them to even a score I keep with them
Women - I can never seem to let go of wounds I have to have around women; I expected more than them to leave; the Spirit of behavior I did was to hurt them; they made me jealous by leaving so it's their fault
Pocketbook - I think everyone cheated me out of whatever I have decided is mine; I believe a system that says people robbed me when I was really the one that did that to them

My Part

How Am I...
Dishonest - Half of this wound stuff is made up; the other stuff is really what I did to others because I could
Selfish - I take no responsibility for all the times I intentionally hurt people with what I said and did, but I would like to be able to
Self-seeking - I only see things my way; I say this is just how I am, but it is truly just how I act; Spirit and principles are the only way out of me and when I justify doing; I believe I can do better
Afraid - Of always being a victim of the belief systems I created for myself before now

5 Fears

1. Fear of having faith that these are no longer real
2. Fear of having to act my way into better living
3. Fear of not having valid excuses to stay where I am
4. Fear of the spiritual side not being real and won't showing up when needed
5. Fear of me not being good enough to pull this off and being willing to change

Resentment to God

For making me work this hard to get out of the game; for not just letting me die

Corrective Measures

1. Find two ways my exit wounds play out today and call them out in real time

Expansion Pack

The expansion pack is a living, breathing prayer that goes with me in Spirit. This is where I come to Spirit and we begin to ask for things to be easy in the middle of something being hard. These are the things I want to force to change on the inside, not what is happening on the outside. Mike always said things might just be hard or scary because you say they are, and that in reality it isn't true. What I think or feel might be valid, but not relevant.

Expansion, or a shift, is a marker for me that indicates moving into principles from a place I find that dominates me. This domination stems from one of my darker behaviors. It is something I always do, but it's killing me more than helping. That's how I know I need to change—the pain becomes greater than the payoff. This is the crux of the case for how I justify all my behavior coming from the dark side.

An example of the expansion pack in motion is progressing from my insane expectations of others into something else. Expansion over time and moments happens through asking myself why do I think I need to have expectations. The answer that Spirit provides is: because you think you do and you still think you get something out of pushing on people to be who you think they should be for you. I then remember that I always have motives. Why do I think I need to have motives? Spirit says: because you have told yourself that you have to have them. Spirit tells me to consider the possibility that I have just not remembered that motives are not necessary. But then I ask, why is it so hard? Spirit always has an answer. Spirit says: because you say it is. What if you could ask me to remember that it isn't hard, and you are just awesome at creating things with expectations tied to them? It's simpler than you think.

People say the universe rearranges itself to accommodate one's picture of reality. When I think things are always unfair, the universe has to bring more unfairness to me. When I say I'm always jealous, the universe brings me more things to be jealous of. There may be no truth in any of that, but I am way more careful to look at my belief systems and see how insanely attached I can get. I always seem to attract more of what I don't want, probably because I focus on it most of my waking hours.

The expansion pack is a contract based on my Spirit having final say to things I think I feel. This contract also says that I am willing to believe anything I think, hate, or criticize is only half as bad or half as big as I think it is. This is the expansion shift. Spirit and principles like integrity, brotherly love, willingness, or humility are the target for my expansion from the shit I see or the unfairness I live in.

I ask God, could you help me to be willing to be willing to believe anything is half as unfair as I think it is? Could you make this shift feel cool in me? I have to ask the God dude. It's like in The Matrix. instant expansion upon request. Are you willing to believe it is? I just pretend to remember it is already done.

I expand my need to be authentic and honest, my need to lessen my opinions.

Expanding my need to be tolerant, to have integrity, be in gratitude, needing to not be a victim, needing to be humble. Remember, and so it is done. I don't need self-pity; I need to pretend that that's true starting now.

Inventory

How this affects my...
Self-esteem - On the surface, I thought this was bullshit; I thought I could pretend because no one was telling me I had to do this or that
Pride - My pride actually stood down; seems I've been waiting my whole life for the instant change and pretend door to open up
Security - My security comes and goes just like my feelings; what if I made up the bad feelings because someone told me to? What if my feelings could be ascended?
Ambition - I have no ambition anymore; I'm tired of what I have known; I understand expansion is already completed, I'm just required to remember
Men - Maybe If I change first, some will also, if they don't, why do I need to care? What if I could remember I am way more tolerant than I ever thought I could be? What if I remember that I already am?
Women - The expansion pack for me with women is letting them know they don't have to change a thing; my opinions are not important, what is important is me not needing to think they should change anything
Pocketbook - I should get paid to be a better person

My Part

How Am I...
Dishonest - I lie about being confused and angry when it comes to changing over to principles and spiritual law
Selfish - I don't like to be pushed out of my comfort zone; if I have to go down this road, I expect people to do the same but treat me better instantly when I get a learning curve??
Self-seeking - I even try to push the principles around; I find I try to control my Spirit dude which is really funny when I think about it
Afraid - I'm afraid to put in the effort for my belief systems to be changed yet I forget the pain and misery that drove me here and keeps me here

5 Fears

1. Fear of letting go of what I know
2. Fear of people taking advantage of me like I do them
3. Fear of me refusing to get honest about the things I think are still working for me, like manipulation

4. Fear of God refusing to work with me on my terms
5. Fear of radical change

Resentment to God

That this is all God has to offer; that service, honesty, inventory, and amends makes me want to throw up in my mouth a little bit

Corrective Measures

1. Two times tomorrow, pick two things that you will do that you usually refuse to do (i.e. not trying to be in control of the way something is done, not sharing opinions for a hour, not criticizing when you always do that)
2. Ask yourself why you think you're supposed to hate any part of the expansion pack; pick things and ask yourself why you think you don't like growing into it and doing it?

Resentment Warrior

Getting vs. not getting (what I want)

This is a radical piece. I thought I had to understand it, but I really don't. My mind never will, and that's perfectly fine. My Spirit says it's in me, so I believe it is—one moment, one decision at a time. Getting what I want is easy. I pray to get things that I want to a Santa Claus God. I even visualize these things, like "The Secret" tells me to. Manifestation will get me what I want, right? I ask God to wave His magic wand and create the highest possibility of the performance, effect, and embodiment of things coming easy for me, for what I believe I should have. I even ask for the force of grace to move things my way. Then, my Spirit executes His plan for me on the path that will present itself. Anyone else have trouble with this working?

The force of getting my way and how I control this has many old belief systems woven within it that don't include me getting what I want. All kinds of feelings, judgments, self-pity, and self-righteousness come deep within and through the experience by my Spirit Dude, especially when I don't get my way when I believe I should.

It never comes to mind that if I don't get my way it was probably an experience and path that God and Spirit have created for me. The purpose of this is to humble me and get me ready to go down a path of some version of humility I've not seen before.

Not getting my way instantly brings up a lot of shit about what I think and feel. The same shit from the last time I didn't get my way rears its ugly head. These are my favorite dark dude running buddies. They're fierce. They want my life and for me to think they are still real and alive today in this moment. They are the "grass is greener" guys, the "I deserve more" guys, the "I'm better than this" guys. Inside of me a fierce anger and rage is always waiting for me to blame something. Other lurking entities are jealousy which arises because someone is getting what I want and I know it, and blame for everyone involved in me not getting what I want. Don't forget the shock of things not going my way.

I blame all of this on God at the highest level. Why can't I somehow make people want to give me what I want? Can't they just read my mind? I was so used to manipulating people that when I didn't, I was angered by still not getting the results I was looking for. The blame I feel for what I think I did wrong, how I failed to get what I wanted, and how it's my colossal fuck up ravages my thoughts. I put all these together, walk around for a while, and make people feel my shit energy until I get tired of it. At least until the next time.

Not getting things that I deserve has all kinds of old contracts wrapped in it that are a bottomless pit and block me from the other side. There is my Spirit Dude waiting and asking to offer me patience, humility, and giving my stuff away. My Spirit tells me: what if getting is the same thing as giving, just a different experience, and it's meant to bring things I have forgotten to remember in my spiritual nature?

I never had the thought of being the Spirit Dude, but I come to the table with these belief systems that say it isn't going to happen and that I don't even have the courage to stand. There was a part of me that said Spirit Dude stuff was for wimps and quitters. But when there's nothing left and you suck at killing yourself, you try anything. I had never even heard of this kind of stuff, except in church, and I knew the building would burn if I stepped inside the chapel. Who would have thought that being a decent, good dude was already within me? I certainly didn't. No pressure.

I learn nothing when I get my way. When I doubt, or lose things or people, the God piece says "have a seat, get a pen and paper, and I'll show you moments and a path to move through these defects in real time. You don't have to remember anything that's ever happened in your life to be present and willing."

Consider the possibilities, one principle at a time, as we move through you one issue at a time here and now. Pretend that God's Spirit is already embedded in you. This other stuff is not what I came for. If angels weren't present in my life, I would never see that all this stuff might be smaller and easier than I think. How could I see who I am myself when I was trained so well to be a junkie, liar, and a thief?

A little less angry than one minute ago, and a little more humble than I've ever been in my life, how could I ever see humility unless I had none? How would I see jealousy if I was never jealous first? How could I be less demanding if I did not have the courage to be much more demanding in the first place?

From the beginning, Mike was making me write this stuff out. The language was different than I expected, especially coming from Spirit through a Black Panther junkie heroin addict who was opinionated as hell. It was a totally different experience hearing how this man spoke and how he made me write. Everything to this day is written out, whatever the complaint or bitch is, including the **Resentment to God** for not getting something. Somehow, we decide, in this writing, that this shit just won't do. I'd rather kill myself. He would sit with me and say, "I want you to imagine your Spirit being big enough and within you with everything it represents to you, good or bad."

Now imagine you and your Spirit getting on a Zoom call with the Spirit of God. Now think about having these calls every fucking night. God would say, "ask me your junkie ass questions. Let's play ball." Then he would say, "how do you think you would answer your questions? Through principles, with your claims that you don't even have the option not to hate. Leave your hate over in the garage for a minute, we'll pick it up later. Now, school can be in session, maybe even with a part of you you haven't seen before, so you think. What if this part of you has never been far and available? Or not?"

When I don't get my way, all sorts of alarms go off. I believe I have to push back on others or entire systems of selfish people that get in my way. The way I see it, they must be the problem. The other side, the one that Mike brought to me, was that I have a big part in not getting my way through expectations and motives. My part is the expectation, dishonesty, or judgments I have of how I think I deserve to get my way. This, in turn, means that others do not get their way. I like to conveniently forget that.

Maybe it was someone else's turn to get something their way or what they needed, and for you to be the one that gives it to them because you didn't want to. How cool is that?

What would it look like to have the integrity or the humility to see what is right in when I do not get my way? What if that's the crux of the Spirit world for me? What if that's the goal? It's that simple, I just complicate it with my bullshit.

The funny thing is, for some of us, it makes total fucking sense. Spiritual school has commenced. I was going to live out of the covenant I made with God, or not. Welcome to moments of Spirit in real time done by a piece of shit like myself. I might even not be a piece of shit when I'm doing this. I'm not, until I stop doing this and I am again.

Inventory

How this affects my...
Self-esteem - I program myself to be angry and defensive by not getting what I want
Pride - I will not be a victim; others don't see me not getting my way
Security - God is not with me when I don't get my way; I'm close to God only when I win
Ambition - I will lie, cheat, and steal to win; I'm only ok when I get my way
Men - I treat men like shit when they get what I want
Women - Women are supposed to stand down to me and let me get my way, especially in the bedroom and in the house
Pocketbook - I always deserve more; I'm kind of sick like that

My Part

How Am I...
Dishonest - If I can't have it, no one else should have it; I really think like this
Selfish - Is there really any other way to be? I think this is normal
Self-seeking - I tell myself I'm ok, but even I know that isn't the truth
Afraid - I'll never be able to change and live by principles

5 Fears

1. Fear of not winning
2. Fear of not getting my way
3. Fear of not telling anyone about this
4. Fear of depression that comes with this
5. Fear of being kind

Resentment to God

For making believe that not getting my way is so painful and difficult and not letting me remember that it isn't

Corrective Measures

1. Let two people get their way tomorrow when I want the opposite without saying anything about it and keeping my mouth shut
2. Make an amend to someone who you have trampled on so you could get your way

Haven't remembered yet

So, one day, there was a moment I believe my Spirit got sick of listening to all my anger, intolerance, complaining, self-pity, and more. Spirit told me to sit, and that a technique was about to be revealed for my Spirit to the God Spirit and the God Spirit to my Spirit. We're going to pretend that these things have already been changed on some level and that I have just not remembered. He said that none of what I think is true.

I can use this process in me for anything that has become a problem in my life. Everything seems to be a problem for this drug addict having to become a better understanding dude. I love the word dude to describe many aspects of my personality. This process saved my life, I am willing to pretend my way out of something I get stuck in.

When I am angry, Spirit says that I have the choice to imagine that I'm only half as angry as I think I am. What if you have not remembered that you are not? What if anything bad that happens today is only half as bad as I think it is? What if you just haven't remembered and that whatever it is, is not that bad at all?

When I'm insulted, Spirit says, what if the insult is not half as bad, and what if you just have not remembered that you are not insulted? When people cut you off in traffic, what if you're only half as mad as you think you are, imagine that and what if you just have not remembered that you are not mad in real time? When I'm pissed at my kids for something they did that they do over and over, and I tell myself that this time I have had it, Spirit reminds me. What if I am only half as pissed as I think I am? What if? And what if in this moment I just remember what it is not? When I seriously get offended about something anyone says, especially when I think I'm supposed to get offended, what if I'm only half as offended as I think I am? What if I pretend to remember that I am probably not offended, I just am obsessed with thinking I am? What if I pretended for a moment with Spirit that I am not?

What if I have not remembered that I don't hate everything? What if I haven't remembered I don't have to judge everyone? What if I remember that I don't need to judge at all? What if I remembered that I don't have to be right to be OK? What if I remembered that I don't need to have an opinion? What if I remembered that I am not insecure, right in the middle of some insecurity? What if I remember people are not out to get me when I think they are?

I have to get right in the middle of one of my mental storms to be brave enough, along with my Spirit, to be willing to be willing to believe the storm is only half as big as I make it out to be. I need to be willing to believe it is not a storm at all, it is just a path, should I take it.

Inventory

How this affects my...
Self-esteem - I am a byproduct of my past; I really don't want to remember because it's all about burning down the past and stepping into a much better, decent part of me
Pride - I don't want to remember because there are dark parts of me that still work well in my life that I don't want to change
Security - My security and insecurity count on me to deal within or change; I'm not willing to bring someone in that will make me move or change my behavior, I am totally screwed until I do
Ambition - I may not like the problem in me or the same old behavior, but it's what I know
Men - I don't want to remember men are not the enemy; someone else will have to go first here; I can't change or add value to my own life
Women - I just have not remembered yet to treat women better; I have not remembered that I'm a gentleman; I have not remembered that I don't have motives
Pocketbook - I have not remembered that money is not everything; I haven't remembered that it is not money that makes me suffer, it is how badly I need it

My Part

How Am I...
Dishonest - I have not remembered that I'm not dishonest, that I might even love being honest someday, just not today
Selfish - I have not remembered or seen today the part of me that is unselfish, but I have seen it; I just don't think I liked it, but it does feel familiar
Self-seeking - I have not remembered self-esteem is an illusion that I don't need; I have not remembered that I have principles and don't have to like them, just pretend I don't hate them
Afraid - Of remembering that there is one purpose in the rest of my days; I am afraid I have the energy and knowing to proceed in spirit

5 Fears

1. Fear of remembering my past means nothing on this path
2. Fear of not hating everything
3. Fear of not feeling sorry for myself
4. Fear of being very useful and available for instructions and purpose outside of what I want to do
5. Fear of things I don't want to remember or do

Resentment to God

For waking me up now; for not allowing me to continue to be what I love, like lying, cheating, predator, con man

Corrective Measures

1. When in the moment of a strong emotion, like anger or self-pity, ask my Spirit to help me remember that it's only half as big as I think it is
2. Two times tomorrow, pretend that you have remembered and see what comes in

Hesitation Warrior

Limits

The idea of limits is one of my greatest cons. Limits are how I prepare the answer of "no" to either myself or others. I will only do as much as I say, and sometimes not even that much. I have convenient limits, and if I am pushed past them, I quit. I use limits as an unstated ultimatum. I have used this belief system about limitations up until today to hold myself and others hostage in any given situation.

I use limits against people in relationships. I tell myself that I will do only as much as you will, but even that isn't true. In my mind, limits lurk on the edge of what I think is fair. I believe it is incredibly complicated, which means that it is a byproduct of another facet of my need to control.

Where and when did I set these bars to my limits? I can't even explain any of them. Why is it that I have no problem taking out the trash for the members of my family four times, but on the 5th time I lose my mind? What is that about? When did that show up? It seems like I keep score, and sometimes don't even know I'm doing it. Suddenly, seemingly out of nowhere, I tell myself I can't take it anymore. I have a belief that I'm always on the edge, I'm overloaded, I have a lot on my plate. But when I sit down and recognize what I do daily, I realize it's really not that much. Taking out the trash, going to work, being a spouse and a grandparent are really part of life. I expect to expend no energy, which is the epitome of being unrealistic.

Why do I know so much about everything I won't do? Why do I know so little about what I could be willing to do? When I say I have limits, these constraints come out of belief systems that say I won't change. What if my limits are only half as big as I think they are? What if I just have not remembered that I don't have limits? There are things within myself that I have determined that I won't do or will do based on where I come from. I create and justify imaginary thresholds that allow me to revert to old behavior when I don't get my way. Mike told me that I had not been here before. He directed me to join him on a path where we would bring up one limit, address it, and do something to see if it is actually still real. I took Mike into all my parameters so he could tell me how to move through it with force. The greatest thing Spirit and God gave me is the courage to do this coupled with their force to help me go places within myself that I used to be too scared or resistant to go to alone.

When I wrote a letter to God asking Him why I have limits, this is what I received in response: limits for you are how you set a bar to how and when you feel used or not. You have limits because you say you do. You think you have been abused by people who have asked or demanded you to do more than they will do. You have been taught this is wrong. On many levels, you want to see not being pushed past what you think or want to do is wrong. In reality, this is how leaders are formed. Limits are a gift because by nature, you have signed on to being lazy and doing as little as possible. If you do get pushed to the limits you have set, you believe everyone else should, too.

This immaturity of yours in Spirit world would limit where I need you. To be a Spiritual warrior for me, you need to expand and go as far as I say every day. You are always stretching and toning these muscles. Find the gratitude that you can be pushed by principles and serve my children. Your mind and soul are capable of being pushed way beyond what you think and the emotions that you have from the past. I am teaching you that limits are within yourself. When your heartbeat and breath go out—that's the one to worry about.

Inventory

How this affects my...
Self-esteem - I decide how much or how little I will do; my limits are preset within me, how that happened, I don't know
Pride - I love telling people how much I'm willing to do; I know they might ask for more which justifies my quitting
Security - I have to make my own decisions of what I will or won't do; I don't tolerate being manipulated and expected to do more
Ambition - I will only do as much as the next guy; in my mind if I do more I automatically decide this is unfair; there are definitely things I have no limits on doing
Men - Men don't limit what they do for me or expect of me
Women - As far as what I will do for women or allow, it is endless, if they will give me the attention I need and want; once I have a woman, my limits will become known; during the chase all bets are off
Pocketbook - I have way less limitations if you pay me; I am totally for sale for the most part

My Part

How Am I...
Dishonest - I say I will do anything to the right person for the right price, but I won't, all of this is a lie
Selfish - I put limits on people and what I want, I have none on myself; I will change my mind if I feel like it, but not if anyone asks me to
Self-seeking - I have no loyalty; I do have demands of what I should have done for me; if I do something for someone else, I demand they praise me for it in abundance.
Afraid - Of being alone when people get tired of my bullshit and see through me

5 Fears

1. Fear of that I make it too hard to begin change
2. Fear of people not trusting me
3. Fear of never doing more than I want

4. Fear of being utterly selfish
5. Fear of asking for help and identifying what I can be through the Spirit of God

Resentment to God

For letting me get so fucked up, selfish, and stuck in what I know

Corrective Measures

1. Do something extra for someone, either in the home or at work
2. The next two times someone asks you to do something you don't want to do, say yes and pretend you don't hate it

Blame Warrior

My Part

Let's be clear: it is horrible finding my part in things I have experienced. It is a whole different universe of any past I thought I lived. To recognize my part is like a different language than I have spoken. Finding where my actions come into play the biggest piece of my relationship with my Spirit and the Spirit of God. First, I must be granted the courage and honesty to go down this path. This comes from the Spirit of God alone, and I have to ask for it. Doing this cuts across anything I grew up with or came out believing in the game. It plainly had to be done. I find my Spirit has to be present to find it and acknowledge my part in the harms I have done throughout my life. This is true especially in the way my belief systems tell me how I should be.

My sponsor gave me an avenue to find my part, which would eventually give me a reason to live. This method comes into all the four column pieces that I've put in this book. My dark belief system says this is all bullshit and demands I don't look at this stuff. He makes it clear that he wants my life to stay the same: miserable, depressing, and without purpose.

First, I make a list of what harms have been done to me by someone or an institution (like marriage or the police). What follows is a few examples beliefs I have implemented and my part in them.

Belief: People don't lie to me.
My Part: I lie and I'm unforgiving.

Belief: People don't tell me no.
My Part: I tell people no all the time with no consideration of what they need from me. I lie about why I tell people no, and question why should I do for people what they won't do for me. Things I ask for are purely selfish and unwarranted, I give nothing.

Belief: People should want me in their lives.
My Part: I give nothing in relationships worth wanting or having. I never shut up about my opinions. I have consistently burned people. Why should they let me into their lives to begin with?

Belief: I deserve more.
My Part: I believe that I deserve more but I give little to begin with or even in return. Why should I get everything without giving? This is the selfishness that is killing me without deep-seated principles coming into my behavior.

Belief: I like being dishonest and hate when others judge me for that.
My Part: I expect honesty and caring behavior, yet I don't feel the need to reciprocate. My part is thinking and expecting people to treat me honestly.

After 14 years of working up to looking at my behavior today, I find my part in belief systems on a regular basis. Unhealthy contracts crop up consistently, and it takes monumental effort to continue to burn them down by finding my part. The alternative is worse, so I keep chugging along.

Inventory

How this affects my...
Self-esteem - I have a need to be able to blame people for what I think and feel about a situation; I don't want or need to be responsible for what you think I do wrong towards you
Pride - People just need to get over anything I do that is harmful and inappropriate
Security - What I need to be OK is for people to buy into my selfishness and dishonesty and however I choose to treat them
Ambition - I can't feel responsible to find my part in anything, I wish I could, but I don't; my part thinks it is not my responsibility to worry about
Men - I really owe men nothing different; I think they will all screw me over like I do them
Women - Women only want me around when I tell them all the lovely things they want to hear; they don't want to be around the real me, at least I know when I see my part
Pocketbook - I would much rather take the earn; my part is I don't think I ever get enough even though I give as little effort as possible

My Part

How Am I...
Dishonest - I lie and dismiss my part as being problematic; I won't look at my arrogance, undermining behavior, or my controlling nature with what I do to justify my part or not having a part at all
Selfish - I refuse to see anything wrong about how I come at the world; I just like to complain about what I don't get; my jealousy is as important as breathing
Self-seeking - I don't really care about how I affect others; I care about no one's feelings except the women with whom I'm trying to create importance
Afraid - I will never find it important enough to change small things; afraid of old belief systems about all this not allowing me to find the courage to live in principle

5 Fears

1. Fear of being totally honest
2. Fear of my Spirit not waking up because of or in spite of me
3. Fear of looking weak
4. Fear of being responsible for my part and harming others
5. Fear of not being afraid enough to make life changes every day

Resentment to God

For bringing me to a point in my life where I have to surrender my will and right to be right

Corrective Measures

1. Admit to two people my part in an amends I said I was never going to make
2. Pretend to take accountability for what my part in a situation is and don't blame someone or something else; pretend it isn't painful to do so

My Dark Side Warrior

My Regrets

Do I have regrets? Probably. They were never in my design. Someone who is powered by glorious selfishness does all the horrible things I did. Everything I thought I needed to do and things I said because I felt I needed something was second nature. Am I willing to make amends for my behavior and do what is needed to make things right to the person or institution I harmed? My answer had to be yes, I'm willing to pay anything forward.

Regrets are horrible. They keep me suspended and living in what is done and over. They seem so real and justified when they show up. They are old contracts with things I have done, but I think if I could do them again, I imagine what I would do differently. Regrets are part of this depression thing. Sometimes I can get depressed in my current state. Better yet, I can dig up some old regret and it can activate the depression contract I get into.

One day I was on a roll and my Spirit hit me with this: Michael, could you be willing to be willing to believe that in this moment all your regrets might be only half as big and dominant as you think they are? Consider the possibility that you just have not remembered that they are no longer real. That is, unless you decide that you need them to be. You just have not remembered that you may not need them any longer. The people in your regrets probably never think of you. Most, if not all, have happily moved on and you no longer affect them.

I had never thought of that before. I still thought they sit around talking about how I screwed them over. Self-importance would be an understatement.

I asked my Spirit dude about this. He is so cool in how he breaks me down. He said to me, you did not have any regrets, remorse, or guilt when you did all this stuff before yesterday. What makes you believe you have regret, remorse, or guilt now? Just saying. It is very cool to think you feel bad, but look at the things you do. Can you really feel bad when you continue to behave in the cycle? Guilt and regrets seem convenient to talk about in front of an audience or to make you feel better momentarily, but it doesn't show in your behavior.

One of my favorite things to talk about is the Pay it Forward Plan, like in the movie. I never cry, but I cry every time I watch that movie at the end. I was taught at 44 years old the only way to deal with the regret was to pay it forward. That is what the 12 steps, four column resentment inventory, and amends do for me.

My wish was to ask my Spirit to come alive and walk through each regret I think of and find a way to make it possible to make right my mistakes. The goal is to find a way to make this type of regret right by not doing the same behavior to hurt people. Part of how I do the things today in real time makes up for old regrets I cannot change.

Inventory

How this affects my...

Self-esteem - Deep inside, I have to make up regrets; any regret I have or think I have can easily be replaced by me justifying any damage I did

Pride - My pride says that I don't really feel guilty for anything that could be a regret; pride is the dark voice that says regrets only come up in the process of getting off drugs and liquor

Security - I just need to detach from regrets to be OK; I need to dig deeper into my no remorse pattern

Ambition - Ambition says regrets are just ways I have to clean up and get better; I have to get better at being self-righteous, controlling, and lying

Men - I expect men to have great remorse for all the things they do to me today and have done in the past

Women - I expect women to have remorse for how they have judged me, avoided me, and things they said about me in the past and even now in real time; don't they know how sensitive I am or controlling they need to let me be?

Pocketbook - I have a little remorse from the people I have robbed or stolen from; they all deserved it a little for not just giving me what I wanted anyway

My Part

How Am I...

Dishonest - I only have regrets for things I got caught doing and for having to go to jail on charges like possession

Selfish - I should not have to regret anything; I should be able to sweep it under the rug and call it the best I could do; I really like having no remorse

Self-seeking - I expect people in my past to have regrets for the bad things they did to me; why won't they make it right like I have to?

Afraid - Of Making things right with people, I really screwed up in the past; afraid of being accountable and doing the next right thing when I don't think I have to; afraid of completing 12 steps each day in real time

5 Fears

1. Fear of letting people off the hook
2. Fear of finding my part
3. Fear of humility
4. Fear of honesty within myself
5. Fear of forgiving myself for my regrets, things I wish I could have done differently

Resentment to God

For not allowing me to fix or control me and things I have done in the past

Corrective Measures

1. Write a prayer to God to ask my Spirit to remove the past and find one purpose for what I've done since then
2. Two times pretend the regret is half as big as I think it is in a letter to God and that I haven't remembered that it's gone yet

Resentment Warrior

Pretending

I pretend to know a lot more than I know I do in reality. I've always been a con, finding a thrill out of making things up along the way. Inside, what no one can see or know, is that I pretend to care about people. In general, I pretend to feel guilty, but I never do. I pretend I'm going to give things back to people that give me their time and (especially) money. I've been a liar and a thief so many times and haven't had a problem with it any of that. I pretend to be loyal, until I'm not. I have become so good at pretending that it has taken on a life of its own, like an inside joke that I share with myself.

I con myself into believing I can and will be a better person. I found that although there is a popular opinion that we lie to ourselves, I never lie to myself. The only reason I know this is because I do exactly what I mean to do and when I want to do it. Pretending is just lying. My motives with people are to just get as much as they will give me and then disappear and go on to a new set of people that will believe me. This is what the game and life in addiction taught me.

I sold weed for many years because I learned that everyone loves their drug dealer. They begged me to come and always had money for me. These "clients" needed me every few days. I thought that was my version of love. I never pretended to be happy. I was stuck in a cycle of being suicidal or being incredibly high. Sometimes, I was both. I settled for not being unhappy. I lowered my expectations to live less unhappy than I was. I have never, in my life, had to work hard, but I pretend that I do. When people find out that I don't, they get a little jealous, and they judge me for what I did to others. That is the tough one to get over.

Jealousy is or can be a difficult contract to move through. Most people I have known at times can be jealous. I only think the worst about people that get or have more than me. I found if I'm not around a bunch of jealous people, I tend to not be so jealous. I'm very selective what people are in my life. Today, I remember that these people have to be better than me for me to grow. Without being challenged, I will be stagnant and eventually move backwards.

There came a time in my recovery when I needed to act like I was willing to pretend to move towards principles being the most important thing in my life. I had to pretend to care about which others needed me to be in their lives, at least half of the time to begin with. An example was that I had to pretend to not need to talk about people negatively. This had to come from the depths of my Spirit, not my mind. I had to pretend to not need to control what people said and did. Pretending and asking my Spirit within to not need to complain about anything was also necessary. I needed to do these things at least two times a day in real time. Although this seemed impossible, I began to pretend to not need to be so angry about things that don't go my way. Replacing the anger with the thought that maybe I was just a little irritated helped enormously. The things I refused to do, when coupled with pretending to do something just a little different, were really doable. I believed I had to remember that all the shifts have already happened within and through Spirit and are true on some level in this moment already. With these words and a new belief system ringing true, moments of change started showing up within me. This was all through Spirit, not by going through my mind.

Inventory

How this affects my...
Self-esteem - It allows me to lie about anything; gets me into the best circles
Pride - For some reason, I take great pride for conning people to get things
Security - My security is so shallow that this is really a good thing for my security
Ambition - My ambition is to get good enough at pretending that no one will ever suspect
Men - I lie, cheat, and steal from men but they better not do this to me
Women - I pretend to be sensitive and care about puppies and things in order to get women to like me and end up in bed with me
Pocketbook - I will lie to get more when it comes to money or prestige; pretending to be smart and committed going into relationships and jobs is something I'm very good at

My Part

How Am I...
Dishonest - I have no guilt or loyalty to people and relationships; it's not about where I am loyal and my relationships, Spirit says it's only about where you are not
Selfish - I only think about what I want or think I need
Self-seeking - I'm usually only after things I want to take that people don't want to give to me, like I used to rob my drug dealer to save money, then I would help then find what I stole… priceless
Afraid - Of being caught in the act of being something I'm not; of being called fake and a liar even though I was

5 Fears

1. Fear of not pretending and being honest and authentic
2. Fear of being alone
3. Fear of not being or feeling guilty
4. Fear of not wanting or needing to change
5. Fear of not knowing the truth from the false

Resentment to God

For allowing me to be so good at pretending and treating people like they were nothing

Corrective Measures

1. List three ways that I could pretend are positive and do them twice each
2. List three ways that I pretend as a defense mechanism and don't do them at least twice each

Secrets Warrior

Principles

Acting like a selfish prick really wore me out after 30 years. I was really good at it. Now, being really, really principled seems like it wears me out as well. Then, I checked with myself and agree that it doesn't. I'm willing to believe that having to tap into Spirit and working outside of what my old belief systems require or where principles lie is easier than I think it is. Principles are a shock to my self-seeking system.

Regarding honesty, I'm on a path where I need to tell you where I have been dishonest and have lied. For this path with Spirit, I make amends with the people I can find that I harmed, stole from, and lied about. I want to think this is scary stuff, but it really isn't. I have done way scarier things in addiction. I asked these people if they need to say something about what I have done and prompt to just listen and not talk back. The worst part is that I have to ask them what I can do to make it right. Then I have to do what they tell me.

There is an opposing principle for each of my defects. The aspect of discipline arises for me when I list all of them and make amends as quickly as possible in a short period of time. This is all part of the covenant I made with God. It sets the record straight to any and everything in my past. This has to be done face to face.

Practicing principles kind of sucks sometimes. Being who I was in the game was killing me, but I'd be lying if I said I didn't enjoy it. My Spirit Dude has to come into me and we have to come together in order for me to get into this principled mode.

A few of the principles I practice are: impeccable honesty, faith, hope that I can walk this path when I don't want to, courage to represent the Spirit of God, willingness to stay on path and allow others what they need from me, humility to take a knee when others say I do things that I think harm me instead of them.

I never wanted to need to be this guy, but I became tired of the old, controlling me. Forgiveness, discipline, and brotherly love are things I must live by today. I do this because I don't want to. I have surrendered in all the ways I resisted so I could have a better life.

Inventory

How this affects my...

Self-esteem - Principles ask way too much of me to change; I like to change slowly and drag things out

Pride - In principle I'm not supposed to be in pride; my pride is asked to leave the room by my spirit for a day

Security - My security is out the door; my securities become insecurities; insecurities come only when I get apart from my Spirit

Ambition - Since I am not in Spirit allowed to lie, cheat, and steal, ambitions are whatever is going on at the time

Men - I don't think all men are pieces of shit in principle, just God's kids
Women - I begin to resemble a gentleman; conning women is not principled, I go make it right and let them know I can and will do better, it's a crazy concept
Pocketbook - I pretend to not need to worry a lot; I become grateful for the problems I don't have

My Part

How Am I...
Dishonest - I lie when I say I practice these principles all the time, in actuality today it's probably around 65%
Selfish - I judge and hate on people for thinking they need to practice principles to me
Self-seeking - If I act humble towards something or someone and I have to tell people about it, it doesn't count; Spirit told me I don't get credit if I brag
Afraid - That I will get tired of this path and principles and end up somewhere I don't want to be, I don't want to be the old version of me again

5 Fears

1. Fear of having to do more than others in principles
2. Fear of giving up
3. Fear of my own dark side taking over
4. Fear of overcomplicating with God in Spirit
5. Fear of needing to not take from people; fear of my deep judgment

Resentment to God

For pulling me out of a great drug induced life only to be offered to take me and serve a powerful God, why don't I get to do what I want now that I'm free of drugs?

Corrective Measures

1. Identify two principles I despise and write inventory on them
2. Write a prayer to God asking to hate the principle half as much as you think you do. Ask, what is the motive for hating something like honesty?

Purpose

I have done my best to find a purpose in my life that fits and is continuous. My purpose has been to be the best con artist, to control people, to get what I want, and have as little responsibility as possible. In other words, to lie, cheat, and steal, and above everything don't get caught. If I could do this, it was a good day. After 30 or 35 years, the consequences caught up to me. My consequences were that no one wanted to have anything to do with me. Everything I was involved in was illegal. Not to mention the deep consuming depression that even meds would not help. My wife was in rehab. Only one of us could afford to go. She and all the women in rehab gave me a big ultimatum: get to a 12-step meeting for cocaine and meth or get out of the house. I thought, how bad could it be? Then I was shocked when at the meeting they told me I had to work the 12 steps.

So, I did. I still do every day because of my bad behavior. My Spirit-driven purpose has little to do with the purpose I make up for myself. My purpose is actually yet to be determined, even though sometimes I think I know what it is. Mike convinced me that my purpose will always be woven within this covenant I wrote to giving my life, thoughts, and feelings to the Spirit of the principles.

I'm not crazy. I work on two principles a day. My purpose is to unthink and unfeel. Mike told me that what I think and feel has to be bullshit. This is true because it comes from me and my belief systems that have been killing me.

When I get sad, I'm probably not getting something I want. It's usually about a woman. When I'm angry, I'm probably not getting something or I think somebody is being disrespectful toward me (like I normally am, right?). When I'm judging someone, that person is doing a better job at something than I usually am, which makes me jealous. All my feelings are attached to my expectations of how people should treat me or that I should be getting more than the next guy. There are thousands of different versions of this running through my head. They all come back deep in the night. I want more, so I should get more and do less. This is Spirit world.

Inventory

How this affects my...
Self-esteem - My real purpose is to take up as much of people's time and energy as possible
Pride - I really have no pride or purpose; I just make people think I do because I say so
Security - I talk about purpose because people say I need to know what mine is; my purpose is to get things so I can feel a false sense of security
Ambition - My ambition is what people think I will do; I demand an audience until I actually have to perform (then I cut and run)
Men - Purpose with men is a lie; I lie about everything so they will look up to me; I avoid men and try to do my damage to women

Women - My purpose with women is purely and most of the time sexual. I'm a predator and lie to women about anything to get them to love me
Pocketbook - To get what I deserve and more; to not get caught when being a thief, I'm always a thief on some level, whether it is money or women, I believe I need to take things to be OK

My Part

How Am I...
Dishonest - My purposes based on what I can take, what I do reflects my purpose; I used purpose as an excuse to harm people because they harm me
Selfish - I don't really care what other people's purpose is, mine is more important
Self-seeking - I am great at convincing people that their true purpose is to agree with me and help me more than themselves
Afraid - Of the purpose that I have and seek; that my belief system about all this is crap and won't hold up for long, then what do I do?

5 Fears

1. Fear of having no real purpose
2. Fear of needing to change everything
3. Fear of thinking I am only cold hearted and will just be alone
4. Fear of being of service to God and his kids unconditionally
5. Fear of truly facing myself with my Spiritual Father and not running

Resentment to God

For not letting me die in meth addiction, for wanting me to serve his children, for not making me better than that

Corrective Measures

1. Imagine your purpose in principle where you have none (what would a purpose to God's children be?) two times tomorrow.
2. Write a letter to Spirit: why do I find my purpose more important to people I don't care for?

Set Aside Prayer

This was the first prayer my sponsor, Mike, had me write. Nothing else has ever shifted me immediately out of dark belief systems to something else. This prayer helped me to understand that my old belief systems are not even real and that in this moment they are already not present. I have written different versions of this prayer as I have wandered down the road of spiritual possibilities within me.

My bad side and my I-don't-need-to-be-bad side run together, side by side. I believe they always will. My Spirit dude says He just gives me the courage to not need to be the dark dude.

He also says that I have the freedom to live in that dark space if I so choose. I believe He does this in order for me to not forget that that dark part of me is alive and still wants my life.

The following are two set aside prayer examples.

God, please set aside everything I think I know about my old belief systems, about control, about how I think people should treat me, about humility, about honesty, about respect, about being lonely, about being right, about myself, and especially about you, God. So that I may have an open mind and a new experience with my belief systems, with control, being controlled, taking control, with how I think I need people to treat me, with my humility, honesty, respect, with loneliness, with needing to be right, with myself and especially with you, God. So that this can be fully manifested into my picture of reality. And so it is.

God, please lay aside what I think I know about disrespect, being demanding, self-worth, justice, expectations, harm, motives, anger, jealousy, rage, responsibility, fairness, and happiness. This is a path for me to find where I am hung up on me and how I use the past to fortify what I do, think, and feel. It won't do anymore.

I can plug anything into this prayer. Wherever I think I'm suffering, when added to this prayer, the topic or issue becomes much smaller and more manageable.

I say this prayer two times a day, once when I wake up and another time before I sleep. When I do this for two weeks, life changes. If I miss one time, I will start the clock over. I have so many belief systems that I carry over from life before I began this that it will always be relevant.

Inventory

How this affects my...
Self-esteem - This Is making me question where all my shit behavior is; I just have to look in the mirror
Pride - I think I'm quite comfortable where I am on the outside only because I've never been ready to allow me to change anything
Security - It makes me question get honest about how suicidal I am; this shakes up all any security and insecurity I think I have or don't have
Ambition - I don't think I can really go any farther; I've just been hanging on to the way I am, but I will deny this until an angel finds me
Men - My disgust and hatred of men consumes me; I need my Spirit dude to give me courage to confess; I really want no part of this
Women - I stereotype women; my current obsessions with women are at an all-time high; I want to have a problem with this and not be afraid
Pocketbook - The expectations I have with people and money are killing me; God please lay aside everything I think about money so I can have a new experience

My Part

How Am I...
Dishonest - There are some things I don't want to change because they are still working for me; like control, anger, and power
Selfish - I believe I need others to change first; any excuse will do for me to myself
Self-seeking - I brainwash any self into thinking I have to care about this to commit; caring was never necessary, I did not want to do any of the stuff that I do
Afraid - Of the unknown, of my excuses; afraid of anything that looks hard and requires change in the moment or having my Spirit change me

5 Fears

1. Fear of God and change
2. Fear of changing my belief systems
3. Fear of being honest with myself
4. Fear of humiliation (my actions say otherwise)
5. Fear of laying aside where I think and feel, I think this stuff is me, but it is really just how I act

Resentment to God

For starting to disassemble all that I think is true, both good and bad, for making all of my drug use and behavior come to this bullshit

Corrective Measures

1. Write my own version of the lay aside prayer to encompass the things with which I am struggling today
2. Say the prayer twice a day, for two weeks straight, and start over if I miss

Demands Warrior

Suffering

Anytime I find myself in suffering, it is an intricate masterpiece. Suffering is my favorite individual sport. It is best when I suffer alone. When other people are involved, I seem to suck the life out of them to avoid my own deep suffering. It has taken me years of being in my suffering without drugs and alcohol to feel and write my way into the core of this relationship I have with suffering.

I've had to have a person, who has changed their suffering and lives through the other side in spiritual principles through this Spirit, to translate my suffering in real time. The big question started out to be, why do I think I have to suffer and am I really suffering? What if it is real and I like it, since I'm not willing to do my part to change some of the core elements? I could easily and reasonably change my suffering by doing one or two things differently in a given day. But I don't.

Some of the breakdown occurs in the middle of what I think makes me suffer. I became very used to it up until now. Even if it is bad, it feels so familiar, like a friend. It came up so glaringly because I realized that I never put credit or spotlight on times when I don't suffer. I only acknowledge when I do suffer. I never saw that before. This is where some principles were brought in to create moments where I see that I don't suffer. Even if I pretend I'm not suffering, I don't seem to get to the dark place of suffering. I do this through the simple act of saying and imagining a few principles being possibly present. These include impeccable honesty, integrity as an outcome for my behavior, faith as an old friend passing through a patch of suffering, and humility when I have no expectations of suffering versus not suffering (just being a little irritated).

So, after writing and asking if suffering is real or if it's just a word I use when my many expectations are not met, I ask myself a question. Why do I think of these elements that bring me to the sacrificial table inside my suffering and listen to the darkness that makes me hold the knife to kill myself with? The pool of my suffering is really like no other. It draws life only because I gave it life. It tells me I have to obey.

Then in comes the option of my Spirit. Spirit tells me, I give you the option of waking up inside Spirit and principles so that Spirit can battle all the lies that my mind says are true. The lies are: self-pity, defiance to anything, Spirit, control, entitlement, caring, resistance, resentment, principles sucking, pride, dishonesty, controlling, thinking people have to like me, my part in things doing as little as possible, loneliness, my dark side, and complaining. I am suffering because I think things are supposed to go my way, not yours. As a servant of the Spirit, that is a lie. Serving Spirit dictates that things never go my way and that I remain grateful regarding and graceful on the journey.

I had to get beaten down around the question: why do I think I'm the only one that should get my way? An answer I walk away with in life in real time is: what if all the lessons of things that you don't think go your way, what if they are going the way intended by God in Spirit to move you into what you were really designed to be? What if, in Spirit, the good and bad stuff is really the same thing? They both will bring an experience; they just have different consequences. In suffering I try to control the consequences. I rate them as good or bad. What if I change my perception and believe that if the bad is the good and the good is the bad? I see that as the way my Spirit hands it to me. Is just something to play with.

Inventory

How this affects my...
Self-esteem - I think I've suffered enough
Pride - Others should have to suffer as much as I did
Security - I need you to suffer equally for me to be OK
Ambition - I want to manipulate my way out of pain
Men - Men don't know the definition of suffering
Women - I need to control the way women see me suffer
Pocketbook - The more money, less suffering

My Part

How Am I...
Dishonest - I say I'm suffering even when I'm not, to steal thunder
Selfish - I don't care if anyone else is suffering, it actually makes me mad because I get less attention that way
Self-seeking - I induce suffering so people pay attention to me
Afraid - Of not suffering, being cool

5 Fears

1. Fear of not being the center of attention
2. Fear of not complaining
3. Fear of not having chaos
4. Fear of trusting God
5. Fear of having expectations put on me

Resentment to God

That my past suffering doesn't preclude me from suffering more

Corrective Measures

1. Two times this week don't complain when I think I'm suffering
2. Help someone else who is suffering without offering an opinion

Taking a Knee

Taking a knee is a way for me to not engage in having to be right and just saying OK to anything. It is sparing people what I think I need to say in real time.

I learned to take a knee to my Spirit, God, when I'm in a situation or conversation or someone or something activates my dark nature to start pressing back. When I think someone has lied to me, is trying to take something I want, is getting something I want, or even trying to be right about something that I'm already thinking I'm right about, I automatically think I'm about to do battle. I start defensively. I reason to myself that there are things I naturally want to argue about and think I have a right to.

In this covenant I have with God, my Spirit, and principles, I have chosen to go down a path where I surrender my dark dude's reactions and stop for a moment to take a knee. I do this in situations when I don't want to, especially within myself. Instead, I stop and connect to Spirit. Or I just pretend to act like what my Spirit dude will have me be. It is fascinating how I can go from mad to I really don't need to be mad right now.

This is totally an inside job. I find this need to surrender in my Spirit in action and not needing to be right even though it feels like it's killing me on some level. I had a choice of either going back to being an angry drug addict or begin to take a knee in life. I had every right to get back to being controlling, hateful, defensive, non-judgmental, and holding super grudges. I decided go try another way for a while as an experiment.

This take a knee idea was either going to become the core of my behavior to everything I opposed or not. The God piece said He did not care either way. I was going to pretend to act as if it was already dialed in within me. I was going to have to determine how hard or easy it was each day, in each situation. I was going to have to write my part for when bad situations happened. I had to seek why I needed this to be hard and pretend that it might be easier than I originally thought.

Inventory

How this affects my...

Self-esteem - This cuts to the heart of my dark dude and demands, in a kind way, that I shut up and sit down

Pride - I need to speak up for myself and not battle mentally and emotionally

Security - My opinions and pushback have to matter and be recognized to be OK; this is a dominant belief system

Ambition - I don't think I am supposed to stand down to any adversity or lies about me

Men - I don't need to bow down or take a knee to any man; I cannot look weak

Women - Women are supposed to see me take a knee or surrender what I need to say to men; women should take a knee to me

Pocketbook - I have to fight to get ahead, there is no other option; I have to make people give me what I deserve when they won't give it to me

My Part

How Am I...
Dishonest - I don't take a knee unless I have motives to get or take something
Selfish - I blame people for not admitting I'm right, which I believe makes them wrong; I'm very peaceful when this happens
Self-seeking - I need people to value my opinions and my way of doing things
Afraid - That I can't surrender to Spirit and principles within myself; I'm afraid I'm too set in my ways to change my path in mind

5 Fears

1. Fear of serving the Spirit of God
2. Fear of being honest in principles in my behavior when I don't want to be
3. Fear of falling in love was not wanting to fight with people
4. Fear of taking a knee to being humble
5. Fear of staying a fearless spiritual warrior when my dark dude side shows up every day

Resentment to God

For not making decisions easier through my covenant, he says he does not do that, but he offers me the courage to be a spiritual warrior

Corrective Measures

1. List two ways you refuse to take a knee and do something different for a day
2. In an argument or disagreement, one time just stop and say, "Okay, let's do it your way". Do this without sarcasm and pretend to not hate it so much deep inside of yourself

The Cool Factor

The cool factor was a gift that showed up from my Spirit deep in the night in my room. I was surrounded by depression and anger for all the things that were not OK in my life. This was just another normal night for me at this point in my life. I hated everyone and everything and resented that I had to be a different person than I had always been. I was living perpetually in the headspace of wishing I could use drugs again without consequences.

The dark stuff that bleeds over from long term addiction to my sobriety is hard to explain. It's a continual torment of all the bad things that happened to me as well as the bad things I have done. It always comes deep in the night, on a loop that replays like a Quentin Tarantino movie that is being showcased on HBO for a month. I only seem to remember the horror, the gore, and the grimy feeling that it's left me with. Even still, I would try to recall the good times and positive feelings around using.

The cool factor is something I learned that, in a nutshell, is just all pretend. Spirit and I made it up. It is a request: could it be cool to pretend to not be angry when I am deep within my anger? Could it be cool to not hate the God piece for a minute sometimes when I do? Could it be cool to not be disrespectful to my wife for how I'm about to be? Could it be cool to not be consumed by self-pity when that's all that I can see? Or could it be kind of cool to be a little humble when I do not want to be?

When I say cool, I mean cool like my Spirit dude is cool. Cool like the Fonz cool, back when the Fonz was cool. I asked the Spirit of God for the cool factor to show up with whatever I am struggling with. This takes so much pressure off the part of me that won't get past the intensity of whatever character defect I'm sitting in.

I'm asking something to be cool about me shifting from the same old belief system I've always had to something new, unfamiliar, and uncomfortable. Even though my character defects and belief systems are killing me, there is some sort of comfort in them because they are a known factor. It's like sitting in a shitty diaper as an infant. No baby likes their diaper changed, even though they feel better afterwards. The shit is warm and comfortable and soothing. Sometimes I just can't see that life would be better if I get a fresh diaper change and that if I don't, I'll get a rash.

I am set in having to live in old belief systems like anger, control, jealousy, self-pity, intolerance, etc. The cool factor allows me to ask: what if I'm not, I just don't have the magic language to get myself out? Could it be cool to not need these defects for a day? Could being honest be more cool than being dishonest? Can we make this real today? Could it be so fucking cool within my Spirit to not feel sorry for myself when something crappy happens today? Could it be cool to call my mom today and not bitch about anything she says? That would be a miracle, by the way. Could it be cool to find some gratitude today from my life, and could that not suck?

The cool factor was a vortex between me and my Spirit. A place I could imagine my way out of old belief systems instantly and could pretend that the change is happening right now. There were nights I was in tears because I could see myself out of years of these patterns that had been set in what I thought was cement by using the cool factor with my Spirit.

Some examples are as follows:

1. To make it cool that God is in me.
2. I did not ask for it to be cool to be honest, I asked God in the moment in my room for Him to make it cool to not need to be dishonest
3. I asked God if it could be cool to not need to be so afraid of anything I don't understand today for two minutes.
4. I'm normally an asshole in how I think and treat people when it pleases me (I actually love this). I asked God if He could make it cool for me and my Spirit to not need to be an asshole? Could you make it cool like never before for me to feel compassion, to be in love with even though I'm not? Can we pretend?

I could do this all night and sometimes did. For the first time, I could feel some light on my soul. I found a way for it to be so cool to not need to be a slave to my dark side in these moments. I had never felt free from them before using this mind ninja tactic.

I'm about to pretend with my Spirit to find a way to move over to the Spirit side of me more often. I felt like I had been training my whole life to be a dark natured person until I found it a little more cool to not need to be so much. Don't get me wrong, the dark side of life happens the moment I think it does, which is often. I can pretend it is cool or not need to believe it is so real.

The God piece said to me, "what if it could be cool to not be overwhelmed with your thoughts, feelings, and behavior? What if you are already willing to believe this is true, what if you just have not remembered yet? What if none of this is true and what if it does not have to be? What if it was cool for you to just want it to be?"

Could it be cool to not need to avoid my mom? Not need to not call her? Could it be so cool to experiment to not needing to know the outcome of a few big things today? Could it be cool to not need to think and just go into things today without plotting and scheming? Could I fall in love, just for a minute, with it being so cool to not need to criticize a couple of times when I always like to?

I could write these questions all day. For some reason, putting this in a question makes it more palatable. A few word changes and different ending punctuation marks were all it took for my perspective to shift. I started to bring the cool factor into every area of my behavior and old belief systems. I started to get into it being cool to not needing or wanting the things I think that I have needed or wanted. It changed me. I never imagined I could get out of the me that I had created and the game had grown.

I can pretend to change anything in a cool kind of way. I don't pretend to believe it's real, but it's cool to believe it is on my spiritual path. I only have to buy into it for a minute to feel the radical change.

Inventory

How this affects my...
Self-esteem - I can't really believe in things that I pretend to change; I have to believe that the way things are happen to be real and have to be inside me
Pride - I believe I have to be hard on myself because someone told me this is the world and how it is for you
Security - Wouldn't it be cool if I did not need security for a day?; I could just wing it and not hold the results against anyone or God
Ambition - Would it not be so cool if I could just pretend things are not half as bad as I think
Men - Wouldn't it be cool if I did not hate men for a day and not judge anyone for what I think they should do
Women - Wouldn't it be cool for a day if I could see women as equal and did not expect them to do anything for me
Pocketbook - Wouldn't it be cool to not need more than I get for a day; cool to wish the best for people, to pretend I want that even though I don't

My Part

How Am I...
Dishonest - Could it be cool to be more honest and dishonest?; could it be easy to want to be?
Selfish - What if it could be cooler to wish to not be selfish than to do the same selfish thinking today, because I'm in love with being selfish
Self-seeking - Could it be cool to be selfish in my actions when I'm in selfish belief systems, to go against my selfish nature and do things for other people without motives
Afraid - Of letting go of what I know, even for a minute

5 Fears

1. Fear of instant change being real
2. Fear of changing belief systems that I think define me
3. Fear of believing in the Spirit more than myself and the power it has to change me
4. Fear of the principle of change
5. Fear of leaving people behind if I move forward

Resentment to God

For trying to make it too easy for me to believe that I can change; for change having to be as hard as I think it should be

Corrective Measures

1. Find two things I can't stand and make them cool for two minutes
2. Start a conversation with someone you can't stand and make it cool to accept and respect them and their opinions

Tolerance

At the core, tolerance is about what I believe is my God given right to judge how everyone acts and whether or not this is for or against what I believe is right. How people think and treat me gives me clues to how I should react. They are predetermined and I like to think they are unchangeable. My inner storm is a lack of tolerance at any level. My anger, self-pity, and defiance are set off when things go too far off what I think I am supposed to tolerate.

I am the one that sets the bar of tolerance, and it tends to be arbitrary most of the time. How patient and tolerant I am depends on how I feel about you, what mood I'm in, or what my expectations are in that moment. I tolerate different people or situations incredibly differently than others.

Mike let me know that we were about to go into the depths of something that is all me. This was my intolerance. This was the beginning of my sobriety journey into Spirit. The goal was to hopefully find out that I am not intolerant as a whole, but I use it as an excuse I create to make me think I am more important than other people. It might just be a behavior and standard I like to believe is true. It was killing me and keeping me from letting my Spirit wake up, so tolerance was next up at bat.

Entitlement is where my darkness thrives. I cannot handle changing this or seeing this alone. Another problem with tolerance is that I lie about it. I tell people I am tolerant with my words while I betray the truth in my actions. My intolerance is surrounded by my love for dishonesty and unwillingness to tell anyone the truth about the depth of this defect. I certainly do not wish to find my part every time I am intolerant. I don't know why; I just don't want to. The truth is, I'm not even willing to find a way or ask the Spirit of God to give me the courage to find a way to get broken enough to find the root of my intolerance. If I do request this in prayer to Spirit, the road to tolerance becomes easy and the next right thing for me to pretend to be willing to do becomes clear. This only happens once my ego has been shattered. It becomes way more doable if I take one moment of intolerance at a time and pretend that I am tolerant. Again, this is the bite-by-bite method of eating the elephant that is my intolerance.

Mike and I had to prepare for intolerance that would come today and every day. Intolerance and judgment show up as the same thing, but I had never realized that. We wrote a four-column piece every day for six years to find the connection between them because I swore they were unrelated. The corrective measure for the next day was always made to someone or to do something I hated. It seemed like it was killing me, but it was saving my life.

Inventory

How this affects my...
Self-esteem - I need the control to decide what I tolerate and what I deem acceptable, down to the smallest thing
Pride - My insecurities and fear are based in the control I have to have; I judge what is good or bad for me to accept
Security - My security and control are based on my ability to decide what I believe is tolerable or not when it comes to people and what I expect
Ambition - Tolerance has everything to do with how successful or unsuccessful I am
Men - Men need to not look down at anything I do or take; I expect this of them no matter what
Women - I don't need to tolerate women; they are expected to tolerate anything I say or do
Pocketbook - If you pay me a lot, I can tolerate a lot; I'm a little money whore and I like it

My Part

How Am I...
Dishonest - I'm dishonest about my intolerance; I hold grudges but I'm silent about them
Selfish - I expect way more from people than I'm ever willing to give or do
Self-seeking - I assume everyone is out to get me; I cannot explain my mood swings with this, I know the problem is me
Afraid - That I am set in my ways with this, I don't do the Spirit of God thing and should not be asked to engage in principles

5 Fears

1. Fear of asking for help on a deep level
2. Fear of being tolerant when I know I'm wrong
3. Fear of not having the courage to ask for Spirit to assist
4. Fear of allowing people to go first and be right
5. Fear of not blaming people for what I do to them

Resentment to God

For not allowing me to fix or control my life; for not being big enough for me to find within myself

Corrective Measures

1. When I think I am being intolerant, write a prayer to God asking to remember that I'm not
2. Go do an act of service for someone that you are intolerant of

Complaining

I say I don't know when I'm complaining, but that's a lie. I do know exactly when. I also lie about not knowing why and blame it on outside circumstances, like my upbringing. This is also an untruth. I was designed to complain. Being an expert complainer is the only thing I like about myself; it's a gift and I'm awesome at it. The only thing I do better is complaining when I have to hear others complain. I leave no room for them to know I'm right and squash their opinions deftly with my own. If I could only convince them that I'm more important, they would not need to complain. I don't really think much of myself, yet I complain about people that don't respect me. That's the crazy loop I'm in when I'm in love with complaining.

Complaining is the never-ending story of my life. I say I'm not complaining, or would not have to, if people would just stop what they are doing or thinking and give me the attention my complaining deserves. It sounds ridiculous, but it seems so real. What am I complaining about in real time? It depends. I actively search for reasons to complain. I complain when I need attention and must be heard. I complain when I need something but don't know what it is. Complaining is like throwing out a fishing net hoping to get something tangled in it. I complain when I get tired of myself and just need some company. Some other examples of why I complain: when I'm angry and want to pick a fight, about a bad day or a good day, when others around me complain too much or more than me because I can't have that, on a bright sunny day because I can't stop myself, the weather, politics, the kids, really anything you can imagine. I had to take one of these items each day and just shut up about it. It was one of the hardest things I ever did. My Spirit today says that I will let you know if it's time to complain. In the meantime, just bless everyone.

I never had someone breakdown my motives behind complaining before this program. Even when complaining, I have specific goals which are what I expect to gain from this behavior. Motives behind complaining could include being combative with my words versus your words, getting people to feel sorry for me and my situation, not having to care about others' situations, minimizing other people's complaints, opinions, or integrity, or just to stir the pot.

My truth in complaining is that I have adopted a love for doing it. I don't tolerate when other people complain or get negative. I say I have no tolerance, but what if I do? Now that my Spirit tells me this is all bullshit, I'm willing to be willing to believe I just like to hurt people like they do me. What if I change my part, the why I do this, for a day and throw in a couple amends for doing this to others?

They say this transformation can only come through an awakened Spirit in a person. Someone must be at the end of their own tolerance for the complaining nature within them to start such a radical change in behavior. This is how it began for me. I hated it, but I did this every day with two people I constantly complained about—that is where the Spirit of God found me, in the change. This is consistent ever since God made it clear that He is the one changing me in real time.

Inventory

How this affects my...
Self-esteem - Complaints give me something to do when I get down on myself
Pride - Makes me feel better about myself when I don't
Security - Makes me feel like I know something about what I complain about; makes me feel right
Ambition - If I complain long enough, people will get tired of not giving me what I want, let's wear them down
Men - I automatically complain about men because that's all men do
Women - It seems that women do nothing but complain about many things I do; I won't do anything their way because I don't want to
Pocketbook - Complaining might get me shit for free, but I refuse to entertain anyone else's complaining

My Part

How Am I...
Dishonest - I lie about complaining when I'm complaining; my mother says she is just "expressing" and I learned it from the best
Selfish - I only want to hear about what people will do about my complaints
Self-seeking - I can't stand to hear other people's complaints; I rarely do anything about them
Afraid - That people will get tired of listening to me; that people will just talk about me and no longer invite me

5 Fears

1. Fear of not complaining to others
2. Fear of not wanting to hear what people say
3. Fear of the spirit of God not making it easier to change
4. Fear of not waking up and changing
5. Fear of becoming humble and lessening my complaining

Resentment to God

For making me pay the price for my own decisions, I should not have to learn from my mistakes, they should be taken off the table today

Corrective Measures

1. Make amends to two people I have complained to and ask them about themselves without interjecting
2. Make amends to two people I have complained about

I'm only ok when things are ok

In reading this chapter, please keep in mind that I'm only talking about the insanity I create and go through when it comes to what has to happen for me to be okay for a minute. This is much more about what I do to make things agreeable to me, what I have to do and say to make people want to do things my way. There's always an "or else" attached to this. I only register things as my way or not my way. If things aren't my way, I truly believe that I have no other option but to con people into wanting and needing to make things better for me. I do this through manipulating them into acknowledging that my way makes it better for them because it's better for me. I have a belief system that emphasizes I'm supposed to be okay. However, I learned that it can't last because inevitably, I will think of something else I need in 5 minutes.

What even is the concept of being okay? It seems to be a dark belief system I created and nurtured. If I'm not okay then comes, depending on how serious the need or expectation, self-pity. I don't seem to know how to handle not being okay. Come to find out, being okay or not okay are the same thing, like good or bad. What if each, aligned with my God Spirit dude, is the same thing as the other? They both have an experience, up or down on the same path. They just have a different outcome.

I don't learn much when things are okay. I don't really learn anything or grow as a person in Spirit when things go my way. But when things are not going my way, or blowing completely up,—that's where I'm going to challenge my Spirit to give me the courage and grace to move through principle and show me a way to act honestly through things I hate to do. Staying uncomfortable in what I was told to do allows me to become better, although I hate it.

Being comfortable has become boring for me. I've come to love the storms in life. I had to find a couple of people in my circle that have had the heart and courage to run to the storm, not to a safe place. We're like storm chasers—it's for the thrill and the education that each storm provides.

I justify my behaviors when I decide something in my path is not okay. I decide that it lies upon my shoulders to make changes happen that are more agreeable to me. I love to start demanding things. I love being self-righteous. I become fake and I start lying about what I need. I try to dominate people and dictate what people should do for me. I stop caring, if I did even to begin with. My resentments start flaring out of control. I have been a slave to this dark dude. This is just over one big thing where I need something to be okay in order to be okay. I can find this in so many places. My Spirit says, what if you are only half as not okay as you think you are? What if you just have to remember that everything is okay already on some level?

Inventory

How this affects my...
Self-esteem - I close my eyes and don't want to deal with the things that are not okay because this is what I do
Pride - I'm only grateful when things are right, why not when things are down or edgy?
Security - I want to take all the credit when things are good and give all the blame when they aren't
Ambition - I don't see a thing wrong with what I say and do; I really believe I have no need to change
Men - I'm only okay when men do what I say and don't argue with me
Women - When things are okay, I found myself to be a wonderful leader; I only love the women that do what I say
Pocketbook - money should get me out of all my problems

My Part

How Am I...
Dishonest - I blame other people when things don't work out, even if it's clearly my fault
Selfish - I don't care if things are working out for other people; I get no satisfaction when things work out for other people
Self-seeking - I don't seem to be able to be happy for other people when things are going okay; I just don't care unless my life looks perfect
Afraid - Of not having enough spiritual power to move through this

5 Fears

1. Fear of asking God to come into this and God not helping me change this
2. Fear of continuing to do this without the power of the Spirit
3. Fear of waking up to this change that has to happen
4. Fear of not loving the things that don't work out and being uncomfortable in them
5. Fear of really talking about this in depth

Resentment to God

For not allowing me to make this relationship with God whole, but I really believe that it's coming; for making me think I have to be upset when things aren't going my way

Corrective Measures

1. When I think something is not okay, or going wrong, write a letter to God to find out what is right about this situation
2. Write a gratitude list about what things are going right in my life

Motives

Motives are a serious component of my personality. Everyone has them, but most of mine come from my con, controlling, I-can't-be-less-than a place deep in my ego. Motives are wrapped up in everything I do, even though I convince myself they aren't. I chose different motives at different times to gear up to make shit happen my way, regardless of whether they were good or bad. It doesn't even matter if they're good or bad, or who is judging them. The fact is that they push my behavior and eat my emotions for brunch. I chose different motives in varying situations to gear up to make shit happen my way; good or bad doesn't even enter into the equation.

I'm a con by nature. I'm probably only half as good at it as I think I am. No one can know that, though. When it comes to motives, the question is why? What I do on the inside to get what I want with the least amount of effort? This is the concept of my motives; it is about the push that it takes to live in this world. At least from where I'm sitting.

The why? Because I can and I love it. My motives give me purpose which I otherwise don't think I could find. To me, they're like smoking my own crack or being able to suck my own dick. I had a beautiful dark nature to simply cause harm. I backed this behavior up with the years of abuse I suffered and wrapped it up with a big dose of addiction. I then rationalized and justified it until it was all I could do. I tricked myself into believing I couldn't not do these things.

My motives are my permission slip to fuck shit up and create chaos. What I usually don't realize in the moment is that I provide the chaos in my life through self-sabotage and destruction. Most of the time I'm also creating disasters in the lives of people I care about, or at least pretend to care about. My own motives stress me the fuck out sometimes because I think I can't change them, that they're stationery and immovable. This is another lie I have taught myself to believe, right down to my core.

Motives emerge in the way I can talk down to people, lie to cause confusion, and use smoke and mirrors to manipulate all the actors in this sitcom called my life. Lying and motives go hand in hand; lying is amazing. When I'm knee-deep in motives and can't figure out how to force someone's hand, I can't lie enough. It's like cotton candy to a 9-year-old. It doesn't work every time, but it's worked enough for me to keep doing it. I play the odds and I typically win. When it doesn't work, I blame myself on the quality of the lie itself or the missteps I took while delivering it. I never look at the subject of lying as an issue in its own right.

There's a motive behind everything I do, but there is a more sinister side to this concept. That aspect is that I have an agenda for everything before I even step into the room, plus I have no problem hurting anyone and everyone to make it happen. My motives play into my judgments, expectations, and control. And I learned this all when I was a 15-year-old kid. Not bad. The problem is that here I am, decades later, still believing and living in this bullshit. I think it works for me when it clearly has not for years.

How do I get what's good for me? Is the question du jour every day when it comes to motives. This is with family, kids, employers, coworkers, grandchildren, dealers, strip clubs, etc. Doesn't matter who you are, my motives are coming and coming hard, like a freight train, bearing down to make you either get off the tracks or get run the fuck over. My motives win or else watch out—there will be hell to pay. A motive is the energy I use to get people to stand down and want me to win, even though I'm a fucking idiot. I use motives and my ability to con to insert other ideas into innocent bystanders' heads so that my wants become their ideas.

I've been consumed by motives every day of my life, including today. What will I not let happen today? How do I begin to shift my motives in real time? How do I step down to let another person be right or get what they want when I don't want to?

This is what my Spirit and God had to say about this: I talked to them just like the man in The Shack that lost his daughter. I ask questions with answers I've never heard before that free me from the burden, the prison that I think through. I lost my soul and my Spirit but not in this moment, not today. The work I do with this Spirit Dude does not suck half as much as I thought it would. I committed to it for a couple of years and then, at that point, I finally found gratitude for how hard it was/wasn't in coming out of the game.

Inventory

How this affects my...

Self-esteem - My motives work for me, and the arrangement is that I come first, always; I doubt this will ever change

Pride - This is the only way I can be comfortable in my own skin; my motives are not negotiable and I answer to no one

Security - I need people to agree and to understand why they agree for me to be ok

Ambition - The ambition is the driver for my motives and ambition is my excuse; I've never had to ask myself for permission

Men - I tell men as little as possible; men see through me; I avoid men when it comes to my thoughts and ideas

Women - I just want women around so I can look at them and so they can entertain and serve me

Pocketbook - I hope to do as little as possible to make money; it's much better now, but I'm still lazy as shit on some level

My Part

How Am I...

Dishonest - I lie about my motives because I think it would freak people out; I always make myself sound good and talk about things I have no intention of doing

Selfish - I only like people that like me; I take everything the wrong way if my motives are not accepted (don't question me or there will be a problem)
Self-seeking - I only care about myself, I really believe this is the best I can do; I think I suffer when I don't think of me first
Afraid - That I will keep trying to do this work alone; that I won't find someone to push me; of letting the right person in to move some of this stuff out

6 Fears

1. Fear of humility
2. Fear of being judged
3. Fear of believing my own bullshit everyday
4. Fear of not finding the courage to move through this shit
5. Fear of believing there is nothing wrong with me
6. Fear of not being afraid (cause I'm dying)

Resentment to God

For not allowing me to fix or control my life

Corrective Measures

1. Find two people tomorrow that I don't care for and say to them "I see you and I think you do good things"
2. Be honest about 2 motives in real time when you don't want to and that you totally fucking disagree with

Relationship Warrior

My Defects

My defects are the things I do best. They are also active per my choice. Taking my behavior, how I judge things, and how I treat people close to me illustrates this love affair with my defects. It has to be true, taking how I show up into account. This is the dark side of how I came to be motivated by bottom-feeding. I do distasteful things and I'm really OK with them. Never mind that I lie about them to get people off my back. That just comes with the territory.

Some of the defects I have as an addict seem to become more important after being sober for 14 years. They haven't gone away; they show up differently today than when I was in active addiction. Some examples are selfish behavior, judgment, hatred, anger, jealousy, self-pity, self-righteousness, and dishonesty. This is not a comprehensive list, but a glance at the highlights of a long list. Largely, most of my defects can fit into the above categories. Each major defect has tendrils of other defects that feed into the madness.

The truth is, I never have a real problem with these until my Spirit asks me to. The Spirit of God would ask, how is all this behavior working for you? If I want to commit to God's team with my Spirit, these behaviors will not do. God gives me the option to continue and says that He doesn't care either way. It is truly up to me, and that freedom creates more interest. Although, God did add, that He designed me and has been training me to do better towards His children. He gave me that point of information without strings attached, which I greatly appreciate. Knowing that I have the free will to do better, or not, is captivating.

At that point, I wrote a contract with the Spirit of God that I would serve him and the principles for two years. He said, let's pretend this will be half as hard as you think it will be. The point was to not avoid self-pity, but to get deep in it and imagine pretending that I am not in it at all.

I never experienced not being in my self-pity or anger when I was consumed by it. So, I would sit down and surround myself with something I'm angry about and then ask, what if I was only half as angry as I thought I was? I imagined the no-anger dude sitting right on the lap of my anger. Spirit would then say, now what if you can realize, right here and now, that you just have not remembered you are not angry at all? What if the need to be angry has left for a minute? A second? Less? Or longer?

Spirit said that if I want to have my anger back, I can. Just ask Him for it, or not. Players' choice. My defects to this day dig being handled by my Spirit. It is an easier path. Instead of me managing them and being devoured by them, I push the easy button and bring Spirit into them all. The Spirit in me now has something to do all the time, and I have a new hobby. I kind of like when me and Spirit can kill defects together.

Inventory

How this affects my...
Self-esteem - Defects are how I lower the bar on my behavior and my need to not meet your expectations of me
Pride - When you are a liar, predator, and thief, you don't need pride, just a good lawyer
Security - I think I feel more comfortable in these defects than to move into spiritual principles; principles have expectations, I don't do expectations, but what if I do but I don't know it
Ambition - My ambition is to one day not to need to always be my worst-case self
Men - I don't put up with men's defects, I force them to put up with mine
Women - I don't put up with women's excuses or to hear them talk about their defects, I just don't care
Pocketbook - Whatever I can't make, I will take; I love serving my defects in this area of my life, they say everything is allowed and to control people to get what I deserve

My Part

How Am I...
Dishonest - I say I want to change some defects in real time, then I make excuses not to
Selfish - I want others to change first; if you get honest with me maybe I will too, but maybe not; this is my pattern
Self-seeking - I don't really care what people think of me, my behavior says that I don't; I strive to cover up my behavior so I don't have to listen to your judgments about it
Afraid - That my Spirit will not grant me the need to change

5 Fears

1. Fear of not being dishonest or deceiving
2. Fear of the Spirit of God not protecting me from myself
3. Fear of not having a guarantee that things with my Spirit life will be better
4. Fear of not feeling sorry for myself
5. Fear of not being committed to being selfish; what it feels like to not need to be

Resentment to God

I'm not sure how to say the **Resentment to God**, but I know I think I should have one

Corrective Measures

1. Write a list of the defects I acted on for one day
2. Make amends to the people who were affected

Resentments

I don't even know where to begin with resentments. They're a combination of so many factors. They seem to begin early in life, and many of these have come to be the same today as they were then. They are great conversation pieces at church parties or when hanging out at my dealer's house. Very versatile. Resentments are a combination of belief systems of how I say things are, my issue with control, hurt feelings, expectations of how things should be or should have been, hatred from holding onto things that have happened to me, and defiance of how I will act if this same situation comes about.

My life is a choose your own adventure book where all the pages are preset, and the choice depends on which resentment is most active. I believe I have freedom to live life in free will, but in actuality my resentments predetermine my fate. I have no control because my belief systems have made it so.

Mike said that there was no other place to start but here. The first three steps in 12-step work were merely statements. Getting free of even a minute amount of resentment is where Spirit shows up. Spirit reveals to me my true self and how I act in my part of the situation. What I love about my resentments is keeping them, one at a time. I treat them like fledgling plants that need love, water, and sunshine to grow. I nurture these resentments and then question why they eat my lunch and consume my headspace. I can blame everyone else for my stuff and never have to hang onto a thing. Mike always asked, "how is that dark space working for you?"

In the end, some spiritual force of grace, some Spirit of God, had to be invited into my cold, black heart to give me the courage to ask to start blessing all the people I hated and judged in secret. Over 14 years I've had to do this four-column inventory on just about everything and everyone. I always find my part, one issue at a time.

The resentments were mostly the same. They centered on whichever person did whatever to me, my dad that beat me, the institutions that fucked me over (law enforcement, Jesuit prep school, people that stole from me and I stole from, my wife and kids, etc.). Most importantly, resentments were about principles. I had major issues here. Honesty, brotherly love, integrity, forgiveness (fuck forgiveness but people damn sure need to forgive me for my actions, fairness, the list goes on), etc. All my resentments were just categories. Death, justice, disappointments… I could go on for days. I was mad at everybody and everything and felt great about it. But inside, I was dying. I wanted to kill myself because of the pain I was putting myself through.

I wrote my resentments for people to show that the courage we use to see ourselves lies within the resentments themselves.

Inventory

How this affects my...
Self-esteem - I should not have to do anything to be respected and trusted; being a liar is totally acceptable to me
Pride - Everything I think and feel about life should be true; no one should question my judgment of them; I can do whatever I want up to this point
Security - People should be standing in line to get my forgiveness; everyone should have to pay their dues for what I think they did to me
Ambition - I demand to get anything I want and I don't need to give a thing back; I really believe this should be true
Men - Other men's resentments are unwarranted; I did what I did to them and it was on purpose and they deserved it and should shut up about it
Women - Most of my resentments to women are sexual, like turning me down or laughing at my approaches or not sleeping with me; they're lucky I put up with them when I do
Pocketbook - I should get reparations for what people have done to me; I blame all my problems on not having money, when I get it I can't keep it which is everyone else's fault

My Part

How Am I...
Dishonest - I will never admit how much of this stuff I caused; especially resentments towards me or other people's problems because I did nothing wrong
Selfish - I don't really owe anyone an apology or explanation for the lifetime of resentments I caused; I have to believe this to live
Self-seeking - It always has been and will be about me; no one has ever helped me change this about me, maybe someone will
Afraid - Of being resentful forever on some level; of starting a principled life within myself with my Spirit Dude

6 Fears

1. Fear of being humble
2. Fear of admitting things I have done to cause resentment
3. Fear of not being afraid
4. Fear of what making things right with people from the past
5. Fear of not having so many resentments
6. Fear of trying and finding a way

Resentment to God

For breathing me into this world and not take care of me like I think I should be taken care of

Corrective Measures

1. Find two people or institutions you are resentful towards and write what your part is in the issue you have (ex. My part is judgment of them, I expect they treat me better than I would ever treat them)
2. Letter to God asking why do you think you have to resent people and think you love it

Trauma Warrior

The past

The past seems to be how I determine what decisions I will make today. I like to go with what I know and what feels comfortable. For this reason, I continue to hold all pain, sorrow, and excitement from previous experiences and use them as current emotional references. These old experiences lurk under the radar, forcing my hand without me even knowing it. The one area where it is most visible is when I speak about my fears.

As a drug addict, I grasp onto blame for every shitty thing that has happened in my life. It is always front and center and skews information in the decision-making process of anything in the present. The beatings, drug deals gone bad, sexual abuse, being robbed... I hold these events against people today, even though they have long passed and I have totally healed.

The mental and emotional garbage I hang onto steals my life. If someone beats me today, I say I've always been beaten. What I don't see is the times it happened and the times it didn't. It's easier to take broad strokes; it enables me to blame and skirt responsibility longer.

I found it was time to only see the in-between times. I chose to focus on my life with all bad events excluded. If I focus on all the times there were no beatings, molestations, arguments, etc., I can see that my life hasn't been all bad. I tend to have a love affair with the life that my existence has always been horrific, the worst of the worst, and way worse than anyone else's.

In the Spirit world, the past begins today. The issue is what to do with all the anxiety, fear, and anger I have held onto. Spirit said to find a guide, a person of the same gender, that went through the same things and found the courage in their Spirit to allow God to burn it all down. This person had to teach me to live and die today like it was my last day. Even though it was not easy to find this person, I prayed for their approach. The person I found I did not like. The things he said would be in the form of writing and corrective measures for what would and would not be acceptable in my life today. I had to get into action to change who I was. My thoughts alone wouldn't do it and I couldn't do it by myself. Engaging in these corrective measures were miracles for me. There was an old part of me then, and even today, that had to die and be born in the form a personal surrender of what I think and feel. I looked forward to searching the past and seeing it as just where I've been not having to do with where I'm going.

Inventory

How this affects my...
Self-esteem - I'm stuck thinking and feeling who I have been in my past; my self-esteem is about what happened and what I should do today; this is the area of my life where I contemplate suicide

Pride - My pride is incredibly deep rooted; where do I find the courage to take a chance on who I can be spiritually?
Security - My past holds me down from waking up, but I continue to believe it's all I have and know
Ambition - The past failures are what I focus on; someone had to help convince me of my successes so I can see I can be better
Men - Men don't hold the past against me, that's my job
Women - Women don't judge me for my past; I will make sure they only see what I want them to, but that doesn't mean I don't judge their past and take pleasure in doing so
Pocketbook - I go to what I have had to complain about what I have today if it's less

My Part

How Am I...
Dishonest - I use the past to fortify what I refuse to do or allow today; I exaggerate and lie about my past to justify my behavior; I live in the past a lot
Selfish - I don't care what other people have gone through; I hold their past against them
Self-seeking - I only hear what I want to; I act like I care but I'm not really capable, at least that's what I tell myself
Afraid - I'm afraid of acquiring the courage to live and make decisions today based on principles in the present

5 Fears

1. Fear of the past controlling my life today
2. Fear of seeing the past is only bad
3. Fear of waking up and being held accountable for my actions and beliefs
4. Fear of no empathy for others and what they have been through
5. Fear of the path to release myself including pain and suffering from the past

Resentment to God

For not removing my memory and pain of the past; for not making it easy to move on; for making me grow up from it

Corrective Measures

1. Make amends with my past
2. Write a blessing prayer to anyone I blame for causing me pain

Trauma

What a heavy word! This is a word I had to change in my personal vocabulary to be able to move forward from my past and be free. I had to change many words because the way I think of these words, especially this word, keeps me in a prison and pigeonholes me. It causes me to keep relieving the events that I called trauma over and over again without an end in sight. I changed the word to big challenges, like back injuries, death of my daughter and mother of my granddaughters, overdoses (me, my wife, friends), childhood events, car wrecks, beatings, sexual assaults, molestations, rapes, and the years of drug addiction. I had to quit calling these experiences trauma because they happened a long time ago. Using the word trauma insinuated that it was still happening in the present day. I was reliving the shit out of all the terrible things in my life, and it was killing me.

The word itself is incredibly charged. It's a buzzword today, and I've noticed that people say it about a wide range of experiences. Texas had a winter storm recently that people called traumatic. It can be whatever it is for them, but the word trauma held me back.

It's a word that cannot be challenged. Any trouble I get into would vanish if I started listing the various traumatic experiences in my life. Nothing beats the "I was raped/abused/molested" trump card. It's always a winner. The problem is that, as a drug addict, I figured that out early. Using my horrendous life experiences to manipulate people to get what I wanted or get out of them what I needed became second nature.

I wanted to quit reliving my life cycle of what has happened. I would only focus on the negative things. I wanted to find a way to bless it all, be grateful for where it all brought me, and start life here, today.

I use the word trauma to arrange it in my memory bank and identify the belief systems that came out of each experience. The word trauma is always associated with something bad. I used to revolve my life around these events, but it wasn't working anymore. I was stuck and needed a way out.

Most of the trauma I had experienced was deep in the past, even in recovery. I never recognized that these events were over. I kept bringing in the old drama and emotions into current situations and blowing everything up. Living out of these belief systems made everyone wrong, harmful, dangerous, and out to get me. I thought I was protecting myself by living in suspicion of everyone and everything. I was a paranoid fuck and it screwed up my life and relationships little by little, every day.

I was no longer willing to allow the past—trauma—to dictate anything that happened today, even if it looked the same. I wanted something different, so I made everything different in my perception. I started to see that the new traumas had nothing to do with the ones I had experienced before. I found this contract that I had bought into that told me to act, react, and feel the same way as I had in the past. I had to put each and every trauma to bed, explaining to myself that nothing now is related to the past. The players and the game have both changed.

I found I could never grow beyond what had already happened if I didn't let go of it. There is no option for growth spiritually if I keep holding onto these things and living life through the same eyes. Spirit just wasn't present in the old things that happened, and if I kept living there, I couldn't be with Spirit Dude. I had to choose. The old stuff did not allow me to be unencumbered, humbled, or allow me to bring God's blessings to big challenges that were way out of my control. Those belief systems made me shy away from God, thinking that if He didn't help me then, he wouldn't or couldn't now.

For instance, I went through a monumentous neck injury. It took 9 months for me to relearn how to walk with all the rehab that goes with it. I was learning to walk again, but not the way I did before. I started out mad as hell and full of self-pity. I had a busy life, and this just didn't fit in my schedule. I had to put everything on hold for months. It was inconceivable that I had to do this, but there was no choice. God turned up the pain times ten so I couldn't create another option or a work-around. It was clear that painkillers weren't going to be part of the experience—not because I didn't try them, because they just didn't work. Bummer. My Spirit showed up and said that we were going to find dignity and humility with this, because I knew it wasn't going away for months. There was gratitude that it would be over someday, for people who brought me food like never before. I had insane gratitude that my legs were starting to work while in physical therapy. Spirit said that I needed to embrace some pain. Laying in that bed, my Spirit was hanging out with the Spirit of God. We were right there together like old home week. Everything was good except that I couldn't walk. It's the only time I've ever been in so much pain that I couldn't even jerk off. What a concept. What I went through to go to even the bathroom was unreal. I screamed the whole way every single time. When it was over, my Spirit told me that we weren't bringing anything forward in anything that happens and that it would never be relevant again. I was to find the humility to shut the fuck up and move on.

Trauma seems to choose me without an invite. When it does show up, it brings an experience that I don't want. The God piece, at that point, tells me that whether or not I like it, it's here and we're going to learn something. So, join me for the ride. It isn't supposed to be pleasant. Nothing monumental comes from easy experiences. Adversity and pressure break people down to build them up. I needed those experiences to be the person I am today. I'm no longer mad about them—I needed them to catapult me into my life.. These principles (honesty, integrity, humility, etc.) are living moments where I get to do something the opposite of what I normally do. I have to be willing to be willing to pretend to let the experience be mine. I always wish it was someone else's, but it was chosen for me. There is no use in fighting these experiences, because once they're here, they're here. The only way they're moving on is to deal with them. Bitching doesn't eliminate the issue or shave off time.

Big challenges choose me on a spiritual level, I believe, because I have what it takes to deal with them. I am awake to and have the courage to move through what is needed. I also have the ability to shut my mouth about what I think is good or bad about it. I've been blessed with the capability to have compassion for the people around me that are going through hardships. Today, I can do this without comparing or judging or anything that comes with it. I can just sit back and be helpful without spewing my shit. It's a fucking miracle.

Inventory

How this affects my...
Self-esteem - I make myself keep reliving trauma, sexual and physical and mental stuff, to justify and brag about how much stuff I've been through so I can create excuses ahead of time
Pride - My trauma, my stories, should trump anyone else's; I make sure that people recognize how much I've suffered but I don't really care about their past or present suffering
Security - I can't imagine not bringing up the abuse from my past; every new person I talk to is a new audience and a way to steal attention
Ambition - I've always dwelled on old trauma and used it as an excuse to not move forward in areas of my life, especially recovery, and punish people today
Men - I expect men to listen and feel sorry for me and what I've gone through, even if they've had the same experiences
Women - I use trauma as a way to get women into bed, hang out with me, invite me to do things, and feel sorry for me
Pocketbook - I should get paid for the trauma and suffering I've been through; if I got paid for it, maybe I could move on faster

My Part

How Am I...
Dishonest - I exaggerate my trauma and refuse to acknowledge my role and downplay what I've done; I keep shoving this shit into conversations with people even though it's inappropriate and people don't need to hear it, I use it as a powerplay; I get offended when they won't play into it
Selfish - I really have no mercy or care about what other people have gone through, especially childhood stuff, because mine is worse and yours doesn't count because it wasn't as bad (no matter what)
Self-seeking - I have no intention in moving past this trauma shit, it's who I am
Afraid - Of seeing the strengths I have that I could have only gotten around the horrible things that happened to me, the things that only adversity could have brought me

5 Fears

1. Fear of not caring and getting past trauma shit
2. Fear of pretending to dissolve these issues in real time with the people that were affected by me
3. Fear of not hating on people or situations
4. Fear of giving up my free pass, get out of jail free card called trauma
5. Fear of not blaming and hating on things years after they have happened, of moving on, of not having opinions from these experiences

Resentment to God

For not letting me die; for not protecting me from things that I shouldn't have had to go through; for making all my opinionated bullshit meaningless

Corrective Measures

1. Create a gratitude list for what gifts I received from my traumatic experiences
2. When someone else brings up bad things that happened to them, don't share mine or compete or try to steal thunder

Triggers

When thinking about this topic, my Spirit told me that this will hurt a little bit. I had to somehow make these triggers, these ideas, half as big as I think they are. I can't deny that they carry some weight on me and my Spirit.

I found in this process of becoming humble, honest, and having integrity, that I use this excuse called triggers. When certain things happen, I am programmed to preload and justify how I'm going to react. Drugs, sex, whatever it may be. The God piece says, what if you're triggers are not real? What if you don't have them, you just made this shit up because someone told you? What if you just think you do, so it has to be true?

A trigger is like me texting myself that it's time. It's a word to describe me deciding in the moment that I'm going to use again, that it has come back around. I was never not going to use. Then there's the bullshit of feelings and triggers. That's just a can of worms I'd rather not open, even inside of myself. It doesn't change anything, even though I lie to myself and everyone else to say it does.

My triggers are an impressive way for me to justify old behaviors and act them out in real time. It's a built-in excuse and a trump card blame game. The universe has to rearrange itself to accommodate my picture of reality. I make triggers true today by believing they are. What if I picked a different word? What if my Spirit could take out a word and kill these? What if I could just erase the idea and replace it with a different word to describe the picture? And what if it was half as big as I think it is?

My triggers are things I love to do as lifelong drug addict. Getting out of drug belief systems and deep, addict-fueled wants seems to be a lifelong journey. When my triggers come up, like the smell of meth, the smell of weed, strippers, etc., I have to run.

Early on in sobriety, my sponsor convinced me to no longer go down the same roads that I always drove down while I was in that lifestyle. He said that I had to pick new roads because the old ones are full of triggers. Strip clubs, drug dealers, the works. Mike said, why would you want to go down those roads? They have everything you're trying to get away from in one convenient place. Makes it easy to avoid, no?

I don't care what anyone has to say on this topic. I know my dark dude and he is very convincing. He makes it okay for me to get back into my triggers and then follow through. He loves when I shoot myself in the foot. I will end up in the places that will take me back to the game if I am not diligent.

People say that if you are spiritually fit, you can go anywhere. I might start out that way, until I'm doing that stuff. Then, all bets are off. I know myself. Also, who decides if I'm spiritually fit? I can't trust my own mind, so I'm not exactly sure who gives me the stamp of approval. I'd rather not take a chance than bet it all and lose. For example, I know people who said they were spiritually fit. Then one day, they decided to go to a rave. They never came back to the rooms of recovery. Never saw them again, ever. I don't know what happened to them, but I'm not willing to take the same risk they did. Maybe after the rave they decided to move halfway across the country and are living wonderful, sober lives. I highly doubt it.

The idea of being spiritually fit is a cluster fuck of an idea. It's great on paper, but in practice it's a slippery slope. The determination comes from my brain, which I cannot ever trust because I have a disease of my mind called addiction. In reality, it's usually my dark dude showing up. At least I know who he is. I never know when the spiritually fit 'dust' will wear off. Then, the idea of spiritual fitness; does that mean that I can shoot meth and not be off to the races if God is on board with the idea? Doesn't make much sense to me. I'm not here to debate people, I just don't want to go back to that life.

Anyone that tells me that I can go wherever and do whatever needs to get out of my life. Wanting to go to the rave to begin with is the first red flag to me not being in a good place. It's my defiance cropping up. If people tell me not to, so I will. And that's where the dark dude shows up and takes control. I can feel him pulling at my strings when my defiance rears its head. I hear of sober people going to mock bars, drinking mock cocktails. The thought process around this is convoluted. I went to bars to get fucked up and meet women, to hook up and ghost them. So does everyone else. That is unspiritual, drug-life behavior. Why would I want to continue that behavior sans drugs and booze? The bottom line is, I don't. I could fool myself into thinking that I want to have a good time with sober people, but my motives are to get mine. I will just wait for the ticking time bomb that is in my head to go off. When that happens, I'm out the door and off to the races.

I am willing to assume that I cannot and will not ever be spiritually fit enough to be around meth, cocaine, or the people that sell it or do it. This goes double for strip clubs and women that look fucking awesome. It's my kryptonite and that'll never change. It makes my mouth water.

My prayers to Spirit were always to leave my triggers gigantic so I could see them in front of me. I never wanted to be blindsided by some tiny bullshit and accidentally shoot meth again.

I don't trust the darker part of me, so I plainly do not go to the places that I used to love. If I loved it, I probably didn't need to be there. I only truly loved three or four things when I was in the game. That's just me. I can go to parties with normies where they drink, I can go to pool parties or beaches where there are copious amounts of boobies and bikinis, but I'm miserable seeing and smelling all the weed and watching people drink and party. Honestly, I get miserable and angry because I can't and I'm a little pissed cause they can. I'm jealous and my self-pity (on the highest level) shows up to the party and starts whispering in my ear.

My Spirit said, why do you think you want to be all fucked up and mad when you go to places like that? Where you can't do what you did, but everyone else is, and where your mouth waters like crazy? I wrote a lot of substantive inventory about why. I wrote about my love affair with wanting to be around all this stuff without taking part in the festivities. I had an elaborate funeral to put all this stuff down, put it to rest. My Spirit asked: why don't we just know ourselves and quit messing around with that stuff? Maybe make some fucking peace with it?

I wrote a gratitude list for all the pleasurable drug time I had since I was 15. Then I closed the coffin and asked God, 'what would tomorrow look like if I never looked back?' Right then, the burden was lifted. I cannot be who I was before or go to those places. But, in principle, do I want to be the person who does?

Inventory

How this affects my...
Self-esteem - I blame my troubles in recovery on triggers and people that trigger me and all the other shit on my head; the ups and downs that I think sobriety causes me are to blame, not me
Pride - I label these triggers to be an insane problem and I blame it on God; I will stay sober if I don't have to suffer
Security - In a fucked-up way, my triggers are very exciting; at times, they're the best part of sobriety because they are all I really think about, until I ask my Spirit to come into it
Ambition - I never intended to run from triggers because I was never going to change my behavior
Men - Men are a trigger because they talk, have opinions, and don't respect me; my anger with men is a huge trigger because I want to react; thinking I have to be right is a huge trigger
Women - Coming out of the meth world, porn, strip clubs, etc., my lust is an insane trigger for me having to do anything about women
Pocketbook - I would pay anything to have 'trigger night' once a week, a hall pass to do anything I love

My Part

How Am I...
Dishonest - Thinking I'm spiritually fit when I say I am; if I think it, it's probably a lie
Selfish - There's a dark side of my trigger that says I'm going to do whatever I want and no one can tell me what to do
Self-seeking - I am back to doing what's good for me, there will be no boundaries until I go down
Afraid - Of never having the goddamn courage to be honest about my triggers in real time

6 Fears

1. Fear of pretending to be afraid of not coming back after triggers
2. Fear of not being able to kill myself successfully
3. Fear of my Spirit not helping me find a way to fall out of love with the triggers in the game
4. Fear of thinking that I know what I'm doing
5. Fear of how many people I'll take out with me
6. Fear of not being able to battle my dark dude

Resentment to God

For not giving me the power and control to change my belief systems; for making it too easy for me to quit this path, and for that I blame God

Corrective Measures

1. Write out a list of things I call triggers that I continue to participate in
2. Tell on myself about these things to people in my support system so I can stop doing them with accountability

Trust

Over the years, I've held people hostage by how I expect them to be. I tell myself that I can't trust people if they don't live up to my expectations or do what I think they should. This goes both ways.

Since becoming sober over the last 14 years, I've had to take on a new level of trust. The definition of trust and what people need me to be in order to have trust in our relationship was something I thought about deeply. I see trust as an expectation that I put on people. In order for me to trust you, you have to be there for me no matter what and drop whatever you're doing when I say I need you. I expect you to treat me as #1 and vice versa. Although, I don't really treat people as number one, I just say I do but still expect to be treated as the real top dog.

My trust with family and friends has had to evolve because of the expectations I had surrounding trust. They were unreasonable and unkind to others. I tell myself that I only trust people I have known for a long time and have passed fictional tests I have created for people to prove themselves without them knowing the challenge. When I trust someone, that means that we have experienced storms together in our lives and are bonded in this way. What that means to me is that as life goes on, we have agreed to prioritize each other.

One of my favorite examples about trust is if I am moving and you said you would help. I'm counting on you because I trust in you. If something happens and you call me and say you can't make it, one of two things happens. If I really cared about you, I would understand and find other people to help me. This is me today. But back then, I would get angry and offended in the insinuation that I cannot trust you to do what you say. I would beat you down in our relationship for weeks to come with this supposed show of disloyalty. This illustrates the expectations that come with trust in my mind.

I recognize that during anytime in the future when I say you can still trust me, you probably aren't so sure. I've done this over and over. I use things against people for leverage and betray trust by being insensitive and unempathetic. I show people in my life that I cannot be counted on. I trust people in my life if I need something, but if they can't give it, I hold it against them. I also expect trust if I don't show up, give nothing, and act like an ass about it.

I have grown spiritually, and principles today dictate that I cannot use trust like a bat. I'm grateful to be enlightened when it comes to trust and letting people off the hook just because I can.

Inventory

How this affects my...
Self-esteem - I feel like I have to blame people, places, and things for my trust issues; it's safer than blaming myself
Pride - I refuse to believe I do anything wrong to people that justifies their distrust; I negate their feelings by saying it's all in the past and I should be forgiven
Security - My deep-seated need to trust is outweighed by my need that trust is an expectation you put on me
Ambition - I don't believe trust matters unless I need to trust someone to get something; trust is based on my motives alone
Men - I only trust men that make me more important than themselves
Women - The only thing I trust about women is how I can manipulate them into doing my bidding
Pocketbook - I only trust what I can see; I believe I should get more than I do for what I do

My Part

How Am I...
Dishonest - I tell people they can trust me; if I lie to you, chances are I will do the same again; I deny when I'm caught in a lie and con you into trusting me again
Selfish - Deep within I really don't have the courage or desire to change
Self-seeking - I don't trust anyone really, because my expectations of them are non-existent; don't trust me, I will find a way to have to let you down, it's inevitable
Afraid - To lower my expectation of people, I set people up to fail; this way I don't have to be loyal to anyone or anything

5 Fears

1. Fear of being accountable for what I say and do
2. Fear of letting people make mistakes
3. Fear of humility
4. Fear of brotherly love
5. Fear of not being and acting superior when I'm not

Resentment to God

For letting me become so jaded, for not giving me the freedom to be a different way

Corrective Measures

1. When a friend needs something, do it without question or motive
2. When someone can't do something for me, say it's okay and mean it

Unheard/Belittled

I have this dark, inner voice that was created way back in Catholic school as a child. I was taught by nuns that you have to speak up to be heard. I always, always have a deep need and craving for attention. This was illustrated in both relationships with women and men, just with different flavors and motives. I was a quiet, insecure kid until I met methamphetamines—that took care of that.

This is another subject that became center stage. I felt unheard, ignored, and belittled. I learned that I could be this way to anyone in response to their behavior or just because I wanted to be this way. Ignore me and I will ignore you. It turned out to be a lonely, dark place to visit. At least I felt justified in my pain and retaliation. My dishonesty and blame over being unheard and belittled was a very isolated place. My reasoning was that if I could ignore people, not listen to them, and put them down, I could have a life. If I could do this behind people's backs and not get caught, I could feel good about my life on some twisted level.

I was a small, skinny kid and I got picked on a lot because I had a big mouth. I also went to a Jesuit all boys Catholic High School. I took joy in being a vandal. If people teased me or bullied me, I just keyed their car. If my dad beat on me or hurt me, I could just throw his tools in the neighbor's pool. If my neighbor wanted to molest me a little, he would have to pay me money to stay quiet. Being unheard and belittled was going to have consequences that I decided upon and doled out without anyone knowing.

In recovery, Mike led me down a path that asked why at this time, at 45 years old, do I believe I need to not be ignored? The answer was because I have a belief system that I have had for years that it has to be important to live knowing how it feels to not be. I also had a belief system that dictated me belittling others and making them feel unheard. Why do I find it important to belittle people, why do I need to ignore people? Because I think I'm getting something out of it. The question then always comes, what if I'm not?

Inventory

How this affects my...
Self-esteem - I demand people hear me
Pride - What I say is more important than what you say, so you better listen
Security - Your behavior needs to meet my expectations for me to be okay
Ambition - To be the loudest motherfucker so I can control everything and everyone
Men - I disregard what men say because I think they're stupid and I'm always right anyway
Women - I don't listen to women because they have a motive
Pocketbook - Don't try to buy me off, but try to buy me off because I'm secretly open to negotiation

My Part

How Am I...
Dishonest - I say I want to be heard but I don't do that for anyone else
Selfish - I will not stop until you hear me; I will always keep coming
Self-seeking - I manipulate conversations to fit my agenda
Afraid - That not being heard isn't that big of a deal

5 Fears

1. Fear of meeting my own needs
2. Fear of humility
3. Fear of relying on God
4. Fear of being irrelevant
5. Fear of not being the most important person in every room

Resentment to God

That I'm not the most important person ever

Corrective Measures

1. Two times tomorrow make an effort to listen and hear someone else
2. Two times tomorrow don't share my opinion without being asked

Unimportant

I'll begin this chapter with a question: why do I think I need to be important? My answer usually boils down to the fact that I believe that I have been incredibly unimportant for years, especially as a child and teenager. I believe, by reviewing my actions and what I do now, I can make myself suffer by manifesting everywhere I can to push to be important. It's like riding a bike. I'm ready to make all the people I come across feel how important I need to be. My unimportance and how I believe I have to be treated otherwise is set in my mind.

There came a day when, at about six years sober, I needed to find my importance. At least, I thought I did. I was willing to become the person that had a job, and that was to let people know I was important. I thought I should demand this. There was a part of me that made this a main aspiration in life. I knew that being important revolved around how people treated me. This guy inside of me that came out started blaming people that could not prove this to me or were more important than me to begin with. Being unimportant and demanding importance lets people know I had to be the most important within myself. I felt that that they were responsible to do this for this insecure person. I thought I was fooling everyone with my show of importance, but people knew I was grasping at straws. The self-pity and self-righteousness was amazing. I was dying and cutting cords with people all around me. I refuse to put up with this behavior in anyone else, so why should I expect them to?

This overwhelming feeling of being unimportant set off all my old belief systems of entitlement to God, including blame. I thought people should read my mind and know what they should do for me all the time. If they could and would, they would show it by making me more important than themselves. This stuff is priceless for me to move through today.

I say I can't control my demands. My Spirit has to execute this for me. I will continue to double down expectations in real time. This is all self-inflicted hurt that I can never see. So, this unimportant nature has been lurking in my obsessions and dark side for a long time. I believe that is why I have gotten so comfortable with my secrets around this topic. It's kind of like Schmiegel in Lord of the Rings.

There came a day that a man found me. For nine years, we had to become willing to be willing to believe that me and my Spirit God dude were going to war and that He would kill this belief system for me for the rest of my breathing days. Unimportance still exists in me, but it does not if I stop acting like it does. Maybe it has just become very small at times.

Inventory

How this affects my...
Self-esteem - I will go overboard to make myself important when I think I should be relevant
Pride - I make me important by making other people unimportant
Security - expect to be important and do nothing to earn that respect from others, I have to do that to be OK
Ambition - I'm fucked up in the head and Spirit about what I do to make myself unimportant
Men - I blame men for making me feel unimportant even though I dislike them and do nothing for them
Women - Fuck me and I feel important, if you don't I feel unimportant
Pocketbook - Money makes me feel important and I always feel I deserve to get paid more

My Part

How Am I...
Dishonest - I should not be responsible for my own importance, you should do something for me to make me important; I'm lazy and unforgiving; I expect to be treated importantly by doing as little as possible; I have a big part in my own unimportance; I create it with my expectations
Selfish - I don't let anyone be more important than me; I'll battle you to be more important
Self-seeking - I make myself more important than I deserve to be and have no problem hurting others to do it
Afraid - Of letting others be more important, being unimportant and being okay in my unimportance

6 Fears

1. Fear of humility
2. Fear of showing brotherly love
3. Fear of making others feel better and more important than me
4. Fear of anger when I feel unimportant
5. Fear of prolonged self-pity
6. Fear of earning my way out of importance by doing something of importance that's not for me

Resentment to God

For not letting me be as important as I don't deserve to be

Corrective Measures

1. Two times tomorrow make someone else feel special
2. Two times tomorrow don't bring the conversation back to me and make my ego stand down

Pride Warrior

Vindictive

Being vindictive takes a lot of energy. The deed, whatever it was, has already been done to me. This topic is about my retaliation. Being vindictive is kind of a cool, exciting experience. I could get caught in this, maybe resulting in going to jail. I don't even think about this stuff in the moment. I never think about getting caught because the motivation of doing things to pay people back is like no other. Nobody better do these things to me because I will tell on them and make them suffer.

When I think of being vindictive, I think of all the planning and hours of conversation with myself. The best part is when I convince other people to help or to pay them for their assistance. I like that--it feels a little professional, even. This dark dude voice comes in and tells me that we still do this kind of crap today. He is always kind enough to tell me he wants my life. That wakes me up and sends me to Spirit to find out alternative ways to deal by acting in principles.

It's the same old stuff from God. This is your path if you wish to go big, let's go ahead and make the amends to this person or group. The amends looks like this when it comes to being vindictive: I don't mean it, but I'm willing to pretend for my Spirit. I love my mentor Spirit dude.

An example of an amend for vindictiveness would go like this: I made a list of people that I despise and you are on it. I owe you an amend for hating on you, for talking behind your back, for thinking you have to trust me a certain way, for really wanting to hurt you and be vindictive or retaliate. I can do better than this and I believe you deserve better. Is there anything you need to say to me? I promise to shut up and listen. Is there anything I can do to make this right?

Being right or wrong has nothing to do with this process. My Spirit says that this is what angels and spiritual warriors do. It's about what aligns with principles.

Inventory

How this affects my...
Self-esteem - I really like dishing out the pain as long as it does not disrupt me
Pride - This seems like it is just part of my nature that I really don't want to change; I blame the hobby of vindictiveness on people victimizing me
Security - I notice I feel better about the parts of me that I think are cheated, made fun of, or denied when I can be vindictive and hurt people back some way, even if it is just with fueled words
Ambition - I will lie, cheat, and steal and be vindictive to get and stay ahead; there is a mean-spirited side of me that I approve of; I call it option B and it's always available and ready to go

Men - I got this thing with men where I am so much more sensitive and faster to react against them; I'm sure I take a lot of things out of context to justify being vindictive towards them
Women - I found this dark part of me towards women that they owe me attention and need to do what I say and ask for all sexual stuff; I believe it's cool
Pocketbook - My reaction to being vindictive can be bought;, money isn't amends to me for having been hurt by others; I have no shame in being a sellout

My Part

How Am I...
Dishonest - I don't get honest about what you said or did to make me need to hurt you back; I never tell you to your face because what you did is not up for discussion; I don't argue fairly
Selfish - I'm selfish because I do not tolerate people reacting vindictively with the things I've done or said on purpose, but I expect them to tolerate this behavior in me
Self-seeking - I make up excuses for the things I say and do to make people go off on me; I don't believe other people's accusations; I minimize what I do until death
Afraid - Of not having the courage to take a knee and believe the hurtful things people say I've done; but what if I do, my Spirit says what if

5 Fears

1. Fear of not reacting
2. Fear of finding my motives
3. Fear of letting my Spirit remove the belief system behind vindictiveness
4. Fear of finding things very wrong about why I have the vindictive gene in me, what if I don't?
5. Fear of wanting to be the opposite: the courage to be kind, understanding, forgiving in real time today; I always say I will start tomorrow but it does not work

Resentment to God

For not allowing me to hurt people back for free, it's just easy to blame God first

Corrective Measures

1. Make amends to someone who I judged because of their vindictive behavior or to someone I was vindictive towards
2. Write a set aside prayer pertaining to what I think I know about everything that comes with being vindictive

Waking Up

Waking up happens in the moment. When I get completely dishonest, this is the moment I realize I need to get honest and fix this. This experience is me waking up to how my Spirit would handle the situation. Anytime I find myself getting super opinionated or controlling of people, places, or things, and recognize what's happening, that is me waking up. When I can say you deserve better than all my opinions, and matter of fact, you can be right, I'm waking up from a place that I'm not willing to be anything more than my defects. Waking up to a moment where more is expected from me by God in the Spirit place is what I live for today.

When it comes to controlling, I will justify that I can do anything I want in order to control and get what I want out of people. Control also means I don't have to do anything for anyone. Being controlling is awesome for me, I really love being defiant. But it really doesn't work out anymore with this Covenant to Spirit. When I'm controlling, the wake up happens when I get around to making the amend for being a controlling ass and letting you know I can do better.

The wake up is going from my normal dark defective behavior and stopping that for a few minutes. I always have to tell on myself to the person I'm abusing so that I can wake up for a minute when I stop. Other wakeups for me: being condescending to not being condescending, being a thief to stopping and not being a thief for even 30 minutes.

The wake up is a huge shift that happens when I move into a principled behavior in the next breath. It is the movement from complaining a lot to not complaining by just not talking for a few minutes. These are baby steps to most people, but it rocked my world. Another big one was moving from desperately wanting to kill myself to not killing myself today. The principle is to wake up and serve Spirit. Although these are small, brief changes, I couldn't bear to swallow any more than this. Any more and I would have surely contracted a case of the "fuck its".

Inventory

How this affects my...

Self-esteem - I fight waking up because part of me thinks I should not have to and find the way I was

Pride - Waking up kills my pride; my Spirit and principles forced me down a different road

Security - This shakes my security up completely; what was or is off the table and what could be is unknown in my behavior

Ambition - This shows me the option of two roads to go down: the old ways that I know (like control), or the new ways (like honesty and humility)

Men - Waking up really effects relationships with men; I am no longer able to stereotype a man, I have to have an open mind

Women - Waking up with women is only present in the change in my behavior and how I treat and talk to them; I become a gentleman

Pocketbook - Showing how I wake up to what my purpose is to be unknowingly in service; my motives start to shift from what I demand to make and to seeing the resources I have been given today and working from that

My Part

How Am I...

Dishonest - If I'm waking up, everyone around me should wake up at the same rate; I deny having this opinion

Selfish - I let people know all day how hard this is for me and all the things they should change for me to be okay

Self-seeking - I call bullshit on others waking up; if I can't see it in their behavior towards me, they are liars and fakes; watch me to see how it's done

Afraid - That I will not be able to hold myself accountable to spiritual behavior and new belief systems

5 Fears

1. Fear of the change being too much too fast
2. Fear of new belief systems not being true
3. Fear of quitting this path and going back
4. Fear of I won't be able to find God and Spirit
5. Fear of not finding the willingness to commit to this spiritual path

Resentment to God

For not making it easier for me to do all the work; using principles in my daily life is the only way, as the gauge in my behavior to dictate when I am awake to Spirit or not

Corrective Measures

1. Ask God: What makes your waking up more important?
2. Ask God: Why do I think I need to have an opinion of others that I think should wake up faster?

What Spirit designed me to be

What my Spirit designs me to do changes day to day with what is right in front of me. I'm not talking about the good stuff—that stuff is free. I'm talking the storms, the grey cloud part of life. The moments where I seriously question, do I do the principled thing or the non-principled thing? This thought always comes first. Part of my design in the past was very important, especially the bad stuff. I see I was designed to get beat up by my past: beat up by people, to get molested, and to sell myself when I left home. I was perfectly designed to be a thief and meth addict. I can see this today.

Everything I went through was designed to illustrate how strong I was at that time. It allows me to understand all these things so people can relate to me as needed on their path through their storms. This was all part of the great awakening I've had through it all. It only made sense through an amazing man named Mike who gave of himself to help me.

The purpose of it all, my Spirit tells me, was to see and feel that these events are over. The experience moving from being a hateful victim is that my part mostly was being in the wrong place at the wrong time. That's it. I did heal.

My purpose in Spirit has been brutal within the 12 steps. How I think of people was matched only in my becoming awake and aware to Spirit in the present. I found that I have and do treat people in my life close to the same way as the people that hurt me, abused me, and took things from me physically and emotionally. I have treated many, many people the same way as the people that abused me. I could instantly see it. My behavior, my verbal abuse, and my judgment punished people that had nothing to do with my past. The purpose my Spirit had was simple: spare your guilt and remorse you don't even have, and begin now to let them know you can do much better.

Inventory

How this affects my...
Self-esteem - Half of the time I don't really know who I am, maybe that is what I'm designed to be
Pride - I would like to believe that maybe there is much on the other side of pride, like freedom I have not been able to experience because of it
Security - Today I'm okay with or without the security I know; they say when you know something you block the channel for higher possibilities to occur
Ambition - Ambition just comes and goes naturally; maybe I'm designed to lose that word and go with principles, just half of the time will do
Men - I hate to say it, but there came a time where my Spirit said and brought into me that it was no longer okay to be combative with men because many of them need someone not to be

Women - There came a day that the Spirit of God moved into my Spirit and removed a big piece of my physical obsession with women; I was told I was designed to represent a good, married man that would not seek harming women
Pocketbook - I was designed to find gratitude with what is given, even if it isn't enough in my opinion; tomorrow blessings will fill me, there is no experience like not having enough—it is priceless

My Part

How Am I...
Dishonest - I pretend to be the spiritual dude, especially when I'm not; maybe I'm not designed to need to be arrogant and condescending
Selfish - I always want more than what I am designed to get; I am not that grateful here
Self-seeking - I tend to revert back to the selfish, opinionated guy when I think I deserve more; pretending to be grateful saved my life
Afraid - Of too much being asked of me too fast; I won't pay attention to what Spirit demands of me; I'm afraid to say "no" to the God Spirit in me

5 Fears

1. Fear of surrendering my life each day
2. Fear of making this path harder than it has to be
3. Fear of calling bullshit on this and going back
4. Fear of not having enough humility
5. Fear of not needing to be dishonest

Resentment to God

For not allowing me to fix and control my life; for not giving me enough humility to resent God for something I could never do on my own

Corrective Measures

1. Ask God: Why do I have to take a knee and align with principles today?
2. Ask God: how can I find out what I was designed to be?

Why

I have to be very careful when I ask why. Why is one of the most aggressive words I know. If I'm asking why, I most likely already have the answer and explanation I need you to have. I have an expectation that I've set up, and it usually entails you failing it and me rationalizing why I then have the right to punish you. Most of the time, when the answer to my question comes, they answer people give me is "just because".

When you ask me why, I usually make up a story or lie. Tell me, why did you drink too much? Answer, either because I did or I made a mistake and did not mean for the 10th time this month to do that. You decide which one is the truth.

Here are the classics that no one really wants the answers to: why don't you love me, why did you cheat on me, why don't you want to spend time with me, why won't you listen to me, etc. The answer is because I did and because I can, or thanks for letting me know I can do better.

Why can't you check out the trash without me asking? Because I don't. I take a very condescending stance when other people ask me why. No answer is really good enough because I rarely think I have to tell the truth. When I ask people why, I expect an answer. I should just tell you it won't be good enough and I will not believe you. I am right at all costs. This is the ticker tape that runs through my head constantly.

Sometimes, the question why is meant to get a solution to an epic problem that has been brewing. Personally, when I ask someone why, I want a good enough answer. I'm really just setting you up to argue with or rage at you. It is different when I'm in a good mood.

To my kids, I will ask why would you even think that? Why do you think that's a good idea? To my parents, why do you always have to do things that upset me?

Needing to know why instead of what I should do next is something I hope to find the path to. I would like to not have to accuse you for my benefit when I ask why when things happen.

Inventory

How this affects my...
Self-esteem - The need to ask why is automatic; I like to put people on the spot to see if they will lie or not
Pride - I think I like to have the upper hand asking why; it's all OK until you ask me why, I will usually just make things up rather than tell the truth
Security - Asking people why when I have the answer in my mind gives me a sense of power when I get insecure and full of self-pity
Ambition - Ambitions are much more successful when people don't ask me why I do or did things the way that I did

Men - Men don't need to ask me why; they need to know that I do what I do because I can and answer to no one

Women - I always want to know why women won't do what I say and why they always leave; I wonder why they don't stay when I tell them to; why, I'm really not that bad, right?

Pocketbook - Why can't I get what I deserve, maybe I do; why am I so lazy, because I like to be

My Part

How Am I...

Dishonest - I use the why question to grill people, I really don't care about the answer; I just love to feel superior

Selfish - I rarely ask why to add to the value of anything; it is just something I use to punish

Self-seeking - I like and feed on the attention when I make people answer my "why's".

Afraid - Of explaining my actions truthfully when asked why; lies and perception is all I got; honest accountability is a big fear of mine

5 Fears

1. Fear of not needing to know why
2. Fear of the answers to the questions I ask God when I ask
3. Fear of having integrity when I ask why and not having a shitty motive
4. Fear of giving second and third chances
5. Fear of treating people fairly and with some respect, not being a bully

Resentment to God

When I ask God why, He says because it is; I resent God for not answering my questions, He says that His non-answer is the answer most of the time

Corrective Measures

1. Not to ask why for half a day tomorrow and the whole next day
2. When asked why, do not be defensive and be honest

Words

I love to sling words out into the air. It's fun to hear who talks my language and who will be offended. I used to love to offend people, but today I try to be a little less good at it. Part of me does not need to be so verbally brutal anymore.

I notice my word choice changes based on what kind of mood I'm in. Sometimes, I'm clear with my words and still someone gets offended and takes what I say the wrong way. Is it my job to break down some of my words in real time before I say them to see what the other person is hearing? I didn't think so. That's precisely why I had to start doing it.

My words are like land mines. It seems that someone wants to get hurt when they walk into my field. Who do I want to be more like, the dark dude or the Spirit dude inside of me? I have to decide day by day. The mood I'm in dictates my mouth most times.

I get frustrated with words at times, until I find I don't need to be. Attempting to choose kinder words is progress; I am doing better if I'm even thinking about making these vast improvements. The shift is about the reach towards something better than who I am now.

Although I hate when my words get twisted around, I do the same to other people. I take what they say and turn it into what I think they should mean. I love to argue over word choice and what I think I heard you say. I fight until the death to be right. I listen to people argue over the meaning of what they say to each other. When I'm a bystander, it's fascinating.

I asked the God piece, "why do I have to choose words not to hurt people so much?" The answer was, "because you can in principles dictate your desire to need to. It's going to happen, but it does not need to be so intentional. It's a journey, a path to go deeper in doing the right thing. Or not. Your choice."

I have found a deep belief system that tells me that my words are my power. This contract is wound up within my arrogance, entitled mentality, and expectations to be heard and understood. When I am actively in this belief system, rarely a situation works out without some kind of altercation, especially with men. I'm grateful that my need to be right is surrendering to be a better Spiritual dude.

Inventory

How this affects my...
Self-esteem - I expect people to compromise their words for how I expect to be talked to
Pride - I should not have to compromise what words I use; I say what I mean and mean what I say
Security - My security lives in my motives and my need to not be who I was yesterday

Ambition - I demand to be respected and respect is given by the words you choose to say to me, this does not apply to me of course
Men - I seldom want to hear what men say because I'm always looking to disagree and for verbal confrontations
Women - The only word that upsets me with women is no,; there is a belief system going on in me that thinks they owe me something; I think I need to fight for the yes; you can hurt me and abuse me with your words
Pocketbook - I will use any words needed for you to give me more; I can't seem to get grateful for what I have been given

My Part

How Am I...
Dishonest - I said I did not mean to say what I said when being judgmental, opinionated, and disrespectful, but my truth is that I did mean to use the words I used; I always lie about this
Selfish - I'm intolerant at times and pretend to be offended by words; at the end of the day, I don't care and don't listen to what people say anyway
Self-seeking - I read in between the lines of what people say and hear what I want to interpret
Afraid - That I don't have the power to control myself when I'm in the mood to not control myself

5 Fears

1. Fear of changing how I communicate and let people communicate with me
2. Fear of not being able to remember that I don't have to use words this way
3. Fear of being respectful and kind with no guarantee I get the same
4. Fear of how principles might change me
5. Fear of the unknown when it comes to representing the spirit as a spiritual warrior

Resentment to God

For making words so confusing and making me think it has to be so hard; I know it's not, I just need to choose to pretend to not be confused

Corrective Measures

1. Make amends to someone I hurt with my words
2. When someone hurts me with their words, bless them on their way

Conclusion

So now, on this path, my option is to live and move in real time moment by moment. Bringing a spiritual principle into the old belief systems in my behavior that are no longer working and bringing me mental and emotional pain. Maybe I don't love pain as much as I used to.

I find things I still won't do and should not have to. I have things I still won't tolerate in others but I still do myself. Today I see these things within me in real time. The spiritual warrior in me will find a way to inventory this stuff and somehow find a way to make the amend that I can do better than the crap I do to others. Spirit demands I find a way to get this done in real time. My spirit is demanding once I sign up for this path. It does not feel sorry for me, I do this very well myself.

I was told by my spirit, good and bad, right and wrong are the same thing, each just has a different experience, none better or worse than the others. Know I choose this after a life of drug addiction, dishonesty, extreme anger, defiance, and self-pity. For me this is just something else to do. I seek to be a better man within and how I treat people. My wish is to have the courage to live and move in spirit as much as possible and the courage to come back when I get out of spirit.

12 principles: Honesty, Hope, Faith, Courage, Willingness to do the next right thing, Integrity, Tolerance, Humility, Forgiveness, Brotherly love, Discipline, Spirituality, and Service

I see you and wish the best for you.
blessings,
Michael

Glossary of Terms

Glossary of Terms and Concepts

The Push: the drive to move towards either Spirit or non-spirit behavior/thoughts; a force that originates within us without Spirit and is typically destructive unless it reaches toward Spirit; can be negative or positive and both are acceptable

List of 12 step principles: these encompass all principles and are the principles that are referred to throughout the book

Honesty
Hope
Faith
Courage
Integrity
Willingness
Humility
Justice
Brotherly Love
Discipline/Perseverance
Spirituality
Service

Break it down: identifying and destroying belief systems that we carry in our words and actions; looking at things in a way that we've never seen before within ourselves, usually with help from others; cutting through the bullshit of what I think, feel, and have known up until this point

Inventory: a 4-column piece of writing that breaks down four components of a resentment or belief system; it consists of people, institutions, or principles; this can be about an event/incident, hatred, emotions, etc.; itemized blame of shit to the world that has happened to me and how I carry it; the impetus for writing inventory is being stuck; the goal is to find my part so I can make it right

Components of Inventory: the following items are the aspects to be focused on when writing a piece of inventory

How this affects my...
Self-esteem: What I expect people to do or not do to or for me; how it effects how I think about myself
Pride: What isn't being done to support how I think I should be treated and my concept of pride; how other people view me
Security: What I need people to do and/or not do to be ok

Ambition: What I want to happen; what I expect to go my way
Men: How men do or don't do what I want them to do
Women: How women do or don't do what I want them to do
Pocketbook: How I think about money or try to get/control money; how money fucks me up

My Part

How Am I...
Dishonest: How I lie (either to self or others) regarding the scope of the resentment; how my part of what I do is dishonest
Selfish: My thoughts and motives; how I am a taker and what I expect
Self-seeking: My behaviors and actions; Identifying how I only think about me and what I need
Afraid: Letting go or doing something in principle that is new; the things that terrify me that I haven't even done yet; this is about the shift

5 Fears: Listing 5 Fears I'm afraid of regarding changing

Resentment to God: How I blame God for the topic of the resentment

Corrective Measures Two purposeful actions that are identified for the next day to correct and amend my behavior

Amends: Making right something that I have done wrong; the amends doesn't have to be genuine per say, it's just about doing the action instead of believing in it (that comes later); it's always about something I don't want to correct

Taking a knee and standing down: Finding a way to make the principle in question happen

My Spirit: The space where my breath and heartbeat meet without my permission; the connection that meets God to give me instructions of how to take care of God's children and be a better person; only works when it is connected to the Spirit of God

Spirit of God/God/Spirit/Spirit Dude: The source of all; the overseeing spirit of the universe; a different consciousness aside from when I am just with myself when connected; our origin

The Spirit World: The place where God works from in principles and values; where the change takes place through the individual when they choose to participate in a new way of living; a different plane of life where we strive to live; where the force of grace appears to move the spirit of people who struggle with defects and have been called to operate differently in a spirit

The Path: The journey from defects and negative behavior into spirituality and principled behavior

Dark Dude/My Darkness: Where old belief systems reside, where one operates from before they wake up spiritually; a product of one's past (in addiction, childhood, trauma, etc.); opposite of principles rule (dishonesty, etc.)

APPENDIX A - Amends

Appendix A - Amends

Mom

As part of my recovery, I was told to make a list of people I harmed and lied to. I owe you an amend for avoiding your calls and not getting back to you sooner. I owe you for an amends for blaming you for bad things that happened in my childhood, for blaming you for the unhealthy attraction I had for you as a teenager. For the disrespect today, for all the lies I told you. I owe you an amends for expecting you to act the way I thought you should. I can do better and you deserve better. Is there anything you need to say or anything I can do to make it right?

She said that she wanted me to let her into my life with the children unconditionally.

Don (the man who molested me)

I owe you an amend for all the hate I have had for you for 35 years. For blaming you for everything bad I have done. I used you to justify my behavior during all the years I shot meth. The truth is that I did so many of the deviant things you did. I was a predator to women and I took advantage by offering drugs to get my way. I have been a liar and used people every way imaginable. Is there something you need to say to me? IS there something I can do to make it right?

Police

I owe you an amend for talking horribly about you, for blaming you when I got caught doing illegal things (like stealing a car, selling drugs, etc.). I owe you an amend for being so ungrateful for you protecting me and my family today. I owe you an amend for coming down on you, yet you answer my 911 calls. For the disrespect and blaming all of you for what 1% of bad officers do. Is there something you need to say to me about this? Something I can do to make it right?

Son

I owe you an amend for thinking you are worthless and lazy. For saying this when we fight. For the disrespect and avoiding you at all costs. For constantly staying mad at you for all the things you won't change. For talking about you behind your back. For giving up on you. Is there something you need to say to me about this? What can I do to make it right?

Companies (I had a debt of $8k of old invoices I skipped out on)

I owe you an amend for the stress I caused for you when I decided I was not paying my debt to you. For the disrespect I showed you in the face of you treating me well for 20 years. For thinking I could get away with not paying and justifying to myself that I did not owe you. For avoiding your calls and treating you horribly. I owe you an amend for just being defiant and being a problem to you. You deserve better and I can do better. Is there something you need to say to me about this?

I paid the debt in full.

Individuals I judge and decide I can't stand

I owe an amend to people around me and at work that I judge and determine I really can't stand, even though I don't even know them and determine I don't want to.

I owe you an amend for talking about you and judging you royally. I owe you an amend for my disrespect and judgment of you, for thinking I'm better than you when I'm not. The things I judge you for I do myself. Is there something you need to say to me about this? What can I do to make it right?

Wife

I owe you an amend for the following:

- For cheating on you with your friend for four years
- For all the times I guilted you into having sex with me when you did not want to including after surgery
- For being disrespectful about what you had to say
- For thinking I'm better than you and minimizing what you have to say
- For horrible fights I created and how I spoke to you in them
- For making you have to defend yourself when it was out of line
- For not wanting to listen to all the things you thought were important
- For all the money I stole from you
- For treating you like an enemy in my life

For these things I owe you an amend. Is there something you need to say to me? I will just listen.

Let me know if there's anything I can do to make it right.

She said:

Yes, if you are going to continue to talk down to me please get out of my house. You have some serious issues to get over. Continue to work with your sponsor everyday to bring principles into how you act around me. I will take time to trust you again with sex and everything else, but I am willing to work on my part with this. Also, if you are going to lie, just tell me.

APPENDIX B - Letters to God

Appendix B - Letters to God

Question: Why do I feel so sorry for myself and why am I so depressed in sobriety?

Dear Michael,

Probably because you can and want to be. You are an award winning sorry-for-yourself kind of guy. Coming to a spiritual-type world from a dark self-centered kind of belief system has been a shock. The self-pity you choose to hold on to so tightly may be a byproduct of some of that. Let's face it, you give nothing and do nothing in any form of tolerance and giving to anyone but yourself. Part of this self-pity, and many go through this on this path, is that no one around you is allowing you to manipulate, judge, or push them to do things for you that you used to. The self-pity might also be in part that you are having to feel your sober feelings with nowhere to run. You feel so free because you are certain that you are, and have determined that that is God. What if this experience is something you had to move through to get you to this point? You may have to do something for someone to have a moment without your self-pity. Maybe the self-pity and depression is not yours. Try this: pretend it's not available anymore.

Question: Why do I have to change when no one else seems to have to?

Dear Michael,

No one said you have to change a thing. Neither does anyone else. This path with you and your Spirit only requires your belief systems and behavior to shift into another direction. And even then, only when you want to. You have asked for this. The only requirement for you and me to exist together is that you come from dishonesty, addiction, and old behavior. This experience brought you close to death and the edge of suicide. These life events were required for you to understand why exactly you would be willing to move through all of your crybaby bullshit into gratitude. No one else is required to change or stay on path. Pain is the mother of your change. You have the choice to tay in a different kind of pain so you are not in pain the way you usually are. Find a very strong, formerly addicted sponsor or mentor. You will need assistance in order to find gratitude for what you call unfairness. Get ready and put your grown man boots on.

Question: Why do I feel so much entitlement and why is it not working like it used to?

Dear Michael,

Entitlement is awesome, if you can pull it off. Everyone around you is fighting for the same air, so to speak. You are just used to getting your way because you think you should. You will have many experiences with this. People will let you know, and as you already suspect, you are not that important. No one is. You will only be as important as what you are willing to do and how you will add to the value of lives and situations. I never made growth and change with me as something to be pleasant or liked. You will have to determine what you are doing here, and who you work for each moment, each day. You must find someone that has cleared out some of this garbage and ask them how and why they did, and why it is that they stay. Borrow me from them. There is much less suffering this way.

Question: I hate everything. I get so angry at this principled crap. I don't buy the God thing. What do I do?

Dear Michael,

Why? If you did not fight this path, you would not have been as great a drug addict as you were. Pat yourself on the back for that one, buddy. You have been angry for such a long time, now you just have me to blame for it. Your hate is no better than anyone else's. Matter of fact, your opinions, defiance, self-pity, anger, and condescending bullshit is just average. I know you think you're special, that you are the worst of the worst, but this is woefully inaccurate. You are an average piece of shit, a typical scumbag. Among great addicts, what do you wish your legacy to be? What have you been? Do you want something you have yet to see? It does not matter. All that matters is a few honest, decent things that you do for my children. I always know that there are aspects of our relationship that you hate. You despise principles and the people I ask you to serve. I really don't care what you do. But I am grateful to see you at the table with me. You will only see me on the other side of your anger, so bring it with you. I get it.

Question: Why is the world out to get me? It seems that everybody wants something.

Dear Michael,

You are visible now. You aren't running and hiding in the world of sex and methamphetamines. You can't hide behind your dark dude and your dark nature anymore. The world just seems to be out to get you because you are in self-pity. Your nature and belief systems have taken everything captive. Cheating the world and everything around you because you think you can is your norm. Until now, you have justified it well. I'm not going to put up with you or anyone on a spiritual path unless you change. Maybe the world is not out to get you at all. Maybe the world is entitled not to have to pretend to care at all. Maybe you flatter yourself in thinking everyone has motives for something, and that they tend to be for their benefit and to your detriment. All these questions have to take place first for you in order for us to reach and feel the answers. The answers come when your behavior changes.

Question: Why is it so hard to change everything?

Dear Michael,

You have a belief system that says it has to be. You have fortified this belief system by how you feel, think, and behave. Change has been made out to be everything you fight not to do in the lifestyle in the game. You have had to learn to be set in opinions, to be impatient, aggressive, dishonest, condescending, and controlling. You had to be these things to survive addiction in the lifestyle of addiction and possessiveness. You think it is so hard to change, but you will not allow yourself to see there are moments today that you forget to be these things. There are easier moments throughout the hard moments. What if easy has always been woven into the hard? Things must be hard because you say they are. When you go to sit down in a difficult moment, see that sitting down can be separate from the situation. See what is easy about sitting and separate it for a moment from what you believe is so difficult. Maybe what is excruciating is not wanting to see this or to sit down to begin with. Maybe what is easy is that you already have sat down. You can ask Spirit to find this model in anything, or not at all. The heart is a muscle that you flex, easy as the muscle you may not have to flex. Your Spirit, when engaged, is and can be stronger than old behaviors. You can only find this on the path. All this change happens in time as you do things in the Spirit of grace and ease. If it was easy, everyone would do it. Ask to find the easy in the hard in the lessons that cause you pain, or not.